Geographic Expeditions

Specialists in Travel to Bhutan since 1985

Geographic Expeditions offers a sensationally varied roster of high quality tours and treks, with over 50 departures to choose from. We are also uniquely positioned to develop custom trips for individuals, academic institutions, and non-profit organizations.

For a copy of our astute, amusing and award-winning catalog of adventures, please call us at (800) 777-8183, (415) 922-0448, or info@geoex.com.

GEOGRAPHIC
EXPEDITIONS

www.geoex.com

FRANÇOISE POMMARET—Tibetologist, lecturer and writer—has travelled extensively in Asia and particularly in Bhutan, where she has lived and worked intermittently since 1981. She was a research assistant in the Bhutan Tourism Corporation (1981–86) and then research assistant in history in the Department of Education, Royal Government of Bhutan (1986-1991). Now a research fellow at the CNRS (the French National Centre for Scientific Research), she specializes in history and ethnology and she teaches the history and culture of the Himalayan regions at the School of Oriental Languages and Studies (INALCO, Paris). She is resident in Bhutan working for the Royal University of Bhutan, and continues to be very much involved with Bhutan in the fields of culture and education.

Françoise Pommaret has a degree in the history of art and in archaeology (Université de Panthéon-Sorbonne), as well as in Tibetan (INALCO). Her doctoral thesis was a historical and anthropological study of "people who come back from the netherworld" (delog) in the Tibetan world (for which she won an award from the Académie des Inscriptions et Belles-Lettres).

She speaks English and Dzongkha, and reads Tibetan. In addition to numerous articles—scientific and general interest—she has published several books, including Les Revenants de l'Au-delà dans le monde tibétain (Ed. CNRS, Paris, 1998), Bhutan: Mountain Fortress of the Gods (Serindia, London, 1997, in collaboration with C. Schicklgruber), Tibet: The Enduring Civilization (Thames and Hudson, London, 2003; Abrams, New York, 2003), Bhoutan Au plus Secret de l'Himalaya (Decouvertes Gallimard, Paris, 2005) and, as editor in Lhasa: the Capital of the Dalai-lamas (Brill, Leiden, 2002).

BHUTAN
HIMALAYAN MOUNTAIN KINGDOM

Françoise Pommaret

Photography by
Françoise Pommaret, Yoshiro Imaeda
Lionel Fournier, Seonaid Macleod

Translated by
Elisabeth B. Booz
Howard Solverson

ODYSSEY BOOKS & GUIDES

Odyssey Books & Guides is a division of Airphoto International Ltd.
903 Seaview Commercial Building, 21–24 Connaught Road West, Sheung Wan, Hong Kong
Tel: (852) 2856-3896; Fax: (852) 2565-8004
E-mail: sales@odysseypublications.com; www.odysseypublications.com

Distribution in the USA by W.W. Norton & Company, Inc., 500 Fifth Avenue, New York, NY 10110, USA
Tel: 800-233-4830; Fax: 800-458-6515; www.wwnorton.com

**Distribution in the UK and Europe by Cordee Books and Maps, 3a De Montfort St., Leicester,
LE1 7HD, UK Tel: 0116-254-3579; Fax: 0116-247-1176; www.cordee.co.uk**

Bhutan—Himalayan Mountain Kingdom

ISBN: 962-217-757-3 Library of Congress Catalog Card Number has been requested.
Copyright © 2006, 2003 Airphoto International Ltd.
Copyright © 1998, 1994, 1991, 1990 Odyssey Publications Ltd.

Managing Editor: Helen Northey
Consultant Editors: Howard Solverson, Bikrum Grewal, Toby Sinclair
Design: Au Yeung Chui Kwai
Map Consultant: Professor Bai Yiliang
Maps: Peter Tom Le Bas, Sylviane Janin, CK Au Yeung

Front cover photography: Françoise Pommaret (The Taktshang Monastery in Paro Valley, 1981)
Back cover photography: Brent Olson/Geographic Expeditions (top); Seonaid Macleod (bottom)
Photography/illustrations courtesy of Serindia Publications from *Views of Medieval Bhutan*: 15, 57, 202, 306, 308; Seonaid Macleod 92, 122 (bottom), 143, 170, 218, 226–7, 230; David Keen 103

Production and printing by Twin Age Limited, Hong Kong
E-mail: twinage@netvigator.com
Manufactured in China

(Right) *Traditional painting Padmasambhava (Guru Rinpoche) from the thangka of Wangduephodrang.*

CONTENTS

PREFACE 10

INTRODUCTION 11

NOTE ON THE SPELLING OF
   PROPER NAMES IN BHUTAN 17

NOTE ON PRONUNCIATION 17

FACTS FOR THE TRAVELLER 19
Getting to Bhutan 19
Tour Operators 20
Entry or Exit by Air 25
Airport Tax 25
Entry or Exit by Land 28
Visas 28
Embassies and Missions 29
Customs 29
Money 30
Post and Communications 30
Internet 31
Local Time 32
Health 32
Climate 33
Clothing 36
Equipment and Supplies 36
Photography 37
Electricity 37
Food and Drink 37
Leisure and Beauty Care 42
Shopping 44
Monuments Open to Visitors 50

GEOGRAPHY 51
Geography and Population 51

FLORA AND FAUNA 60

HISTORY 61

THE ECONOMY AND CHALLENGES 76

ARTS AND ARCHITECTURE 81

RELIGION 99
Tantric Buddhism 99
Rituals 101
Ritual Objects 101
   Religious Schools 104
The Religion in Practice 104

FESTIVALS, DANCE AND MUSIC .. 108
Religious Dances 112
Religious Music 121
Secular Dances and Music 121

WESTERN BHUTAN 129
The Paro Valley 129
The Ha Valley 160
The Paro-Thimphu Road 161
Thimphu 163
Suggested Day Walks around Thimphu ... 184
To the Southwest: Chhuzom to
   Phuentsholing 186
Phuentsholing 189
The Road to Punakha and
   Wangduephodrang 189
Punakha 192
Wangduephodrang 195

THE ROAD TO CENTRAL BHUTAN 202
Over the Black Mountains:
   Wangdue to Trongsa 202

CENTRAL BHUTAN 211
Trongsa dzong 211
Zhemgang Region (Khyeng) 213
The Road from Trongsa to Bumthang 219
The Bumthang Valleys 219
The Chume Valley 221
The Choekhor Valley 225
The Tang Valley 248
The Ura Valley 252

EASTERN BHUTAN 255
The Road from Ura to Mongar 255
Mongar 256
The Road from Mongar to Lhuentse 257
The Road from Mongar to Trashigang 258
Trashigang 261
Trashi Yangtse Dzong 263

THE SOUTHEAST: TRASHIGANG TO
    SAMDRUP JONGKHAR 268
Pemagatshel 269
Samdrup Jongkhar 270

TREKKING AND MOUNTAINEERING 271
The Classic Treks 276

NATIONAL PARKS AND NATURE
    RESERVES 280

GLOSSARIES 295
Historical Figures, Saints and Others 295
Deities of Buddhist Pantheon and their
    Sanskirt Names 298
Common Trees and Plants 299

RECOMMENDED READING 301

USEFUL WEBSITES 305

RECOMMENDED MUSIC 305
RESORT ACCOMMODATION 307
INDEX 309

MAPS
Bhutan 22–23
The Paro Valley 132
Thimphu 162
Thimphu City 166–7
Bumthang 220

SPECIAL TOPICS
The Monastic Community and Other
    Religious Categories 63
National Symbols of Bhutan 73
Some Statistics 79
Chortens and Mandalas 83
Three Frequently Seen Religious Series .. 123
The Important Stages of Life 125
Bhutanese Medicine 140
Terms of Address 158
Ceremonial Scarves 159
The Punakha Thondroel 198
The Dzongkha Language 214
Some Bhutanese Customs and Etiquette . 281
Personal Names 286
Archery and Other Sports 288
The Art of Books 293

LITERARY EXCERPTS
J Claude White on A Pitched Battle 157
Samuel Turner on Bhutanese Tea 236
William Griffith on A Day in the Life 246
Surgeon Rennie on An Unpleasant
    Encounter 291

(Following pages) *The spectacular landscape near Lingshi dzong with the Jichudrake and Tsheringang mountains both more than 7,000 metres high.*

PREFACE

This guide book was the first to be written on the little-known country that is Bhutan, and it is necessary to explain the spirit in which it was initially conceived in 1990.

Bhutan is a closed country that receives only a few tourists each year (about 2,000 in 1990, about 9,000 in 2004). It practises a policy of tourism control and puts the accent on traditional values. This guide book is, of course, for these tourists curious to discover an extraordinary country, but also for foreigners who come to work and contribute to its development. This is why this guide book goes a bit beyond the usual information found in this type of book. It is less a catalogue of addresses than an introduction to the Bhutanese culture and way of life, a bridge between the real life of the country and the interest of the traveller. Moreover, it stresses specifically Bhutanese cultural aspects and respect for the people of the country. And while perhaps displaying a certain vanity, it is meant to be the vade-mecum of every foreigner in Bhutan, tourist or resident. More simply, this guide book will have fulfilled its role if it helps to bring about a better understanding between foreign visitors and Bhutanese.

I cannot forget to acknowledge all the volunteer teachers, English, Irish or Canadians, who have put me up and helped during my peregrinations in different regions of Bhutan in the 1980s.

My most sincere thanks go to all the Bhutanese who have enabled me to know this country perhaps a little less superficially, and in particular to my friends Dago, Denma, Kunga and Karma, Kunzang, Namgyal, Norzom, and also to Chorten; to Lopen Chencho, who worked with me in the Department of Tourism in the early 1980s, and who, in his humble way, taught me the traditions of his county so well; finally, to the villagers of Bhutan. The harshness of their life is equalled by their sense of humour and their hospitality.

My debt to the great historians, such as Lopen Pemala, Lopen Nado and Dasho Lama Sangnga, and scholars such as Mynak Trulku, Yongzin Tseten Dorje and Lopen Lungten, is beyond words. Without all these friends and mentors, this guide book would not have seen the light of day, and it is to them that I dedicate it.

Finally, I would like to thank Matthias Huber, my publisher, who first back in 1990 took the risk of publishing a guidebook on Bhutan, has given me the freedom to express myself and has never imposed a standard format.

Best wishes! *Tashidele*!

Françoise Pommaret, Thimphu-Paris, September 2005

INTRODUCTION

'Bhutan? Where's that?' This is the response you can expect if you say you are going to Bhutan. Most people have never heard of it. Bhutan does not often make headlines—it makes a small paragraph in a Western newspaper infrequently. From time to time a full-scale article on Bhutan does appear, but then it reaches only a limited audience, although one cannot help noticing that in the last two years, Bhutan has become a trendy destination.

A handful of people around the world, who form a sort of 'initiates' club, eagerly follow events there by carefully reading the weekly journal *Kuensel*, published in Thimphu and now available on the web. Some of them have visited Bhutan on professional trips, some as official guests, and others as tourists. All of them have come back enthralled by this secret land.

Secluded in the eastern Himalayas between India and China (Tibet), as big as Switzerland, but sparsely inhabited (population barely 700,000), Bhutan certainly exudes charm (magic, its devotees would say). The mountains are magnificent, the forests are dense, the people are delightful, the air is pure, the architecture imposing, the religion exciting, the art superb. There are no beggars, few thefts, little violent crime, and a traveller's personal safety is guaranteed. Public relations hype, you may be thinking; guidebooks often inflate their subject. But the surprising fact is that it's all true. For the occasional visitor, Bhutan is truly Shangri-la, the mythical country hidden deep in the mountains.

In the 1990s misunderstandings have arisen in the south of the Kingdom over the nationality of inhabitants of Nepalese origin. His Majesty the King and his entire government have worked to find a solution to this problem and they are in consultation with the Government of Nepal. but this government has itself its fair share of problems with the Maoist insurgency.

While the Bhutanese themselves are aware that they live in a privileged land, surrounded by nations beset with terrifying economic and social problems, they also know that they are not living in Shangri-la. Their day-to-day reality allows no time for dreaming. The hard life of the peasants, consisting of household chores, work in the fields and care of livestock, is scarcely mechanized as yet. Religious festivals, pilgrimages and secular holidays are the only moments of rest, anticipated pauses punctuating the agricultural calendar.

With 80 per cent of the population engaged in agriculture or raising livestock, Bhutan remains a rural country almost devoid of industry, except in the south. The beauty of the pastoral landscape can seem unreal to travellers from the industrialized world: houses with brightly decorated window frames and shingled roofs, patchworks of green paddy fields, plots of tawny buckwheat, oak forests, a covered bridge, fences of intricately woven bamboo, a man leaning on a wooden rail trampling his harvest, a woman weaving in the open air, a baby laced into a horse's saddle bag, yaks browsing in a grove of giant rhododendron.

Such scenes remain in the memory forever. But it is the symbols of Bhutan's religion which leave the deepest impression: the *chortens* (commemorative monuments) dotting the landscape, fluttering prayer flags, prayer wheels turned by the swift water of mountain streams, the monasteries. Buddhism is everywhere, determining attitudes, moulding thoughts. Red-robed monks, high lamas, the religious men in a village; everybody is aware of their moral and spiritual influence on the population. They preside over all events: weddings, departures on trips, official ceremonies, promotions, not to mention the fundamental role they play in religious initiations, mass blessings and festivals. Their importance is underlined further by the fact that Bhutan is the only country in the world where the Tantric form of Mahayana Buddhism is the official state religion.

The National Commission for Cultural Affairs has been assigned the responsibility of preserving the Kingdom's cultural identity. The commission works with the entire population, rural and urban, to ensure the precious Bhutanese spirit is nurtured in the same way it has been for thousands of years.

Religion, tradition and ancestral custom constitute Bhutanese etiquette, the most visible elements of which are respect for all religious institutions and the wearing of national dress. This emphasis on traditional values is as much a deliberate policy of the government as is its concern with socio-economic development and environmental preservation. These form the base of the concept, GNH ('Gross National Happiness').

These aims, which at first may seem contradictory, are reconciled through the desire to develop local resources and promote self-reliance. The two objectives merge in a totally harmonious way: a monk photocopies the pages of a text he needs for a ritual; a high official, wearing a heavy raw silk garment with a sword at his side, discusses a report on improved rice production or yak-breeding. The

(Preceding pages) *The 'Judge of the Dead' with his mirror in which he sees all actions—in front, one of his helpers weighs good and bad deeds on a scale.*

report has been produced on a computer in the dark offices of a fortress where, across the courtyard, monks perform a ceremony for the guardian deities of Bhutan.

The Bhutanese do not reject their cultural and spiritual heritage in favour of modern imported values. Never having been colonized, always fiercely independent and proud of their traditions, they see no need to adopt ideas simply because they come from more developed and powerful countries. Using common sense, they accept only those concepts that help them to improve their way of life and develop their country within the framework of their own traditions without destroying either the spirit or the environment. Uninhibited, they continue to follow customs that many other countries would condemn as archaic. The Bhutanese have no desire for cultural assimilation. They are different and intend to remain so. 'Gross National Happiness' (GNH), to go back to the expression coined by King Jigme Singye Wangchuk, is not a hollow concept.

The practical information given in this guide book reflects the situation in mid-2005. This information can quickly become outdated and for this we cannot be held responsible.

"Loomno, looking towards Tassisudon", 1839. Engraving on steel by M.J. Starling after William Daniell based on Davis, in Hobart Caunter, The Oriental Annual, *7 vols, London, 1834–40. vi, plate 11.*

NOTE ON THE SPELLING OF PROPER NAMES IN BHUTAN

Recently the government of Bhutan has changed the phonetic English spelling of some significant towns in the Kingdom. These changes are reflected in this edition of the guide book. Previous visitors should recognize the names of towns and should not be confused by their different spellings.

NOTE ON PRONUNCIATION

u   is pronounced *oo* as in boot

ü   is pronounced like the French U

e   is a short vowel as in b*e*t

ph   is pronounced as an aspirated *h* not f

tsh   is pronounced as *ts*

c   is pronounced *ch* as in cheek

NB: Bhutanese spelling is complex and difficult to reproduce exactly in Roman letters if one does not know the rules of pronunciation. The spelling of Bhutanese proper nouns, therefore, varies in Western transcription and the reader may find the same proper nouns having rather different spellings.

Common nouns that are now well known in the West have been kept in their now-standard spelling.

The Bhutanese use the Tibetan and Dzongkha name of deities, which is very different from the Sanskrit name by which the deities are known in the West. A list of the most frequently used deity names is found on page 298, giving the Sanskrit equivalent of the Tibetan and Dzongkha names.

(Left) *Two monks dressed as terrifying deities ready to enter a festival dance.*

FACTS FOR THE TRAVELLER

Bhutan's policy of restricting tourism has three purposes. First, it preserves the natural environment and the lifestyle of the people without upsetting their socio-economic balance. Second, it recognizes the lack of infrastructure and tourist facilities, the rugged character of the terrain, and problems of communication. And third, by charging all travellers a daily package fee for tourist services (hotels, transport, meals, guide, etc.), Bhutan is able to earn the foreign currency it needs for vital expenditure in other areas of development. To date there has been no precise limit set on the number of tourists allowed to enter Bhutan. However, it is understood that if the number of tourists exceeds the Kingdom's capacity and begins to drain resources and harm the environment, the government would cap the annual number allowed to enter.

In the last five years, the total number of tourists has risen from approximately 2,500 per year to over 9,000 tourists in 2004. Moreover, the destination is becoming increasingly popular with Indians. This is still minuscule when compared to the 25,000 visitors that enter Hong Kong every day. There are plans to implement a new tourism policy in 2006.

GETTING TO BHUTAN

Unless invited officially by the government, it is impossible to travel to Bhutan as an individual. One must put together one's own group of at least two persons, or join a group formed by a tour operator before departing one's home country. Tourism in Bhutan is controlled by a governmental organization responsible to the Ministry of Industry and Commerce, the Department of Tourism (DoT). PO Box 126, GPO Thimphu, Bhutan. Tel: (9752) 323251, 323252. Fax: (9752) 323695. E-mail: tab@druknet.bt. Web site: www.tourism.gov.bt. The Department of Tourism fixes prices and makes the rules that the local agencies have to follow.

Privatized since 1991, tourism is now in the hands of a large number of private Bhutanese agencies; however, they must all follow the rules set down by the DoT, particularly as regards price. The daily price includes all services within the country and is officially around US$200 per person per day for all tours—cultural or trekking. Indian nationals enjoy special terms, as do diplomats.

Rhododendron blooming in March at Dochu La in western Bhutan

TOUR OPERATORS

It is possible to organize theme trips in Bhutan (bird-watching, butterflies, flowers, introduction to Buddhism, weaving, crafts) or sporting activities (biking across Bhutan, trekking, rafting, etc.); this list is not exhaustive.

USA

Geographic Expeditions, 2627 Lombard Street, San Francisco, CA 94123
Tel. (toll free inside USA) 800-551-1769; Tel. (from abroad) 1-415-922-0448
Fax. (toll free inside USA) 800-777-8183, (from abroad) 1-415-346-5535
E-mail: info@geoex.com; www.geoex.com

Abercrombie & Kent International
Suite 212, 1520 Kensington Road, Oak Brook, Chicago, Il 60521
Tel. (toll free inside USA) 800-323-7308, Tel. 1-630-954-2944
Fax. 1-630-954-3324; www.abercrombiekent.com

Bhutan Travel, PO Box 757 (883 Jayne Place), Baldwin NY 11510
Tel. 516/378-3805; Toll free phone 800-950-9908
Fax. 516-868-1601; www.bhutantravel.com

Far fung places, 1914 Fell street, San Francisco, Ca 94117
Tel. 415-386-8306; 1800-410-9811; Fax. 415-386-8304
E-mail: info@farfungplaces.com; www.farfungplaces.com

AUSTRALIA

Peregrine Adventures, 258 Lonsdale Street, Melbourne VIC 3000
Tel. 039663-8611; Fax. 039663-8618; www.peregrineadventures.com

UK

Cox & Kings Travel Ltd., Gordon House, 10 Greencoat Place, London, SWIP IPH
Tel. 020-7873-5000; Fax. 020-7630-6038; www.coxandkings.co.uk

Explore Worldwide Ltd.
1 Frederick Street, Aldershot, Hants, GU11 1LQ
Tel. 01252-760-000; Fax. 01252-760-001; www.exploreworldwide.com

Himalayan Kingdoms Ltd., Old Crown House, 18 Market Street, Wotton-Under-Edge, Gloucestershire, GL12 7AE
Tel. 01453-844-400; Fax. 01453-844-422; www.himalayankingdoms.com

KE Adventure Travel, 32 Lake Road, Keswick, Cumbria CA12 5DQ
Tel. 017687-73-966; Fax. 017687-74-693; www.keadventure.com

Steppes East Ltd., 51 Castle Street, Cirencester Gloucestershire GL7 1QD
Tel. 01285-651-010; Fax. 01285-885-888; www.steppeseast.co.uk

The Oriental Caravan
36 Vanbrugh Court, Wincott Street Kennington, London SE11 4NS
Tel/Fax. 020-7582-0716; www.theorientalcaravan.com

Trans Himalaya, 4 Foxcote Gardens, Frome, Somerset, BA112DS
Tel. 01373-455518; Fax. 01373-455594
E-mail: info@trans-himalaya.com; www.trans-himalaya.com

Worldwide Journeys & Expeditions Limited
27 Vanston Place, London SW6 1AZ. Tel. 020-7386-4646; Fax. 020-7381-0836
www.worldwidejourneys.co.uk

BHUTAN

For official information see www.tourism.gov.bt and the Association of Bhutanese Tour Operators abto@druknet.bt. A brief selection of the 180 or so tour operators is listed below in alphabetical order.

Department of Tourism, Post Box 126, Thimphu. Tel. (975-2) 323251, 323252
Fax. (975-2) 323695; E-mail:tab@druknet.bt; www.tourism.gov.bt

Baeyul Excursions, P.O. Box 437, Thimphu. Tel. (975-2) 2324355
Fax. (975-2) 2323728; E-mail: baeyul@druknet.bt; www.baeyul.com

Bhutan Dorji Holidays, P.O. Box 550, Thimphu. Tel. (975-2) 328663
Fax. (975-2) 325174; E-mail: dorji@druknet.bt; www.Bhutan-dorji.com

Bhutan Heritage Travels, P.O. Box 293, Thimphu. Tel. (975-2) 324407
Fax. (975-2) 326666; E-mail:hishey@druknet.bt; www.heritagetours.com.bt

Bhutan Tourism Corporation Limited, PO Box 159, Thimphu
Tel. (975-2) 322647, 324045; Fax. (975-2) 322479, 323392
E-mail: btcl@druknet.bt; www.kingdomofbhutan.com

Bhutan Travel Bureau, P.O. Box 959, Chhubachu, Thimphu
Tel. (975-2) 321749; Fax. (975-2) 325100; E-mail:btb@druknet.bt; www.btb.com.bt

Chhundu Travels, 31 Norzin Lam, PO Box 149, Thimphu
Tel. (975-2) 322592, 322547, 328464, 323586; Fax. (975-2) 322645
E-mail: chhundu@druknet.bt; www.chhundu.com.bt

Diethelm Travel Bhutan/Yarkay
Yarkay Plaza, P. Box 107, Chang Lam, Thimphu. Tel. (975-2) 323483, 322626
Fax. (975-2) 323894; E-mail: dwpenjor@druknet.bt; www.diethelmtravel.com

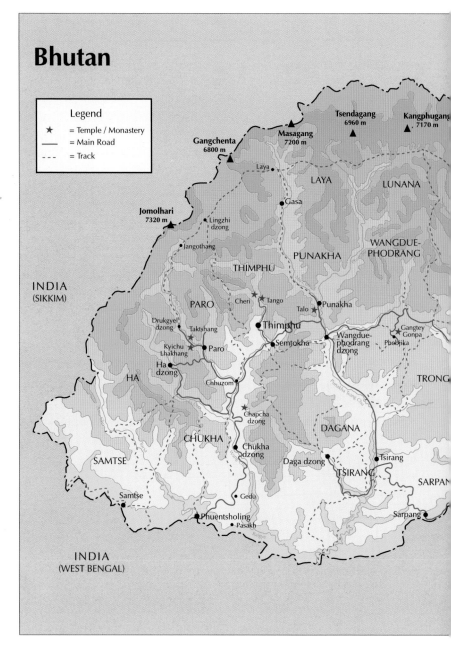

Bhutan

Legend

★ = Temple / Monastery
— = Main Road
- - - = Track

INDIA
(SIKKIM)

INDIA
(WEST BENGAL)

Gangchenta
6800 m

Masagang
7200 m

Tsendagang
6960 m

Kangphugang
7170 m

Jomolhari
7320 m

Laya

LAYA

LUNANA

Gasa

Lingzhi
dzong

Jangothang

PUNAKHA

WANGDUE-
PHODRANG

THIMPHU

PARO

Cheri

Tango

Talo

Punakha

Drukgyel
dzong

Taktshang

Thimphu

Kyichu
Lhakhang

Paro

Semtokha

Wangdue-
phodrang
dzong

Gangtey
Gonpa

Phobjika

Ha
dzong

HA

Chhuzom

TRONG

Chapcha
dzong

DAGANA

Punakha Tsang Chu

CHUKHA

Chukha
dzong

Daga dzong

TSIRANG

Tsirang

SAMTSE

Samtse

Gedu

Phuentsholing

Pasakh

Sarpang

SARPAN

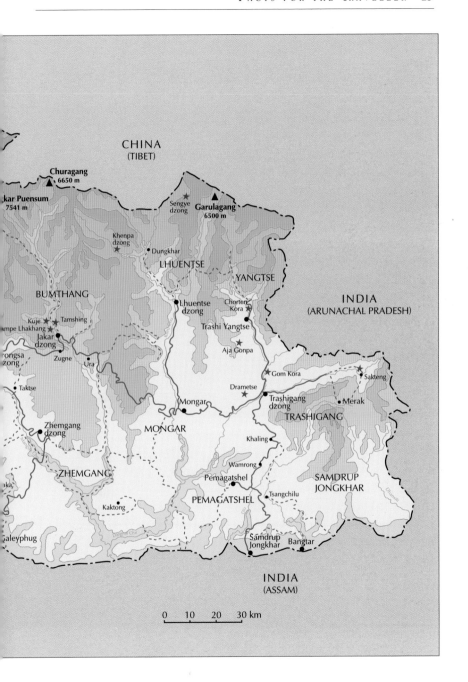

Etho Metho Tours, PO Box 360, Thimphu
Tel. (975-2) 323162, 323693, 322112, 322113; Fax. (975-2) 322884
E-mail: dagoethometho@druknet.bt; www.ethometho.com

Gangri Tours and Trekking Co., Ltd.
PO Box 60–7, Norzin Lam, Thimphu. Tel. (975-2) 323556; Fax. (975-2) 323322
E-mail: gangri@druknet.bt; www.gangri.com

International Treks & Tours, Thimphu. E-mail: intrek@druknet.bt

Jachung Tours & Treks, PO Box 789, Thimphu
Tel. (975-2) 22402; Fax. (975-2) 32274
E-mail: jachung@druknet.bt; www.jachung-bhutan.com

Keys to Bhutan, PO Box 432, Thimphu
Tel. (975-2) 327232; Fax. (975-2) 322490
E-mail: mail@keystobhutan.com; www.keystobhutan.com

Kiga Conferences & Tours, Thimphu
Tel. (975-2) 322221; Fax (975-2) 329153, 351005; E-mail: ki_ga@druknet.bt

Lhomen Tours & Treks, PO Box 341, Thimphu
Tel. (975-2) 324148; Fax. (975-2) 323243
E-mail:lhomen@druknet.bt, www.lhomen.com.bt

Mandala Tours & Treks
Tel. (975-2) 323676, 324842; Fax. (975-2) 323675
E-mail: mandala@druknet.bt; www.bhutanmandala.com

Rainbow Tours and Treks, PO Box 641, Thimphu
Tel. (975-2) 323270; Fax. (975-2) 322960
E-mail: rainbow@druknet.bt; www.bootan.com

Tashi Tours and Travels, Thimphu
Tel. (975-2) 323027; Fax. (975-2) 323666
E-mail:tashitour@druknet.bt, www.bhutantashitours.com

Yangphel Tours and Travels, Chorten Lam, Thimphu
Tel. (975-2) 323293; Fax. (975-2) 322897
E-mail: info@yangphel.com; www.yangphel.com, www.bhutanexplorer.com

Yu-Druk Tours & Treks, PO Box 140, Thimphu
Tel. (975-2) 323461; Fax. (975-2) 322116
E-mail: info@yudruk.com; www.yudruk.com

ENTRY OR EXIT BY AIR

Tourists may enter and leave Bhutan by air, but at least one of these flights is obligatory. Druk Air is the national airline, operating, since 1983, out of Paro Airport. Its name comes from Bhutan's name in Dzongkha, Druk Yul.

The fleet currently consists of two seventy-seat, four-engine British Aerospace 146 aircraft and two one hundred twenty seat Airbus A 319. They fly to Calcutta, Bangkok, Delhi and Kathmandu. Dhaka and Yangon are not anymore reached by Druk Air, but Druk Air flies to Gaya near the holy place of Bodhgaya in Bihar (India) in winter. It will extend its network to Chennai, Mumbai, Gauhati and Singapore in 2006.

Large groups can apply to Druk Air for a charter flight, departing Paro, Calcutta, Bangkok, Delhi, or Kathmandu.

From October to April, flights from Kathmandu offer exceptional views of some of the highest Himalayan summits: Cho Oyu (8,153 m/26,750 ft), Nubtse (7,855 m/25,770 ft), Everest (8,848 m/29,030 ft), Lhotse (8,516 m/27,940 ft), Makalu (8,463 m/27,765 ft), Kanchenjunga (8,586 m/28,170 ft) and Jomolhari (7,316 m/ 24,005 ft).

Mountain flights are available on request and last one hour. They provide spectacular views of the eastern Himalayan range.

A guide and a bus provided by the travel agency meet tourists at Paro Airport, which is an hour and fifteen minutes' drive from the capital, Thimphu.

The Druk Air timetable varies according to the season because of weather conditions. Flight times can also change without prior notice. It is best to check with the Druk Air agent in the city of departure.

All air fares are payable in US dollars (cash or travellers' cheques) whether to the Bhutanese agency or directly to Druk Air. Credit cards were still not accepted in mid 2005.

Druk Air is not an IATA company and reservations are generally made by the travel agency or the organization sponsoring the visitor. It is impossible to buy a Druk Air ticket without having a "visa clearance number" (issued by the Foreign Ministry, through your host agency in Bhutan, to Druk Air offices).

To give an idea of prices, in 2005, Kathmandu-Paro cost US$190, Delhi-Paro US$315 and Bangkok-Paro US$360.

Important: Paro Airport is hemmed in by mountains, and climatic conditions can arise that make flying and landing impossible. Travellers should avoid tight flight connections and ideally should plan for a day between the flight out of Bhutan and their following flight.

All information regarding flight schedules, fares, etc., can be found on the Druk Air Web site: www.drukair.com.bt. Information can also be obtained from the following:

Druk Air Corporation Ltd.
Nemizampa., Paro, Bhutan. Tel. 975-8-27856/857/860; Fax 975-8-271861
E-mail: drukair@druknet.bt; www.drukair.com.bt; SITA: QJCRRKB

Druk Air Corporation
PO Box 209, Thimphu, Bhutan. Tel. 975-2-322-215; Fax 975-2-322-775
E-mail: drukair@druknet.bt; www.drukair.com.bt; SITA: QJCRRKB

Druk Air offices outside Bhutan:
New Delhi, India
Druk Air Corporation
Ansal Bhawan Building Ground floor 3, 16 Kasturba Gandhi Marg, Connaught Place, 110001 New Delhi. Tel. 91-11-335-7703/4; Fax 91-11-335-7768
E-mail: drukair-delhi@vsnl.com; SITA: DELKKKB, DELCOKB

Druk Air Corporation Ltd.
IGI Airport, Terminal Building, New Delhi. Tel. 565-3207, 565-2011, ext. 2238

Kolkota (formerly Calcutta), India
Druk Air Corporation Ltd.
51 Tivoli Court, 1A Ballygunge Circular Road, Kolkota
Tel. 91-33-240-2419; Fax 91-33-247-0050; Airport Tel. 511 9976
E-mail: drukcal@vsnl.net; SITA: CCURRKB

Kathmandu, Nepal
GSA Malla Treks
Lekhnath Marg, PO Box 5227, Kathmandu, Nepal
Tel. 977-1-4410089, 4423145; Fax 977-1-4423143
E-mail: drukair@mallatreks.com.np; SITA: KTMKKKB

Bangkok, Thailand
Druk Air Corporation Ltd.
Room 3237, Central Block, Bangkok International Airport, Thailand
Tel. 66-2-5351960, 5354901; Fax 66-2- 5353661
E-mail: drukair@loxinfo.co.th; SITA: BKKRRKB

GSA-Thai Airways Int. Co. Ltd. 485 Silom Road, 10500 Bangkok ,Thailand
Tel. 66-2-243310019; Fax 66-2-2376124, Reservations: 66-2-233810

Prayer flags broadcasting to the gods surround spring rhododendron in Paro.

PSA-Oriole Travel & Tours Co. Ltd.
10/12-13 SS Building, Convent Road, 10500 Bangkok, Thailand
Tel. 66-2-23504112, 2334714; Fax 66-2-2367186; E-mail: oriole@samart.co.th

AIRPORT TAX

Leaving Bhutan in 2005, the airport tax is Nu500 (US$12) per person departing Paro. For departures for Bhutan from foreign airports, there are also airport taxes, which vary according to the country. This information would have to be sought in each country.

ENTRY OR EXIT BY LAND

One of the two legs (entry/exit) of one's Bhutan visit can be made overland, from or to India. This requires an Indian visa, which would have to be obtained from an Indian Embassy. Entry to or exit from Bhutan is made via the border town of Phuentsholing, which is three and a half hours' drive from the Indian airport of Bagdogra (with daily flights to and from Delhi and Calcutta). The trip between Phuentsholing and Paro or Thimphu takes about seven hours. Overland entry to Bhutan is recommended because it makes the visitor aware of the rugged geography and the relative inaccessibility of the central valleys.

The visitor's visa is issued at Phuentsholing and costs US$20. The visa procedures are the same as for entry by air.

VISAS

Important: Bhutan does not issue visas outside the country. The traveller must provide passport details and a photograph by fax or e-mail at least fifteen days in advance to the Bhutanese Tour operator (TO) or institution through which the traveller is visiting Bhutan. The TO or institution is responsible for the formalities and for obtaining the "visa clearance number" from the Foreign Ministry. It is impossible to board the flight if this procedure has not been completed beforehand. The visa is stamped in the passport upon arrival at Paro Airport or Phuentsholing border post and costs US$20, payable in cash; one identity photograph is required as well.

For any additional information concerning the tourism policy, write to:
Department of Tourism, Ministry of Trade and Industries
PO Box 126, Thimphu, Bhutan
Tel. 975-2-323-251/52, 325-12/2; Fax 975-2-323-695
E-mail: tab@druknet.bt; www.tourism.gov.bt

EMBASSIES AND MISSIONS

Reminder: Bhutanese embassies and diplomatic missions do not issue tourist visas (*see* above).

INDIA

The Royal Bhutanese Embassy, Chandragupta Marg, Chanakyapuri, New Delhi 110021. Tel. 688-9807; Fax 91-11-687-6710; E-mail: bhutan@vsnl.com

BANGLADESH

Royal Bhutanese Embassy, House # F5 (SE), Gulshan Avenue, Dhaka 1212 Tel. 886-863, 887-160; Fax 880-2-883-939; E-mail: bhtemb@bdmail.net

SWITZERLAND

Permanent Mission of the Kingdom of Bhutan to the United Nations, Geneva 17–19, chemin du Champ-d'Asnier, CH-1209 Genève.
Tel. 41-22-799-0890; Fax 41-22-799-0899; E-mail: mission.bhutan@ties.itu.int

UNITED STATES OF AMERICA

Bhutan Permanent Mission to the UN, 2 United Nations Plaza, New York, NY, 10017. Tel. 1-212-826 1919; Fax 1-212-826 2998; E-mail: pmbnewyork@aol.com

CUSTOMS

The export of antiques, *zi* (etched agates), plants, flowers, butterflies or animal products is strictly prohibited. As well, the export of religious objects, whether old or new, is prohibited. Statues, prayer wheels, reliquaries, bells, *vajra* and other religious objects, apart from new *thangka*, cannot be exported. It is best, therefore, to avoid problems and to buy such items in Delhi, Kathmandu or Sikkim. If the object was purchased before entering Bhutan, declare it on the customs form and tell the Bhutanese guide. However, it is possible to export a new religious object purchased from established shops, with a certificate obtained from the Department of Antiquities (under the National Commission for Cultural Affairs). The guide will carry out the formalities. It is strongly advised, in the interest of preserving the country's heritage, not to buy objects directly from villagers. It is wiser to ask in stores for a bill for the purchase of each object, in order to prove the legitimacy of the purchase to customs; an object without a bill can be seized. Keep with great care the form handed to you on arrival. It will be requested on departure. Tobacco products are prohibited for importation.

MONEY

The currency of Bhutan is the *ngultrum* (Nu.), divided into 100 *chetrums*. The *ngultrum* has the same value as the Indian rupee (just to give an idea, about 43 Nu for one US dollar, and 55 Nu for one euro in 2005). The Indian rupee is also accepted as legal tender.

Tourists can change their travellers' cheques or their cash at the BOB (Bank of Bhutan) or at the BNB (Bhutan National Bank) in Thimphu, as well as in hotels. The Swiss franc, the euro, the pound sterling, the Japanese yen and the American dollar are the accepted currencies.

Credit cards are still in little use. Visa and American Express cards are accepted in only a few stores in Thimphu and it is not possible to withdraw money with international cards.

Transfer money by Western Union is possible through the General Post Office in Thimphu (www.bhutanpost.com.bt).

Note: In 2005 Bhutanese tour operators and Druk Air do not accept credit cards in payment for services.

POST AND COMMUNICATIONS

The Bhutanese postal system is rather slow but reliable. The honesty and good will of Bhutanese postal workers are worthy of mention.

According to the 2005 rates, postage for post cards to all destinations (except India, Nepal and Bhutan) was 20 Nu. For letters to Europe, Asia and the Americas it was 20 Nu. as well, and for India, Nepal and Bhutan, 5 Nu. A letter takes, on average, between a week and ten days to reach Europe and Japan, and three weeks to the Americas and Australia. It is best to send packages (up to five kilograms) by registered post. DHL and UPS have an agent in Thimphu, and the General post office now has an EMS Service as well.

Bhutanese stamps are beautiful and delight collectors. (philatelicbureau@druknet.bt, www.bhutanpost.com.bt). At the post office in Thimphu, ask at the philatelic counter to see the stamp albums; you can also buy first day covers. The ladies selling the stamps exhibit amazing patience.

Stamps are also found at a counter in the Druk Shopping Complex and in the handicrafts shop at the Dragon Roots hotel.

It is possible to telephone or fax abroad very easily from Phuntsholing, Paro, Thimphu, Wanduephodrang, Punakha, Trongsa, Bumthang, Mongar and Trashigang.

Small public booths with yellow l'ozange signs are everywhere. Travel agencies in Bhutan have fax machines and e-mail addresses that can be given to families in case of emergency. There are satellite links and communications are excellent. Communications inside Bhutan that are now possible from regional centres have really revolutionized life. For isolated places, wireless is still used.

B-Telecom has a mobile phone network in Phuntsholing, Paro, Thimphu, Wangdue, Punakha Samdrupjongkhar and it is expanding fast. However, because of its large number of subscribers, it is often difficult to get the signal. Foreigners travelling with their own phone linked to a foreign provider might have problems to call.

INTERNET

Internet access facilities are found in Paro, Thimphu and Bumthang and continue to expand. There are some Internet places and the post office offers this service. The rates are reasonable.

Bhutan has several Web sites that are very interesting for anyone wishing to familiarize themselves with the country, and to become aware of changes. All these sites have links with other Internet sites (*see also* page 305).

www.tourism.gov.bt	Tourism Department
www.drukair.com.bt	The National Airline
www.druknet.bt	The national provider, numerous links
www.kuenselonline.com	The national newspaper site, many links
www.bbs.com.bt	The Bhutan Broadcasting Service (BBS)
www.bhutanstudies.org.bt	The Centre for Bhutan studies
www.undp.org.bt	the UN in Bhutan, statistics and reports
www.rspn-bhutan.org	Royal Society for Protection of Nature
www.youthdevfund.gov.bt	Youth developement fund, Bhutan
www.tarayanafoundation.org.bt	Tarayana Foundation
www.qsl.net/a51aa/	Thimphu Ham radio club
www.bhutan.at	Bhutanese art and culture exhibition
www.vast-bhutan.org	Voluntary Artists Studio Thimphu
www.bhutannewsonline.com	General information on Bhutan; hotels

http://bhutan.free.fr: French language site, information about Bhutan, links to Bhutanese websites and is the website of the friendship organization "Les Amis du Bhoutan".

LOCAL TIME

Bhutan's time is six hours ahead of Greenwich Mean Time in winter and five hours in summer. Bhutan's time is half an hour ahead of India's. When it is 12 noon in New Delhi, it is 12.30 pm in Bhutan. Bhutan is 20 minutes ahead of Nepal. When it is 12 noon in Kathmandu, it is 12.20 pm in Bhutan. Bhutan is 1 hour behind Thailand. When it is 12 noon in Bangkok, it is 11 am in Bhutan.

HEALTH

INOCULATIONS

Although no inoculations are compulsory, it is advisable to have tetanus and typhoid shots (TAB). In addition, Hepatitis A vaccine is recommended. The inoculations should be spread out over a period of six weeks. If you expect to stay and live in Bhutan, you should also be vaccinated against polio, diphtheria, meningitis and measles as well as rabbies.

PRECAUTIONS

Amoebae and giardiae (parasites that cause dysentery) are fairly common. Avoid drinking unboiled water or ice cubes, and never eat unpeeled fruit or raw vegetables. Bear in mind that tablets for disinfecting water are not effective against all types of amoeba. Bottled mineral water can be purchased throughout Bhutan.

People susceptible to car sickness should not travel in Bhutan unless they bring adequate medicine. The roads have thousands of curves and turns and the straight stretches can be counted on the fingers of two hands. One long-term resident of Jakar in the centre of the Kingdom claims there is a bend on average once every nine seconds.

MALARIA

Malaria is endemic in the southern region and and no anti-malarial is really effective. In case of an attack, take a dose of Nivaquine. In case of an attack, take one dose (three tablets) of Fansidar. In any event, keep plenty of mosquito repellent, cream or lotion on any exposed areas of skin when you are outdoors and burn mosquito coils, when possible, indoors (available in Thimphu and in the south).

ALTITUDE

The average altitude during a trip is 2,300 metres (7,500 feet) but on a trek it may reach as high as 5,400 metres (17,500 feet). Altitude sickness can be a serious problem for travellers. If you start to get a bad headache, cough, nauseous, loss of appetite or have urine retention on a trek, go down immediately. Altitude sickness can be fatal and must be taken seriously. All trekking guides are well trained in the perils of this ailment.

It is advisable to drink considerably more liquids at high altitudes than at sea level as dehydration is common. If you have heart problems or high blood pressure, you should consult your own doctor before undertaking a trip to Bhutan. A mild sleeping pill can be helpful against insomnia caused by the altitude. Headaches are common during the first days of a trip; it is best to keep away from any alcoholic drinks until you are acclimatized.

MEDICATION
Bring all your customary medicines with you plus a laxative, an anti-diarrhoea medicine (an oral rehydration solution is also very helpful in case of diarrhoea), antihistamine tablets, anti-nausea tablets (in case of mountain sickness), eye lotion, lip salve and one or two syringes with disposable needles. Thimphu has several pharmacies that are well stocked with antibiotics and analgesics. Medicine can be purchased over the counter.

HOSPITALS
The hospital at Thimphu may not be a Western facility but it is the best equipped in the country, with general physicians, specialists and dentists, a laboratory for tests and an operating room, and an intensive care unit. All patients praise its professionalism and levels of sanitation. Simpler hospital units exist in all major centres throughout the country. Medical care is free. The government has succeeded in its objective of providing free medical facilities within reasonable reach of all Bhutanese.

Indigeneous hospitals provide traditional treatments in Thimphu and Bumthang. There is no private practice, or clinic.

CLIMATE
It is hard to generalize about Bhutan's weather since the mountain climate varies enormously from one region to another. It varies with the altitude and can also reach extremes of heat and cold within the same 24 hours at any given altitude.

Southern Bhutan is tropical, with a monsoon season. The east is warmer than the west. The central valleys of Punakha, Wangduephodrang, Mongar, Trashigang and Lhuentse enjoy a semi-tropical climate with very cool winters, whereas Ha, Paro, Thimphu, Trongsa and Bumthang have a much harsher climate, including snowfalls in winter. The north of the country is inhabited up to 5,000 metres (16,400 feet) in summer. The climate there is rough, with monsoon rains in summer and heavy snowfalls in winter that block the passes leading into the central valleys.

In the valleys where most tourist activities are concentrated, the winters (mid-November to mid-March) are dry, with daytime temperatures of 16–18°C (60–65°F) if the sun is shining. By contrast the evenings and early mornings are cold, with night-time temperatures falling below freezing. Snow always covers the mountain tops but reaches the valleys only two or three times each winter.

Spring lasts from mid-March to the beginning of June, with temperatures warming gradually to 27–29°C (80–84°F) by day and 18°C (64°F) at night. However, cold spells are possible up until the end of April, with a chance of new snow on the mountains above the valleys. Strong, gusty winds start blowing almost every day from noon to about 6 pm, raising clouds of dust. (Many roofs get blown off in this season!) The first storms break, and they become more and more frequent with the approach of the monsoon which arrives in mid-June. This brings the rainy season. Bhutan then receives abundant rain, especially in the south, as it gets the full force of the monsoon coming up from the Bay of Bengal, to which its mountains form a barrier. However, apart from the first days of the monsoon when it rains without stopping, the rain falls mainly in the late evening and at night. Temperatures get a little cooler, 23–24°C (73–75°F) by day and 15–16°C (59–61°F) at night, but the sun often comes out from behind the clouds and the days are very pleasant. It is worth noting that, unless you are extremely lucky, it is almost impossible to get a clear view of the high Himalayas from the end of March until the end of September.

At the end of September, after the last of the heavy showers, autumn suddenly arrives. All at once the sky clears, a brisk breeze picks up and temperatures start falling towards freezing at night although bright sunshine continues to keep the days warm. Autumn is a magnificent season that lasts until mid-November.

Watching a religious dance, these young novices relax during one of Bhutan's annual festivals.

CLOTHING

The wide range of temperatures does not make dressing easy. The best solution is to wear several layers, such as a cotton shirt, pullover, wool cardigan or fleece jacket and jacket or wind breaker, which can be taken off or added to as required. Do not bring delicate clothes but opt, rather, for a sport or casual style.

Even in summer you will need a sweater or a light jacket in the evening. An umbrella is required in all seasons. It is more useful than a raincoat and acts as protection not only against the rain but also against the sun, which can be fierce at these altitudes. Comfortable sports shoes are strongly recommended; mountain boots are necessary if you plan to walk up to Taktsang, sneakers are sufficient.

From May to September, cotton clothes are sufficient, plus a woollen sweater or light jacket. From November to the end of April, on the other hand, you will need very warm clothes including long underwear or woollen tights to wear under trousers, and a down jacket or coat. Houses are poorly heated; the electricity is sometimes cut off and rooms can become icy cold especially at night when the temperature indoors can drop to 3–4°C (37–39°F). Hotels are fairly well heated in Thimphu and Paro but can be a little chilly the further east you travel.

Clothes dry fast and you are able to get your laundry returned, washed and ironed, on the following day in all the hotels at Thimphu, Paro, Phuentsholing, Bumthang and Trashigang. Dry cleaning takes a week!

The Bhutanese are conservative and wear their own national costume. Clothes that are too tight-fitting, short or revealing, such as shorts, miniskirts or low-cut T-shirts, cause offence, especially in the countryside and in government offices, and should be avoided by visitors. If you are going to meet a member of the government, city clothes are required (jacket and tie for men, skirt or dressy trousers for women).

Etiquette: Headgear must be removed when entering religious monuments or *dzong*. Moreover, shoes must be removed before entering temples.

EQUIPMENT AND SUPPLIES

In addition to the medicines mentioned under the heading 'Health', it is useful to take the following items: sun cream, lip balm, water bottle, pocket flashlight, pocket knife, sunglasses, headscarf/hat (hat and gloves from November to April), water purifier, insect repellent (from May to September), slippers/socks for visiting temples and ear plugs against the barking of dogs at night. Batteries, toilet paper, tissues, wet-wipes and all hygiene products are easily found in the urban centres and a trekking gear shop opened in 2005 in the centre of Thimphu.

Coffee-lovers should take their favourite brand. Herbal teas and packaged soups are also useful for days when you are not feeling well. Dry sausage, pâté and cheese make ordinary picnics more interesting (but avoid tinned food, as disposing of the tins is a problem).

Unfortunately dogs' barking cannot really be banned and it is better to take earplugs to counter their enthusiastic barking and howling at night.

Spirits and wine are available at the government duty-free shop in Thimphu. These purchases are payable in US dollars (cash). Local alcohol is available everywhere as well as beer.

Bhutan is waging a battle against tobacco and the sale of all tobacco products has been prohibited from December 2004. Smoking is now banned in all public places, indoors and outdoors. This means that, as of March 2005, tourists who wish to smoke may only do so in their hotel room.

PHOTOGRAPHY

All your photographic materials must be taken with you, including film and batteries. In Thimphu and Bumthang it is possible to find some types of batteries and print film, but slide film is more difficult. There are no facilities for the repair of photographic equipment. Video cameras are allowed. It is forbidden to photograph in religious monuments or in *dzong*.

ELECTRICITY

Bhutan's electricity is 220V. Power cuts occasionally occur, even in Thimphu. In the rest of the country, the power supply depends on many factors and can be irregular. Always keep a torch (flashlight) handy.

FOOD AND DRINK

Lack of variety prevents Bhutanese cooking from ranking among the world's great cuisines, but it is nonetheless quite exotic and interesting. There are three conditions for fully appreciating Bhutanese cooking: you should like hot, spicy food, you should like meat fat, and you should like dried meat. However, to set your mind at rest, there are many vegetable dishes that do not contain the last two ingredients though hot chilli peppers are to be found in some form in many of them. In the last seven years, the hotel operators have worked hard with

(Following pages) *Samples of famous Bhutanese textiles:*
'onsham', 'kishutara', 'yatra', *and* 'mensimathra'.

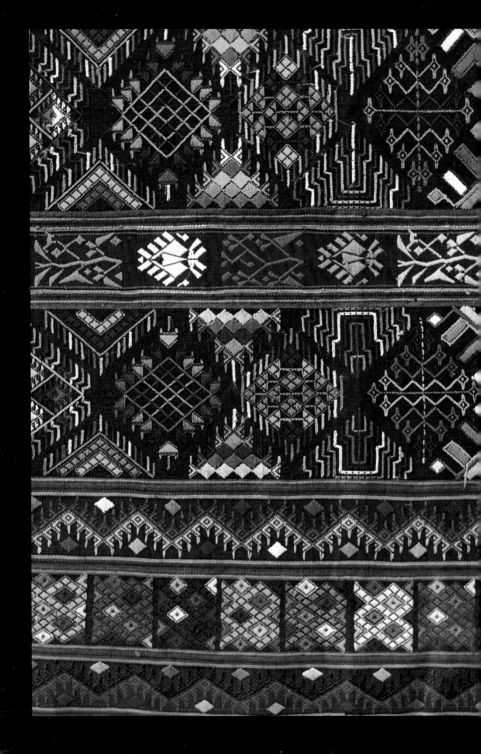

international culinary professionals to trains local chefs to temper Bhutanese food to Western tastes. The training has worked and visitors will be pleasantly surprised to find traditional Western food on the buffet table.

The national dish, *hemadatsi*, is made entirely of chillies (*hema*), treated as a vegetable rather than as seasoning, and served in a cheese sauce. Nowadays, a typical Bhutanese meal consists of a mountain of rice (the Bhutanese eat up to a kilo of rice a day) and two or three dishes with various stews, the number of which increases with the status of the family. The rice may be white or red; the latter is a special variety, not whole-grain rice. Rice is becoming increasingly the staple food throughout the country whereas, until quite recently, buckwheat pancakes (*kule*) and noodles (*puta*) were the main component of the diet of Bumthang in central Bhutan, and maize in the eastern regions.

Melted, soft fresh cheese (*datsi*) is used to make the sauce in which many vegetables are cooked, especially potatoes, mushrooms, asparagus and fiddlehead ferns (*Sp. Dipladsium esculentum*). The Bhutanese are skilled at using wild food products from the forests: fiddleheads, bamboo, mushrooms, taro, yams, sweet potatoes, wild beans, banana-flower buds, even orchids and dried river weed. Soya beans are only eaten in certain areas of eastern Bhutan.

Most stews contain a little meat or small bones. The favourite meats of the northern Bhutanese are yak and pork. Beef and chicken are the second choice, while mutton and lamb were traditionally not eaten. Meat can be eaten fresh or dried and, except in summer, it is common to see strips of meat drying on lines or hanging from windows. Pork-fat is considered a delicacy, and the best of all and the second most popular national dish after *hemadatsi* is undoubtedly *phagshapa* strips of pork-fat, often dried, stewed with radishes or turnips and dried chillies.

Scrambled eggs cooked in butter are the main ingredient of *gondomaru*, while Bhutanese salad, *eze*, composed of hot peppers, soft cheese, tomatoes and finely chopped onions, complements other dishes. Fresh fish is rare because religious considerations rule out fishing, but dried fish brought up from the plains makes a tasty stew mixed with hot peppers. Small pieces of liver dredged in chilli powder, lung stuffed with a special variety of pepper, pig's feet and blood sausages filled with hot peppers are specialities that the casual visitor will probably not have an opportunity to taste.

Many different Western foods such as Swiss cheese, honey and jam are now prepared inside the Kingdom and are readily available in stores all over Bhutan.

Rice is eaten with the right hand, pressed into a small ball and dipped in the stew, or alternated with bits of meat or vegetable. The pungent hot peppers often cause noses and eyes to run, but this just provides proof of a properly seasoned meal. Sweets and desserts barely exist except for *kabze*, dried fritters in various shapes that are prepared for festivals.

Roasted flour, called *pchie* (similar to the Tibetan *tsampa*), toasted rice (*zao*), flattened rice (*sip*) and flattened maize (*gesasip*) are served with tea as an appetizer or for breakfast. They can be eaten dry or dipped in the tea.

Tea is generally considered to be the most widely consumed beverage, but it is worth noting that in parts of central and eastern Bhutan, *ara*, a distilled drink with almost 20 per cent alcohol content, is the most common drink. It is made of all kinds of cereals : millet, maize, wheat and rice.

There are two kinds of tea: *seudja*, which is tea churned with salt and butter, and *nadja*, tea brewed with milk and sugar in the Indian style. If you want black tea, ask for *pika*. Coffee, or rather Nescafé, is a recent innovation and a luxury which is not to be found in village homes.

The herbal tea called Tsheringma, produced by the indigeneous hospital, is very good and widely available.

Drinking pure milk is also a new habit that has not become widespread. Traditionally, milk has always been turned into butter and cheese. *Datsi*, the small, round, soft cheeses on sale in the market, are made from whey and are never eaten raw but are used to thicken sauces. Another kind of cheese is *churpi*, which you will see as a loop of big white cubes strung together. This cheese, made in yak-breeding areas, is nibbled between meals and is unbelievably hard. The last kind of cheese, and the most sought-after because it is the most difficult to find, comes from eastern Bhutan and is called *seudeu*. It resembles a greyish green blob and is sold in leather containers. Its pervasive smell and unappetizing appearance may repel foreigners, except the French. It is never eaten raw but is mixed in small quantities into broth to make soup.

Among specialities of Tibetan origin, by far the most popular are *momos*, small dumplings stuffed with meat, vegetables or cheese and either steamed or fried. *Thukpa* is a noodle soup that many people enjoy in winter. *Shabale* are deep-fried dumplings stuffed with minced meat. The more rarely found *trimomo* is a kind of steamed bun served with soup.

A meal often ends with the passing around of *doma*. *Doma* is a quid of betel, but in Bhutan this is much more than a simple aid to digestion. To offer *doma* to somebody is to express friendship and it is a symbol of sociability. Ready-made quid of betel wrapped in little paper cones can be bought perfectly easily but the true betel-lover prepares his own, which involves a whole ritual.

Fresh chillies on sale at Thimphu market.

Apart from its social significance, *doma* is an intoxicating substance on about the same level as tobacco, and also has harmful effects. The government is now trying to limit the use of *doma* and young people are eating less of it.

In the south of Bhutan, *supari* or *pan* takes the place of *doma*. There, the regional cooking is much less distinctive, being very close to the cuisines of India and Nepal. There are more vegetables, lentils and onions, and the favourite meats are mutton and chicken.

Various brands of Indian beer, as well as the Bhutanese white beer (Red Panda brand), are available in all urban centres, along with whisky, gin and rum produced in Bhutan, at reasonable prices. According to connoisseurs, Special Courier pure malt whisky is good. There is little wine but there are local alcoholic drinks made from grains, *ara* and *chang*, which are not always produced under the most hygienic conditions. A distillery in the Bumthang valley produces, at very reasonable prices, cider, apple wine, and apple and peach brandy, which is similar to schnapps. A gift of a bottle of Jonny Walker or Chivas Regal is most welcome by Bhutanese hosts.

Excellent Bhutanese mineral waters are also available.

For some twenty years now, Bumthang has also been producing, in limited quantity, some excellent cheeses, which resemble Ementhal, Gouda and Roblochon. Gogona valley in the Black mountains also started producing cheese in 2003.

LEISURE AND BEAUTY CARE

Thimphu has a swimming pool (closed in winter), tennis courts, a squash court, a soccer field, basketball court, archery field and a nine-hole golf course. There is also a table tennis club, a badminton club and a taekwondo club. Cricket is slowing catching on.

Appliqué and embroideries from a temple decoration.

In Thimphu, there are two fitness rooms, steam-bath and sauna facilities, as well as hair and beauty salons situated in the Druk Hotel, the Jomolhari Hotel and the Sakteng Club. Aerobic and yoga classes are offered there as well. Several other hair and beauty salons have opened recently and are very popular.

SHOPPING

Bhutan has fine indigenous handicrafts, although not many of them. Objects are fashioned from bamboo, wood and silver, and there are many kinds of fabric and even *thangkas*. Bhutanese handicrafts differ from those of other Asian countries in two respects: they are not oriented to the tourist market, thereby remaining authentic, and they are relatively expensive. Bargaining is not a custom in Bhutan so you cannot hope to get more than a ten per cent reduction. Today however, small souvenirs made of traditional materials are produced for the traveller with neither a lot of money or luggage space.

Outside of Thimphu, Paro and Bumthang, there is little or no choice or even availability of craft items, as crafts shops are practically nonexistent in the rest of Bhutan. You can, while travelling across the country, meet someone who will sell an object typical of the local region, but even this is not guaranteed. Thimphu is without question the place where you can form an opinion regarding differing quality, compare items and find those that are representative of all of Bhutan. One last piece of advice: if you see something you like, you should buy it immediately, because stocks do not exist.

As shops change quickly, names are provided here only to give an idea of what you might find. They all offer a very similar selection but the quality can vary. The weekly market in Thimphu offers a great variety of items, including instruments used for ritual music, but of varying quality, especially when it comes to textiles.

In Thimphu near the site of the weekly market several shops sell Chinese and Bangladeshi utilitarian goods at low prices, such as cups, shoes, radios, but also silk and brocade that remain reasonably priced. The best shop for silk in this area is Tshering Dorje Tshongkhang. For more information, see Crafts, page 94.

THANGKAS

In Thimphu, *thangka* (religious banners), which are new but painted according to traditional iconographic criteria, are found, in particular, at the Handicrafts Emporium, in shops around the School of Traditional Arts (*Institute for Zorig Chusum*) and at Choeki Handicrafts. They can be mounted on brocade or not; the choice is a personal one. Without brocade, prices start about 20 euros; large *thangka* with brocade can cost between 300 and 500 euros.

FABRICS AND CLOTHING

Handwoven fabrics are the pride of Bhutan and will remind textile-lovers of weavings from Laos, from Northeastern India or the from Central America and Peru. Prized around the world, some pieces are collector's items. Handwoven fabrics cannot be bought by the metre or yard.

The cheapest fabrics are plain cotton, while the most expensive are masterpieces, representing many months of intensive work, which are covered with silk designs on a base of either cotton or silk. There are different types of textile for different purposes: belts; the women's national dress (*kira*); the men's garment (*go*); the women's ceremonial scarves (*rachung*); and the men's (*kabne*); ceremonial cloths (*chasipangkhep*); bags (*pechung* or *bundi*); and rolls of woollen cloth from Bumthang called *yatra* which, when sewn, serve as coverlets, sofa covers or jackets.

A woman's *kira* is a simple rectangular piece of cloth 2.5 by 1.5 metres (roughly 2.5 by 1.5 yards). It is wound around the body, secured at the shoulders by two silver clasps and gathered in at the waist by a wide belt. A *kira* is usually made up of three pieces of cloth sewn together to form the rectangle, but it can also be made from a dozen narrow strips which in this case are always of wool. A man's *go* is cut somewhat like a kimono and reaches the ankles. It is pulled up to the knees and fastened at the waist by a narrower belt than the woman's, forming a large pouch over the abdomen.

In 2005, a simple cotton *kira* was worth about 20 euros, a cotton *kira* with silk designs 500 and 700 euros; and a silk *kira* with silk designs was between 1,200 and 2,300 euros. A *go* made of raw silk cost 180–200 euros; a woolen *go* or *kira* was between 100 to 200 euros, and *a yatra* between 200 and 250 euros. A man's belt cost 5 euros, and a woman's varied between 5 euros for the cheapest and 60 euros for a fine silk one. Prices vary considerably, according to the quality of the fabric. In Thimphu, stores that sell traditional fabrics of excellent quality are Tshering Drolkar, Yeedzin Handicrafts, Kurtoe Handicrafts, Kelzang Handicrafts, Druktrin Handicrafts and hotel shops.

Kira and *go*, made of machine-woven Bhutanese fabric, are inexpensive (about 15 euros) garments that make a nice souvenir of the trip; they have little value other than sentimental. They are found in the shops in the Druk Shopping Complex in Thimphu and in the small textile shops throughout Bhutan. These same shops also sell Bhutanese clothing for children. They are inexpensive because they are made of the same machine-woven fabric and make gifts that are appreciated. It is sometimes possible to buy lengths of raw silk, in its natural ecru colour, or dyed red, orange or dark blue, (these are, in fact, mens' ceremonial scarves) as well as shawls. A large choice of machine-woven Bhutanese fabric, as well as silk and Chinese brocade, is available at Sephup Tshongkhang inside the Druk Shopping Complex. For silk and brocade, try, as well, Tshering Dorje Tshongkhang near the weekly market where prices are slightly lower.

JEWELLERY AND SILVERWARE

The most popular products are wooden alcohol-receptacles mounted and decorated with beaten silver, and containers for ingredients used in the preparation of betel nut: these are rectangular boxes containing betel leaves and areca nut (about 150 Euros), and little round boxes to hold the lime.

Bhutanese jewellery is limited but spectacular: large clasps of chased silver connected by a chain, earrings of gold and turquoise, heavy silver bracelets with simple engraving or set with coral and turquoise, silver belt ornaments and elaborate pearl necklaces.

The silversmiths can also make statues, swords, superb traditional teapots or large goblets, but these items are only available on order, given their high price.

The best selection is found in Thimphu and Paro. In Thimphu, the Emporium, Norling and Tshering Drolkar Shop (in the same building as Druk Medical, on the main street, opposite the cinema square), Druktrin Handicrafts at the Wangchuk Hotel, Kelzang Handicrafts in the Druk Shopping Complex, and Norling in the Dragon Roots hotel sell Bhutanese and Tibetan jewellery. This last shop, as well as the Art shop, have an overall excellent selection of handicrafts. In Paro, several shops have opened recently, besides those in hotels, the Emporium, Made in Bhutan (which also sells photos and books) and Chencho Handicrafts in the central square. In Paro the Vajrayana Gallery sell modern paintings by a Bhutanese artist.

As well, one finds "ethnic" jewellery at very reasonable prices; in particular, rings adorned with coral, lapis lazuli or turquoise. This jewellery is either imported from Nepal or India, or made up on the premises to satisfy the needs of tourists who cannot always treat themselves to Bhutanese jewellery or who do not see themselves using it in the West.

WOODWORK

The most beautiful wooden objects are wall decorations and small tables called *chodom*; the latter are often designed to fold and almost always painted. Masks are of individuals, animals or deities represented in sacred dances. They can be made of wood, but also papier mâché, and are always painted. They come in two sizes, normal and small. Lacquered, turned-wood bowls, or *phop*, and the containers called *gofur* and *dapa*, vary considerably in price, depending on the quality of the wood (ordinary wood or burl) and whether or not they are decorated with silver. Wooden decorations and masks are found to some extent everywhere; those found at Choeki Handicrafts and in shops around the School of Traditional Arts shop in Thimphu are of very good quality, but the weekly Thimphu market also offers an interesting choice.

CARVED SLATE

You can sometimes find etched slate objects of excellent quality at the Handicrafts Emporium but their weight can create a problem if you are travelling by air.

BAMBOO AND RATTAN WARES

Common objects for everyday use are the cheapest, and among the most authentic souvenirs you can purchase. In certain shops in Thimphu and in the weekend market you will find tea or alcohol strainers, conical hats, quivers, tall baskets for serving rice, rectangular mats for sorting rice and other grains, or slender bamboo cylinders covered with braided strips and pierced with a hole—they are for carrying alcohol. Rectangular baskets with lids, called *zem*, are meant to be slung over the flanks of pack animals. They are now rare except in small sizes. Finally, there are the famous *banchung*, light round baskets decorated with coloured geometric designs whose two parts stack one inside the other and close tightly; they are very practical for carrying food and can also be used as plates.

PAPER AND BOOKS

Bhutanese paper (*see also* pages 89 and 293) is handmade in large, square sheets with flecks of bark still visible. It is excellent for painting on, for doing calligraphy or for making original gift-wrapping. It can be bought by the sheet at many handicraft stores in Thimphu.

The National Library Shop, a little way beyond the Emporium on the opposite side of the street, sells traditional Bhutanese books at affordable prices, as well as religious postcards. Paper making can be seen and different quality paper samples as well as gifts items can be purchased at the Jungzhi Handpaper Factory in Thimphu.

There are four bookshops where documents on Bhutan can be found: Pekhang, next to the cinema; KMT, in the main street, roughly opposite the Emporium; and DSB and Bookworld, both near the Druk Hotel. They carry fiction, books on Bhutan, Tibet and Buddhism, and even comic books.

It is possible to buy traditional books at reasonable prices as well as religious post cards and calendars at the KMT shop and the National Library shop, which are found a little higher up the main street than the Emporium, on the opposite side. Take note that the opening hours of this shop are flexible, but are generally from 9.30 am to 7 pm.

RUGS

Most of the good rugs that you find in Thimphu are not Bhutanese. Bhutan has always produced outstanding fabrics but never rugs. They were imported from Tibet and China. The best choice of rugs is at Tshering Drolkar and inside the Druk Shopping Complex there are a number of stores which sell Tibetan carpets, made in Nepal or in China. Some carpets have been produced in the south of Bhutan but their quality is not good.

OTHER THINGS TO BUY

Bhutan Handicrafts, near the Swiss Bakery, offers a nice choice of Bhutanese crafts, but also pashmina shawls and items from India.

Cassettes and CDs of Bhutanese music, be it traditional or *rigsar*, that is to say 'Bhutanese pop', are found especially at Norling, opposite the Druk Shopping Complex. The quality of recording is not great but they make nice souvenirs.

Some other interesting things you may find are waterproof black hats, made of yak hair, which come from the eastern region of Merak Sakteng. The appendages that stick out around them allow the rain to run off without getting your face wet. Wallets and other articles made out of traditional fabrics are very popular.

The only non-religious musical instrument, which can sometimes be purchased is the *dranyen* a kind of lute made of painted wood. At the weekly market in Thimphu, it is often possible to buy the long, copper, telescopic trumpets, and the oboes and cymbals that are used for religious ceremonies.

Prayer-flags and bundles of incense are available everywhere. The incense quality is better than that of Indian incense as it is composed of pure herbs mix without added sticks of wood for strength, but that means it is also much more fragile.

Bhutan's stamps (*see also* page 30) are greatly prized by collectors and are very cheap since they are sold at their postal value.

Maps of Bhutan and Thimphu, both of excellent quality, are finally available. T-shirts and sweatshirts with symbols of Buddhism and Bhutan are available. What may not be found in the shops can be found at Thimphu's weekend market.

Darjeeling tea is a good buy. Among the best brands are Lopchu or Makaibari Apoorva. Out of curiosity, take a look at the blackish cones and bricks of tea leaves that are used for making butter-tea.

Boots made of leather or felt are attractive but rather uncomfortable because they are very wide and Western feet tend to slop about in them. There is a specialised shop in Thimphu which custom make them.

Bhutanese machine-woven check material made of mixed wool and polyester can be bought by the metre. Warm and strong, it is intended for school uniforms and costs about 4 euros per metre. It makes excellent winter shirts, skirts or dresses. You can also find printed flannelette (ask for *pooche*) at about 1.5 euros a metre. You can have a shirt made for 3 to 4 euros in 24 hours by an Indian tailor. Unfortunately, these tailors do not know how to make skirts or dresses. Ask your guide where to find these tailors.

The two pieces of a Bhutanese woman's costume, which can be easily worn in the West, are the blouse (*onju*) and the little jacket (*toego*). Neither one fastens, both are cut on the same pattern and one size fits all, more or less. They can be found easily in traditional cloth shops. They are usually made of polyester and cost about 6 euros for the blouse, 15 euros for the jacket. When they are made of silk or imported brocade, the price goes up to 40 euros or more.

Ceremonial white scarves (*kata*) for presentation (*see* page 159) are found, in all traditional shops. The least expensive cost a few cents but they are made of coarse tulle and are not really presentable. The ones called *ashi kata* cost about 2 euros and are of a much better quality. The most expensive, which are offered on exceptional occasions, can cost up to 15 euros.

Various: A visit to the weekly market provides a chance to find everyday items that make original souvenirs that will be appreciated: calendars, prayer books, small butter lamps, yak hair rope, bamboo boxes, ara or tea strainers, wooden spoons and many other things. Curiously, one of the best purchases one can make in Thimphu are fleece clothes, jackets and blankets as well as outdoor clothes imported from Bangladesh.

MONUMENTS OPEN TO VISITORS

When visiting temples, it is usual to leave a small offering on the altar, in a plate meant for this purpose. This allows the visitor to contribute to keeping Bhutanese traditions alive.

Since January 1988, foreign visitors have been forbidden to visit most of Bhutan's temples, fortresses and monasteries. This decision was taken in order to protect the works of art, to prevent any commercialization of the religion, and to preserve the sanctity of its ceremonies. In exceptional cases and for a particular site, written permission may be granted by the Secretary of the National Commission for Cultural Affairs. Please make the request to visit a certain site well in advance through the organiser of your travel itinerary.

The list of religious monuments where tourists were still permitted to enter was as follows in 2005:

WESTERN BHUTAN

Paro district: Ta *dzong* (National Museum), Drukyel *dzong*, viewpoint looking at Taktsang from the small tea-house, Bitekha *dzong*.

At Thimphu: Tashichoedzong (in winter when the monks are at Punakha), Memorial Chorten of the Third King, Temples of Changlimithang and Jigmeling.

Chukha district: Temples of Zangdopelri and Kharbandi at Phuentsholing, Temples of Kamji, Chasilakha and Chime, and Chapcha *dzong*.

Punakha district: Punakha *dzong* (in summer when the monks are in Thimphu).

CENTRAL BHUTAN

Jakar (Bumthang) district: Wangduchoeling *dzong*, Sacred Lake of Mebartsho, Temple of Ura.

EASTERN BHUTAN

Mongar district: Mongar *dzong*.

Trashigang district: Temple of Zandopelri at Kanglung, Temples of Radi, Trashi Yangtse *dzong*, Chorten Kora.

GEOGRAPHY

GEOGRAPHY AND POPULATION

Bhutan's isolation from the Western world can be explained in part by its geography. Located between India and the autonomous region of Tibet, China, between 88°45' and 92°10' longitude east and between 26°40' and 28°15' latitude north, the country covers 46,500 square kilometres (18,147 square miles). Bhutan forms a gigantic staircase from a narrow strip of land in the south at an altitude of 300 metres (985 feet) up to high Himalayan peaks in the north with an altitude of over 7,000 metres (23,000 feet). The population was estimated in 2004 at 700,000 inhabitants and a census was carried out in June 2005. These statistics will be available at the end of 2005. Therefore, Bhutan has a population density of approximately 13 people per square kilometre. The gross national product of US$ 710 per person in 2002 is a notable jump from the US$51 of 1961.

Eighty per cent of the population still live off cultivation and live-stock rearing on only 7.8% of arable land, but this has been decreasing since the mid-1980s, with the appearance of a middle-class, consisting of civil servants and business people, and since the mid-90s, workers in the private tertiary sector, which receives incentives from the government.

ACCESS

The most densely populated and fertile regions are the southern borderlands, the foothills of the Himalayas, with an altitude between 300 and 1,600 metres (985–5,250 feet) and the central valleys, with an altitude between 1,100 and 2,600 metres (3,600–8,530 feet). Until the 1960s, the central valleys were very hard to reach from the south because a formidable mountain wall rises 2,000 metres (6,500 feet) from the plain, cut through with jungle-filled gorges that made travel dangerous and slow. It took five days to cover the hundred-odd kilometres (150 miles) of paths that separated the capital of Thimphu from Buxa Duar on the Indian border.

Paradoxically, until the closing of the border with Tibet in 1959, the High Himalayas provided easy access in several places, with certain passes open even in winter. There were numerous cultural and economic exchanges between the two countries, going all the way back to the seventh century.

In the first half of the 20th century, some of the more accessible regions of south Bhutan were settled by people of Nepalese origin who were used to low altitudes. In 1962, a paved road was constructed for north-south traffic linking Thimphu with Phuentsholing in the southwest, and in 1963 another was completed between Trashigang and Samdrup Jongkhar in the southeast.

SOUTHERN BHUTAN: THE FOOTHILLS

With the coming of the paved road, the narrow southern plain, formerly called the Duars, 'the Gates', and the Himalayan foothills—up to 1,700 metres (5,575 feet)—could now be made productive. The proximity of markets in northern India and Bangladesh contributed to the development of these areas and small trading towns came into existence: Phuentsholing, Geylegphug and Samdrup Jongkhar. Small industries producing such goods as alcohol, bricks, clothes, matches, fruit juice and jam started up in this border region. Two big cement plants, Panden in the west and Nanglam in the east, and a calcium carbide factory at Pasakha, export the major part of their production. Apart from rice grown for local consumption, other crops, including oranges and cardamom, are directed towards foreign markets.

The southern regions are inhabited mainly by peasants of Nepalese origin—high caste people and tribal populations—who continued to immigrate from the end of the 19th century until about 1950. They are full Bhutanese citizens, officially designated as southern Bhutanese, "Lhotsampa". The southern Bhutanese speak the Nepalese language and most of them are Hindu. Although most of them do not, traditionally, belong to the main cultural stream of Bhutan, their importance to the country's development has been crucial and today they participate in all economic schoolors.

A policy of national integration begins in every Bhutanese primary school and throughout the country with the learning of English, the official language and the national language dzongkha.

THE CENTRAL HIMALAYAS: THE VALLEYS

In the central Himalayas, summer rice and winter wheat are grown in the valleys of Paro, Thimphu, Punakha, Wangduephodrang, Lhuentse and part of Trashigang; while barley, buckwheat and wheat are the crops of Ha and Bumthang which lie above 2,600 metres (8,500 feet). Since the beginning of the 1980s, potatoes have made a remarkable breakthrough in areas that are too high or too poor for rice. Thus, Chapcha, south of Thimphu, Bumthang, the glacial valley of Gangtey (Phobjika) near the Pele La (*la* means pass), and the Kanglung region near

Trashigang are experiencing an economic boom thanks to this tuber that has made itself at home in Bhutan. In most of the east, maize is the main crop, with the best soil saved for rice cultivation. Millet is grown everywhere and turned into alcohol. The Thimphu and Paro areas also produce peaches and plums but specialize in apples and asparagus. A large part of the two latter crops goes for export. Oranges and bananas, consumed locally, grow in Punakha, Wangduephodrang, Mongar, Lhuentse and Trashigang.

The raising of livestock—pigs, cattle and poultry—is widespread both in the central valleys and the south, but the purpose is home consumption rather than mass production. Sheep are raised in Bumthang to produce wool rather than meat, as the Bhutanese do not like mutton. Moreover, religious beliefs prevent the killing of animals for meat.

The central Himalayan region is the home mostly peasants and livestock breeders, who are of Mongoloid stock and speak languages of the Tibeto-Burmese family. Their dwellings are normally scattered but towns are now developing around the dzongs (monastery-fortresses) which formerly defended and administered each valley. Their appearance is directly related to the improved network of communications, the growth of an administrative infrastructure and the birth of a middle class made up of civil servants and small shopkeepers.

In addition to the High Himalayas which run east–west, mountain chains also run north–south at a height of 4,000–5,000 metres (13,000–16,400 feet), traversing the country and forming veritable barriers between different regions. Each of the central valleys is thus a microcosm separated from the next valley by a high pass (average altitude 3,000 metres, or almost 10,000 feet), a great hindrance to communications within the country. A main road now links up all the central valleys but it still takes three days under the best weather conditions to go from Ha in the west to Trashigang in the east.

The Black Mountains form the main watershed separating two river basins on either side, where the rivers are oriented north–south, watering the valleys. The rivers are turbulent, rushing through gorges before they empty on to the Indian plains to become large tributaries—the Torsa, Raidak, Sankosh and Manas—of the Brahmaputra. Their hydroelectric potential is enormous and a 336 megawatt power station, Chukha Hydel, has been built with Indian assistance on the Wang Chu (chu means 'river') and three others are being built: Tala Hydel (1,020 MW), also on the

(Following pages) Remains of the Drukyel dzong (burnt down in the early 1950s) guarding an entrance to Paro valley, with Jomolhari Mountain's snowy peak in the background.

Wang Chu; Kuri Chu Hydel (60 MW), in Eastern Bhutan, south of Mongar; and Baso Chu Hydel (60 MW), south of Wangduephodrang with Austrian assistance.

The central Himalayas, inhabited by people who call themselves collectively Drukpas, can thus be divided into three parts with very distinct characteristics, enhanced by the fact that each has its own language which is mutually incomprehensible from the others.

WESTERN BHUTAN

Western Bhutan is made up of the valleys of Ha, at 2,700 metres (8,850 feet), Paro, at 2,200 metres (7,200 feet), and Thimphu, at 2,300 metres (7,500 feet), while Punakha and Wangduephodrang, at 1,300 metres (4,260 feet), form a single long valley. Except for the Ha valley, which has a climate suited more for livestock raising and which used to be very active in trade with Tibet, western Bhutan is a land of rice paddies and orchards.

The relative wealth of the people can be seen in the very large houses that accommodate several generations. The walls are of rammed earth and straw, the upper storeys boasting remarkable woodwork with paintings frequently seen on the frames of the three-lobed windows and on the ends of beams. Wooden shingles, the traditional roofing material, have often been replaced by corrugated iron. However, traditional roofs have come back into favour and the opening of a slate mine provides a totally satisfactory alternative to shingles.

The mountain slopes are covered by fine coniferous and deciduous forests where logging is strictly controlled by the government. All the valleys are rich in reminders of the past: monasteries, temples and fortresses abound, and the country's permanent capital has been located in the Thimphu valley since the early 1950s.

The five valleys which make up western Bhutan are the domain of the Ngalong, 'the first to rise', meaning the first to convert to Buddhism, who speak Dzongkha, the 'language of the dzong', now the national language of Bhutan. Although related to Tibetan, it has many differences, particularly in the pronunciation of final syllables and the conjugation of verbs.

The Black Mountains (Durshing), at 5,000 metres (16,400 feet), have traditionally marked the boundary between western and central Bhutan. The main road, which goes from Paro to Trashigang, crosses them via the Pele La Pass, 3,300 metres (10,800 feet) high.

Castle of Ponaka (Punakha) in Boutan, J C Armytage.

Chapcha Castle, Bootan, 1837, J Cousen from a sketch by Davis.

CENTRAL BHUTAN

Central Bhutan is made up of several regions, all of which speak a language *(kha)* with local variations (Bumthangkha, Khyengkha, Kurtoekha). Its archaic forms place it linguistically in the eastern Proto-Bodish subgroup of the Tibeto-Burman family.

The most southerly district of central Bhutan is called Khyeng, a region blessed with a semi-tropical climate and famous for its dense jungle. The inhabitants of Khyeng understand the forest well and include in their diet all sorts of wild plants: yams, orchids, ferns, rattan shoots, tiny wild mangoes, banana flowers and even poisonous roots and seeds, which they are able to process in ways that make them edible. The people produce splendid bamboo and rattan basketwork.

Trongsa, north of Khyeng, lies along the main road. It is in a gorge cut by the Mangde River with a few cultivated areas terraced on its steep slopes. Bhutan's most impressive *dzong* holds a strategic and privileged position here.

A 3,300-metre- (10,800-foot) high pass, the Yutong La, leads to Bumthang which is a group of four valleys at altitudes of 2,700–4,000 metres (8,850–13,000 feet): Chume and Choekhor are mainly agricultural, Tang and Ura practise yak- and sheep-herding. The mountainsides are covered with dark coniferous forests, rice gives way to buckwheat. Potatoes have made their appearance in the 1970s and are now an important addition to the cash economy. The houses are built of stone rather than rammed earth and are more sparsely decorated than in western Bhutan. Bumthang is very proud of its rich art and history. Its religious traditions are very much alive and each monastery, each holy place, is the subject of long stories that blend myth with reality.

The region of Kurtoe (Lhuentse) to the northeast is separated from Bumthang by a pass at 4,000 metres (13,100 feet), the Rodong La. Kurtoe is closely connected to Bumthang by language and family-kinship, but geographically it belongs to eastern Bhutan. At lower altitudes (1,600–2,500 metres or 5,250–8,200 feet) rice and maize are grown, and this area is best known for its production of fine fabrics with varied and complex designs.

EASTERN BHUTAN

From Bumthang, the motor road crosses into the eastern region by a more southern pass than the Rodong La, the 4,100-metre- (13,500-foot-) high Thumsing La. Bhutan's east consists of the regions of Mongar, Trashigang and a southern part that includes Pemagatshel (the ancient Dungsam region) and extends as far as Samdrup

Jongkhar on the Indian border. This eastern region is the land of the Sharchopas, the 'people of the east'. They call themselves Tsanglas and speak their own language, Tsanglalo. The climate is generally warmer and drier, the forests thinner and the altitudes lower than in the west. It is a region of deep V-shaped valleys, with fields and dwellings clinging to the bare slopes. The main crop is maize, though rice and wheat can also be grown. Numerous cattle, especially the famous *mithun*, a native bull with spectacular horns, graze alongside the roads, roaming freely and rarely put in barns. Most of the houses are built in Bhutanese style, but one can still see some made of bamboo matting and raised on stilts, a reminder of the region's close proximity to Southeast Asia.

The Sharchopas are well known for their piety, and the land is dotted with small temples where *gomchens*, laymen trained in religious practices, live with their families away from monastic communities. As in Kurtoe, the women possess matchless weaving skills and produce magnificent fabrics of raw silk and cotton.

At the eastern tip of the country, three days' walk from Trashigang, lie the high valleys of Merak and Sakteng inhabited by herdsmen, semi-nomadic people belonging to a specific ethnic group with their own customs.

North of Trashigang is Trashi Yangtse, a beautiful rice-growing area. The valley of Bumdeling is a sanctuary for Black-necked cranes. It used to be on the trade path beween Kurtoe and Trashigang.People speak different languages but the most important is called Dzalakha.

NORTHERN BHUTAN: THE HIGH HIMALAYA

Lying above 3,500 metres (11,500 feet), northern Bhutan is the beginning of the High Himalayas. Lingshi, Laya and Lunana are inhabited by yak-herders who grow very little crops and, as such, could be considered as similar to the high valleys of Merak and Sakteng in the east and of Sephu in the Black Mountains. The high altitude limits cultivation to barley and root crops. The diet is made up essentially of milk, butter, cheese and yak meat. The inhabitants are semi-nomadic yak-herders. They spend most of the year in black tents woven from yak hair, but they also build drystone-walled houses, which serve as shelter during the coldest months of the year and as storehouses for the goods and grains that they barter with the central valleys.

FLORA AND FAUNA

The three relief zones (the foothills, the central Himalayan valleys and the High Himalayas) also define three climatic regions: tropical, temperate with monsoon, and alpine with monsoon. These climatic variations, coupled with the huge changes in altitude, make Bhutan a country with an extremely rich flora: within a distance of 70 kilometres (44 miles) one passes from rice paddies, banana and orange groves at 1,300 metres (4,200 feet) in the Punakha region, through deciduous forests and then an alpine forest (at Gasa), finally arriving in the Laya area where yaks graze and only barley and winter wheat can be grown.

The wealth of floral species (5400 recorded) includes 17 species of conifers, 46 species of rhododendrons, junipers and magnolias several metres (yards) high, carnivorous plants, rare orchids, blue poppies, edelweiss, gentians, primulas, artemisia, daphne, giant rhubarb, high-altitude plants, tropical and deciduous trees as well as medicinal plants. Bhutan is such a botanical paradise that one of its ancient names meant 'Southern Valleys of Medicinal Herbs'.

The species of fauna also varying according to the levels of vegetation are abundant (160 species), because the great majority of Bhutanese, for religious reasons, neither hunt nor fish.

Elephant, tigers, buffalo, one-horned rhinoceros (*Rhinocerus unicornis*) and leopards (*Panthera pardus*) populate the thick jungles of the south, while in the rivers, there is the masheer, a fish sometimes likened to a tropical salmon.

The central Himalayan region is the domain of pheasants (*Tragopan satyra* and *Lophophorus impejanus*), red pandas (*Ailurus fulgens*), langur monkeys (*Presbytis geei*), wild boar (*Sus scofra*), deer and above all, the fearsome white-collared black bears (*Selenarctos thibetanus*). The magnificent and elegant black-necked cranes (*Grus nigricollis*) migrate from Tibet to spend the winter in the isolated valleys of Phobjika and Bumdeling. The raven (*Corvus corax*) is the national bird. Traces of tigers have been spotted as high as 3400 metres`.

The high desolate spaces are the domain of yaks (*Bos gruniens*), and horned animals such as the tahr (*Hemitragus jemlahicus*) and goral (*Naemorhedus goral*), the shy blue sheep (*Pseudonis nayaur*), and musk deer (*Moschus chrysogaster*). Snow leopards (*Panthera uncia*) and takins (*Budorcas taxicolor*) are rarely seen.

HISTORY

ANCIENT TIMES

Archaeological research is still in its infancy, but stone implements found on the surface of the ground seem to indicate that the country was inhabited fairly early, probably around 2000 BC.

Secular and religious history in Bhutan are so intertwined that the religious school—the Drukpa—which prevailed from the 17th century on even gave its name to the country it unified and its inhabitants. Thus in the Dzongkha language, Bhutan is called Druk Yul and the Bhutanese people Drukpas. The poetic translation of Druk Yul is 'Land of the Dragon', which can be explained by the following anecdote. When Tsangpa Gyare Yeshe Dorje (1161–1211) was consecrating a new monastery in central Tibet at the end of the 12th century, he heard thunder, which popular belief holds to be the voice of a dragon (*druk*). He therefore decided to name the monastery 'Druk', and the religious school which he founded was likewise called 'Drukpa'. In the 17th century, when the Drukpas unified Bhutan, they gave it their name.

Before becoming Druk Yul, Bhutan was called by various other names: Lho Jong, 'The Valleys of the South'; Lho Mon Kha Shi, 'The Southern Mon Country of Four Approaches'; Lho Jong Men Jong, 'The Southern Valleys of Medicinal Herbs'; and Lho Mon Tsenden Jong, 'The Southern Mon Valleys where Sandalwood/ Cypress Grows'. 'Mon' was a generic term applied by Tibetans to the Mongoloid, non-Buddhist populations who live on the southern slopes of the Himalayas. The origin of the name 'Bhutan' is unclear, but the most plausible guess is that it comes from the Indian term Bhotanta, which refers to all the regions bordering on Tibet.

Bhutan's ancient history is known through written Tibetan sources written later but unfortunately they are not explicit about the population or type of government that existed in those times.

BUDDHISM REACHES BHUTAN

According to Bhutanese tradition, the history of Bhutan began in the seventh century AD when the Tibetan king, Songtsen Gampo, constructed the first two Buddhist temples: Kyichu in the Paro valley and Jampa in the Choekhor valley at Bumthang. In the eighth century, a Tantrist from Swat (in present-day Pakistan) arrived in Bhutan. His name was Padmasambhava but he is generally known in Tibet and Bhutan as Guru Rinpoche, the 'Precious Master'. Here, as in Tibet, he

THE MONASTIC COMMUNITY AND OTHER RELIGIOUS CATEGORIES

Ordained monks are called *gelong*. They live in *dzongs* and monasteries and wear a characteristic dark red robe. They are usually sent to a monastery at the age of five or six, an act that brings great prestige and religious merit to their families. They follow monastic academic courses which in earlier times used to be the only form of education available. After a few years of study, and depending on their aptitude, the monks are then directed into purely scholastic studies or into more artistic religious pursuits (dancers, musicians, painters, tailors).

At present there are about 6,000 subsidized monks in Bhutan under the authority of the Je Khenpo, the head of all religious affairs, who presides over the monastic organization, the Dratshang Lhentshog. His principal assistant at the national level is the Dorje Lopen, who is in charge of religious teachings. The Dorje Lopen is one of four high Lopens or masters, the others being the Drape Lopen, 'master of grammar', who is in charge of literary studies, the Yangpe Lopen, 'master of songs. and liturgy', and the Tsenyi Lopen, 'master of philosophy'. To these four masters, who have the rank of minister, are added a Khilkor Lopen who is the 'master of arts' and a Tsipe Lopen who is the 'master of astrology'. Moreover, in each monastery there is the Umdze or 'choirmaster' and the Kudun or 'master of discipline' who carries a rosary of large ivory beads and a whip.

The state takes care of basic needs, but any money the monks earn by performing rituals remains their own property. The monks carry out daily rituals and perform special ones at fixed times in the *dzongs* and monasteries. They also respond to the needs of people outside and perform the types of ceremonies that are called for either in the monastery or in the homes of the faithful.

Monks progressively take different categories of vows, from novice to fully ordained monk. They are celibate and must abstain from smoking and drinking, but they are not vegetarian and even eat in the evening, unlike the monks in Southeast Asia. A few monks join monastic orders when they are teenagers, but they are rare. Monks can renounce their vows at any time in order to start a family, but they have to pay a fine. They are then called *gétré*, 'retired monk', and there is no social stigma attached to this condition.

The great majority of ordained monks belong to the Drukpa clergy, but ordained monks of the Nyingmapa school also exist. About 3,000 other monks, not supported by the state, live from private patronage.

A *trulku* or *rinpoche* is the reincarnation of a great master whose different incarnations form a line of descendants. All the successive incarnations bear the same name and are thus given a name to the lineage. Such a person is called a *tulku*, which means 'Body of Emanation', but the term by which he is addressed is Rinpoche, 'Great Precious One'. Certain *tulkus* are fully ordained monks and therefore celibate, while others marry and are in no way held in less respect because of their family life. Moreover, once a person has been declared a *tulku*, he remains so all his life even if his activities appear to be incompatible with a religious existence. Being a *tulku* is an inherent quality, almost a genetic trait, like being tall or having brown eyes.

Nowadays, there are about 1,000 *tulkus* in all the countries that practice Tibetan Buddhism. Bhutan has some highly prestigious *tulkus*. The Bhutanese throng to receive teachings or blessings from important *tulkus* who have been granted an intense religious education and have, since childhood, occupied a high position in the religious hierarchy.

Gomchens are a very special category. They are lay-priests most of whom (15,000) belong to the Nyingmapa school. They differ from ordained monks in that they live at home and have a family. They earn their living in secular occupations, as farmers or civil servants, but they have received religious teachings that permit them to perform ceremonies for the faithful. They dress in a *go* that is slightly longer than that of the other laymen. In addition, they sometimes have long hair knotted in a ponytail and have a very wide, dark red ceremonial scarf that closely resembles a monk's cloak. *Gomchens* play an extremely important role in isolated villages where they stand in for monks in all the rituals that villagers need to have performed.

A lama is not another name for a monk, as is often believed in the West. Lama means 'religious master', a translation of the Sanskrit word guru. A lama may be an ordained monk or he may be a married lay religious person. He may be a *gelong* or a *gomchen* or a *tulku*, either married or not (except in the first case). The term 'lama' implies a religious status and is an honorary title given to a man by virtue of his knowledge and wisdom about religious rather than social questions. Frequently the title is transmitted along with religious teachings from father to son. A Westerner should not be too surprised to find a lama serving as the principal of a village primary school deep in eastern Bhutan, wearing ordinary clothes and surrounded by his own offspring. But there are also lamas to be found who conform more closely to the Western image of a venerable religious master.

Nuns, or *anims*, are less numerous than monks in a culture where monastic life is essentially male. There are about 250 nuns, state and privately supported, but their communities are always under the supervision of a monastery of monks. There are a few isolated women's monasteries where young nuns learn rituals and the basic texts. They attend ceremonies when a high lama comes into the region to give teachings or blessings. The state supports about 100 of them.

introduced Tantric Buddhism. He is considered by the Nyingmapa religious school to be their founder and the Second Buddha. All the places he visited and in which he meditated are places of pilgrimage for the Bhutanese, who also worship his Eight Manifestations in almost all the temples in the country. The story of the conversion to Buddhism of a king reigning in Bumthang indicates that, at the time of Padmasambhava, the valleys of Bhutan were already inhabited by a population of unknown origin (but probably Mongoloid if one is to believe the ancient names for Bhutan). They practised an animistic type of religion close to the old Bon beliefs of Tibet.

After this first introduction of Buddhism, the ninth and tenth centuries constitute an obscure historical period. Tibet itself plunged into great political turmoil following the assassination in AD 842 of the Tibetan king, Langdarma, whom tradition depicts as anti-Buddhist. Countless texts disappeared and Buddhism survived only in remote regions. No contemporary information exists now about these troubled centuries. However, later sources give reason to believe that many people, and particularly aristocrats, fled from Tibet and settled in the valleys of central and eastern Bhutan, where they assumed power.

The beginning of the 11th century saw a revival of Buddhism in Tibet which was reflected in Bhutan by the activity of *tertons*, the 'discoverers of hidden religious treasures', in Paro and Bumthang. These treasures were texts or objects hidden by Padmasambhava and other saints, to be discovered by predestined persons at a favourable moment. The Nyingmapa school produced most of the *tertons*.

The end of the 11th century and the beginning of the 12th was a period of religious expansion in Tibet, and several different religious schools came into being including the Kadampa, Kagyupa and Sakyapa schools. The missionary activities of these new schools were also directed towards the 'southern valleys'—today's Bhutan.

SCHOOLS OF RELIGION SPREAD IN BHUTAN

At the end of the l2th century, Gyelwa Lhanangpa (1164–1224) arrived in western Bhutan where he had special links with the Paro valley, having inherited land there from his great-great-grandfather. He was the founder of the Lhapa school, a branch of the Kagyupa school.

In the first half of the 13th century, a religious practitioner named Phajo Drugom Shigpo (1184–1251) arrived in western Bhutan. He belonged to another branch of the Kagyupa, the Drukpas, founded in central Tibet by Tsangpa Gyare Yeshe Dorje (1161–1211) who, shortly before his death, had prophesised that Phajo would convert the Southern Valleys. Shortly after his arrival, Phajo Drugom Shigpo came into conflict with the Lhapas, who by then were firmly established in western Bhutan. Phajo finally won the struggle and, having married a woman from the Thimphu valley, he founded the first Drukpa monasteries at Phajoding and Tango. The Lhapa school continued nonetheless until the 17th century when it was totally crushed by Shabdrung Ngawang Namgyal, who unified Bhutan under Drukpa authority.

In spite of the growing political and religious influence of the Drukpa, many Tibetan religious men, whether they belonged to the Drukpa school or not, continued to come to western Bhutan between the 12th and 17th centuries. Barawa (1320–91), for example, founded a sub-sect of the Drukpas, the Barawas. Others who came were the Sakyapas, the Nenyingpas and the Chagzampas, the latter named after their founder, Thangton Gyelpo (1385–1464), also known as Chagzampa, 'builder of iron bridges'.

SAINTS AND SCHOLARS

In the early16th century, Drukpa Kunley, "the divine madman" (1455–1529) came from Tibet. Drukpa Kunley is without doubt the most popular figure of Bhutanese history and everybody in the country is familiar with his adventures. He belonged to the Drukpa school, and was even a member of the great Gya family from which came the Drukpa hierarchs, who served also as successive abbots of Ralung, the most important Drukpa monastery. Though he refused monastic vows and all organised setup, his wandering life, his eccentric, shocking behaviour and the songs by which he taught the essence of the religion, guaranteed him a special place in the history of Tantric Buddhism. His descendants played an important role in Bhutanese history, especially Tenzin Rabgye (1638–1696) who became the famous 4th Temporal Ruler, *Desi*, of Bhutan.

Drukpa influence finally made itself felt in the centre and east of the country in the middle of the 16th century when Ngagi Wangchuk, a brother of the Drukpa hierarch, and later Tenpe Nyima, his grandson who fathered the future Shabdrung (see below), came from Tibet and founded temples in the east and centre of the country. Up until then, Nyingmapa monks had been the most active in that part of the country.

Longchen Rabjam (1308–1363), the greatest philosopher of the Nyingmapa school, chose exile in the Bhutanese region of Bumthang following a quarrel with the ruler of Tibet of his time. In the Bumthang valleys, he founded the monasteries of Tharpaling, Samtenling, Shingkar and Ogyenchoeling and also carried on missionary activities in Shar (now the district of Wangduephodrang). One of the foremost Tibetan "discoverer of religious treasure"(*terton*), Dorje Lingpa (1346–1405), followed in his footsteps, and he likewise settled in the Bumthang valleys, at Chakhar and Ogyenchoeling.

The most famous Nyingmapa saint, Pema Lingpa, was born in Bumthang in 1450 and died there in 1521. He was the reincarnation not only of Guru Rinpoche but also of Longchen Rabjampa, the philosopher. Famous among Tibetans far beyond the borders of Bhutan for his activities as a *terton*, Pema Lingpa also founded the monasteries of Petsheling, Kungzandra and Tamshing in Bumthang. He was the originator of numerous sacred dances, which came to him in visions, and he left behind him several important writings.

Many descendants of Pema Lingpa scattered throughout eastern Bhutan, where they strengthened the hold of the Nyingmapas. One of them founded the great monastery of Drametse not far from Trashigang, and one of Pema Lingpa's grandsons, Pema Trinley, established the Gangtey monastery in the Black Mountains, on the border between central and western Bhutan. Through the descendants of his son Kunga Wangpo, who settled in Kurtoe, Pema Lingpa is the ancestor of Bhutan's Wangchuck royal family.

This brief outline shows how from the 12th century until the end of the 16th century, Bhutan was an important field of missionary activity for the Buddhist religious schools, but it also shows clearly the lack of political unity which characterized the country.

THE UNIFICATION OF BHUTAN

Under the politically and religiously charismatic Ngawang Namgyal (1594–1651), Bhutan became a unified state in the 17th century. Ngawang Namgyal was a religious leader of the Drukpa school, who took the honorary title of *Shabdrung*, 'at whose feet one submits'. Persecuted in Tibet, he fled to Bhutan in 1616 and, over the next 30 years, succeeded in crushing all opposition and unifying the 'southern valleys' into Druk Yul, 'the Land of the Drukpas'.

Ngawang Namgyal was born into the princely Gya family, and he became the 18th abbot of Ralung, the great Drukpa monastery in Tibet not far from the northern border of Bhutan. He had been recognized as the incarnation of a famous Drukpa scholar, Pema Karpo (1527–92), but this recognition was challenged by the Tsang Desi, the ruler of Tibet's province of Tsang, who had his own candidate. Fearing for his life, Ngawang Namgyal fled from Ralung and sought refuge in western Bhutan. He settled down there, accepting an invitation by followers of the Drukpa school which had been firmly established in the region since the 13th century.

Ngawang Namgyal, using the title of Shabdrung, constructed his first *dzong* at Simtokha in the valley of the Wang River. Subsequent *dzongs* not only symbolized the power of the Drukpa school, since each *dzong* contained a monastery, but also constituted a matchless instrument of government, as each also served as centres of administration for the provinces.

However, before the Shabdrung could bring about the unification of Bhutan, he had to fight against enemies from abroad as well as inside the country. Shortly after his arrival, the Shabdrung had to contend with a Tibetan invasion. Forced back, the Tibetans attacked again in 1634 and 1639 but with no greater success. In 1645 and 1648, the Tibetans made equally vain attempts at conquest.

The enemies within were the 'Five Groups of Lamas'—the long-established religious schools in western Bhutan, headed by the Lhapas, old foes of the Drukpas. The Shabdrung battled successfully against this coalition and firmly established the political and religious power of the Drukpas in western Bhutan. He was not able, in his lifetime, to fulfil his ambition of unifying central and eastern Bhutan, but his wish was carried out shortly after his death in 1651. In 1656, after a difficult military campaign, central and eastern Bhutan were drawn into the Drukpa sphere of political influence and Bhutan took on its definitive shape.

THE SHABDRUNG'S LEGACY

Shabdrung Ngawang Namgyal gave Bhutan a remarkable system of administration and law. He established a state clergy under a religious leader, the Je Khenpo (Chief Abbot) and a political system administered by monks at whose head he placed a temporal chief, the Desi. This dual system of government, choesi, was to be unified and transcended in the person of the Shabdrung and the theocracy lasted until the monarchy took over in 1907. The country was divided into three large provinces—Dagana, Paro and Trongsa—headed by governors, or *penlops*. Each *dzong* was directed by a *dzongpon*. Thus, a whole hierarchy of officials was established. Shabdrung Ngawang Namgyal also gave the country a legal system based on Buddhist moral principles and customary rules in general use at that time.

In 1651, the Shabdrung went into retreat at Punakha *dzong* and died soon afterwards. His death was kept secret for over half a century in case turmoil should erupt in the newly created country while a worthy successor to the Shabdrung was being sought.

In the first half of the 18th century, the theory of the triple reincarnation—the Body, Speech and Mind of the Shabdrung—was finally established. However, only 'Mind' incarnations were recognized as providing official successors to the Shabdrung as heads of state.

From the middle of the 18th century to the end of the 19th century, the *penlops* increased their power to the detriment of the central government. Furthermore, the dual system of government, devised to be run by a strong man, favoured political inertia in the absence of a reincarnation of the Shabdrung's forceful personality. Terrible power struggles took place among the Desi, the *penlops* and the *dzongpons* as a consequence. The combination of these factors led to instability and increasingly frequent internal disputes that ended in incessant civil wars.

THE COMING OF THE BRITISH

Up until the middle of the 18th century, the Bhutanese government had conducted foreign relations only with the Kingdom of Cooch Behar on its southern border and with regions within Tibet's cultural sphere (Tibet, Ladakh, Sikkim). Now it was faced with a new factor in the form of British hegemony in Assam and their expansion into the Himalayas.

In the second half of the 18th century, British missions seeking preferential trade agreements with Tibet and Bhutan succeeded in establishing good relations with the Bhutanese without, however, gaining the concrete results that they hoped for. But the conflicting interests between the two countries over the question of the Duars (the narrow southern plain) rapidly soured these good relations and the expeditions in the 19th century were marked by hostility. Continual skirmishes on the southern border from the 1830s onward escalated until they broke out, in 1864, into a conflict known as the Duar War. In November 1865, the Treaty of Sinchula restored friendly relations: Bhutan lost the fertile strip of land that made up the Duars, but in exchange it received an annuity from the British.

NEW LEADERSHIP

During this time, the progressive weakening of the central government became more marked and, in the second half of the 19th century, it contributed to the emergence of the power of the two main *penlops*, in Paro and Trongsa, who in fact controlled western Bhutan and central and eastern Bhutan respectively. The Penlop of Trongsa, named Jigme Namgyal, helped by a network of alliances and his own political genius, became the strong man of Bhutan after 1865. Upon his death in 1881, he bequeathed the position of Penlop of Trongsa to his son, Ugyen Wangchuck. The new governor strengthened the alliances forged by his father and claimed a decisive victory over his fiercest opponents at Thimphu in 1885. From then on, Bhutan enjoyed its first period of political stability in many generations.

Ugyen Wangchuck favoured increased co-operation with the British. On the suggestion of his eminent advisor, Kazi Ogyen Dorje, he served as intermediary in the delicate negotiations between the Tibetans and the British. In 1904, at the time of the British expedition into Tibet under Colonel Francis Younghusband, he won the confidence and respect of the latter and he was awarded the title of Knight Commander of the Indian Empire (KCIE) in 1905. The British were consequently very pleased and relieved when an assembly of representatives of the monastic community, civil servants and the people elected Ugyen Wangchuck to be the First King of Bhutan on 17 December 1907. Thus ended the theocratic, dual system of government established by Shabdrung Ngawang Namgyal, and a hereditary monarchy was inaugurated.

Monarchy and Modernization

King Ugyen Wangchuck died in 1926 and was succeeded by his son, Jigme Wangchuck, who reigned until his death in 1952. The reigns of the first two kings were marked by political stability and a degree of economic prosperity after the years of internal conflict that had drained the country's economy. A desire to open the country to the outside world, the influence of enlightened men such as Kazi Ogyen Dorje and his son Gongzim Sonam Tobgye, as well as aid from Great Britain permitted the establishment of the first Western-style schools and the sending of the first Bhutanese students to India for advanced training.

The third king, Jigme Dorje Wangchuck (r 1952–1972), is considered the father of modern Bhutan. Inheriting a country at peace, he understood that the world was changing and that Bhutan, if it wished to survive, could no longer continue its political isolation but must start developing. In the 1950s, he abolished serfdom, redistributed land and established the National Assembly.

In 1961, with the help of India, the King launched the first five-year plan of development, with particular emphasis on road-building. In 1962, Bhutan joined its first international organisation, the Colombo Plan, and in 1971 it was proudly admitted to the United Nations. After the sovereign's death in 1972, his son, Jigme Singye Wangchuck, ascended the throne at the young age of 17. Brought up by the late king with an eye to his future role as monarch, King Jigme Singye Wangchuck had no trouble in taking over the reins of state, and quickly dedicated himself to a policy of socio-economic development for the country while maintaining its ancestral traditions and cultural heritage. With emphasis on the well-being of the people, and their ability to profit from the advances of the modern world without losing their sense of identity, the King is challenging the classic process of modernization with a carefully thought out plan that embraces all of Bhutan's heritage.

At the same time, the King began a diplomatic offensive which, while remaining unobtrusive, has nonetheless been effective. By 1989, Bhutan was a member of nearly all the organizations affiliated with the UN. Bhutan has belonged to the Movement of Non-aligned Countries since 1973 and to the South-Asian Association for Regional Cooperation since 1985. It has diplomatic bilateral relations with more than 21 countries including India, Bangladesh, Japan, Switzerland, and other European countries. It also has diplomatic relation with the European Union, and has appointed honorary consuls in several countries.

At the beginning of the 1990s, the country had to face what is referred to as 'the southern problem'. The policy aimed at reinforcing national identity, coupled with the application of the law on nationality (those judged to be Bhutanese were those who could prove they were Bhutanese before 1958, as well as their direct descendants) led to a major displacement of part of the population of Nepalese origin who had settled in Bhutan. These people are now in temporary camps in Nepal, but the number of persons really from Bhutan is the subject of heated debates, especially if one considers the major movements of populations, partly of Nepalese origin, that took place at the end of the 1980s in the whole eastern region of India. After long negotiations, Nepal and Bhutan started, in 2001, a common process of verification in the camps in order to settle the distressing problems of the displaced people but the present situation and the Maoist rebellion in Nepal are not condusive for a prompt settlement.

Since 1998, Bhutan has faced a problem that does not concern it at all, but to which it is hostage. Bodo and Assamese separatists who want to secede from India have taken refuge in the jungles of south-east Bhutan, whence they launch attacks against India. Bhutan has asked them to withdraw beyond its borders; if not, it would be obliged to expel them by force. Talks came to a dead end in 2003 and in December 2003, the Bhutanese army destroyed the camps and expelled the separatists.

THE MONARCHY AND NATIONAL INSTITUTIONS
CENTRAL GOVERNMENT

The system of government is a monarchy. His Majesty the King is the head of state, but since 1998, he is no longer the head of government, having left this function to a prime minister. He is assisted by a cabinet. It is made up of ministers and secretaries of state. Ministers have been, since the major political reform of 1998 initiated by the king, elected by the members of the National Assembly for five years and each minister, in turn, is head of government for one year. Each ministry

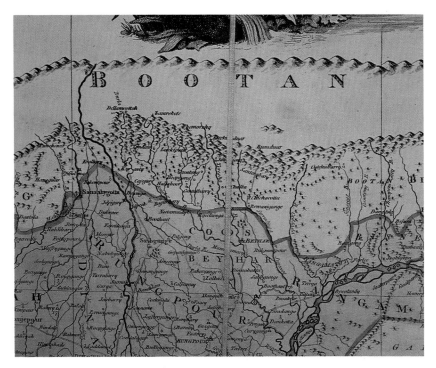

Map of Bhutan dating from 18th century.

is divided into departments or divisions. At the King's initiative, a constitution has been drafted and has been proposed to the people in in early 2005. It is available on the internet and has been widely distributed in Bhutan in Dzongkha and English for comment. Once the changes are made, the constitution will be proposed to the National Assembly and Bhutan will enter a new political era.

THE NATIONAL ASSEMBLY

The National Assembly was created in 1953 and consists of 150 members: 100 representatives of the people, elected for three years, ten representatives of the clergy and 40 representatives appointed by the king from among his ministers, royal counsellors, district heads and other high officials.

Until 2004 the Assembly met once a year for three weeks in the Assembly Hall in Thimphu but the number of issues to be dealt with increasing, it started having two sessions from 2005. The sessions are public. Laws are discussed and voted on and national problems debated.

NATIONAL SYMBOLS OF BHUTAN

The **national flag** was created in 1947 by Mayum Choying Wangmo Dorji and modified in 1956 to take its final shape. The national anthem was composed in 1953. The Bhutanese flag is divided diagonally and depicts a white dragon across the middle. The upper part of the flag is golden yellow, representing the secular power of the king, while the lower part is orange, symbolising the Buddhist religion. The dragon, whose white colour is associated with purity, represents Bhutan. The jewels held in its claws stand for the wealth and perfection of the country.

The **national emblem**, contained in a circle, is composed of a double diamond-thunderbolt placed above a lotus, surmounted by a jewel and framed by two dragons. The thunderbolt represents the harmony between secular and religious power which results from the Buddhist religion in its Vajrayana form. The lotus symbolizes purity; the jewel expresses sovereign power; and the two dragons, male and female, stand for the name of the country which they proclaim with their great voice, the thunder.

National Day is celebrated on 17 December and commemorates the ascension to the throne of Ugyen Wangchuck, the first king of Bhutan, at Punakha Dzong on 17 December 1907.

The **National Anthem** became official in 1966. The first stanza can be translated:

In the kingdom of the dragon,
The southern land of sandalwood,
Long live the king
Who directs the affairs of both state and religion.

The **national flower** is the blue poppy (*Meconopsis grandis*), which grows at high altitudes.

The **national tree** is the cypress (*Cupressus torolusa*), which is often associated with religious places. The Bhutanese identify with it because it is straight and strong and can grow in inhospitable soil.

The **national bird** is the raven (*Corvus corax*) because it adorns the royal hat. It represents the deity Gonpo Jarodonchen (Mahakala with a raven's head), one of the most important guardian deities of Bhutan.

The **national animal** is the takin (*Burdorcas taxicolor*), an extremely rare bovid mammal of the ovine-caprine family. It lives in flocks in places 4,000 metres (over 13,125 feet) high, and eats bamboo. It can weigh as much as 250 kilogrammes (550 pounds).

Royal Advisory Council

Set up in 1965, the Royal Advisory Council is an advisory body that is always in session. Its purpose is to advise the king and also to make sure that resolutions passed by the National Assembly are properly carried out. It has a three-year mandate and consists of nine members who must be approved by the assembly: two members from the state clergy and six members elected by secret ballot by the National Assembly from among candidates elected in the districts. The head of the Council (*Zhung Kaloen*) is appointed by the king.

The Judicial System

Judicial power is held in the last resort by the king, to whom all Bhutanese may appeal. A High Court of six judges was established in 1968 with its seat in Thimphu. Four of the judges are appointed by the king and two represent the people, elected by the assembly. All districts have a local court presided over by a magistrate who is appointed by the Chief Justice, but village headmen still try the less important cases.

The Code of Law is based on the one established by Shabdrung Ngawang Namgyal. While still keeping its Buddhist foundations, it has been adapted to meet modern problems. Bhutan is certainly a country with one of the lowest crime rates in the world. Court cases deal essentially with family disputes or quarrels over property rights. There were no lawyers, each person pleaded his case personally; there were, however, "mediators" for complex cases. These now receive training sanctioned by a state diploma. A major reform of the judicial system is under way, judges are now trained from the legal point of view, and the Code of Laws was reviewed in 2001.

Local Administration

Inherited from the administrative system devised by the Shabdrung Ngawang Namgyal in the 17th century, local administration underwent modifications during the 20th century. The position of *Penlop* was abolished, with the advent of the monarchy, and twenty districts (*dzongkhag*) were created, each led by a head of district, the *Dzongda* (formerly *Dzongpon*), responsible to the Home Ministry.

The *Dzongda* is aided in his duties by an assistant, the *Dzongrab*, who deals with internal administrative matters. The most populated districts have been divided into sub-districts, *dungkhag*, which are led by a *Dungpa*, a civil servant appointed by the government and attached to the *dzongda*. Each district is divided into blocks (*gewog*), administrative units grouping several villages.

A district development committee (*Dzongkhag Yargye Tshogchun*), made up of representatives of the people and high-ranking civil servants of the district, meet to discuss development projects. At the block level, decisions are passed on by a village headman, elected by the villagers of the block, called *Gup* in the north and *Mandal* in the south, who also doubles as a magistrate for minor disputes. There are also, since 1991, block development committees (*Gewog Yargye Tshogchun*). In 2002, as part of the government's decentralisation and devolution policy, both the district development committees and the block development committees were given more decision-making powers as well as certain financial responsibilities.

THE STATE MONASTIC COMMUNITY

The state clergy (*Dratshang*) includes the monks of the official Drukpa Kagyupa school who make up the central and regional monastic communities. The state clergy formerly owned vast land holdings from which it drew its revenue, but since 1968 it has been subsidized by the government. In 1982, the government began buying up monastic land and redistributing it to the most needy peasants.

The *Je Khenpo* heads the clergy and controls all religious affairs. He is chosen from among the most senior monks in the hierarchy and retains his position for life, if he so wishes. He is assisted in his administrative duties by four high-ranking monks chosen by the central monastic community (Thimphu/Punakha). The *Je Khenpo* also administers religious teachings throughout the country. The state clergy is represented in the National Assembly and on the Royal Advisory Council.

The *rabde* regional monastic communities have their seat in the local *dzong* and are under the direction of a high-ranking monk called the *Lam Neten*, assigned by the central monastic community.

The *Dratshang Lhentshog* is an organ of the state clergy, headed by the *Je Khenpo*. It looks after the interests of the 6,000 monks in Bhutan, both Drukpa and Nyingmapa, and maps out broad areas of religious policy. The *Je Khenpo* is aided in these duties by a senior lay official.

Monastic training is very strict and long. Monastic schools have a well defined academic programme; they train monks who wish to do higher studies in theology and meditation.

The *Dratshang Lhentshog* does not have jusrisdiction over the religious laymen who have their private temple or monasteries.

THE ECONOMY AND CHALLENGES

Agriculture and livestock raising are still the main pillars of the economy, with 79 per cent of the population dependent on these two sectors for their livelihood. However, in 1999, agricultural cultivation generated no more than 6.8% of the gross national product (GNP), live-stock rearing 7.5% and forests 10.5%. The low representation by forests is explained by the government's desire not to use forest resources to exploitative ends, but as ecological wealth. 72% of the country is under forest cover and more than 26% is national parks.

The industry and mines sector is increasing rapidly with the operation of a food-product factory, two cement factories, a factory for the processing of calcium carbide, but the wealth of Bhutan comes from hydro-electric plants, which, by themselves, generate 46% of GNP.

Trade contributes 28% of GNP, through, in particular, the export of cement, electricity, and agricultural products of excellent quality: apples, oranges, cardamom, potatoes, asparagus, mushrooms, lemon grass oil. Tourism and the airline, Druk Air, while very important as generators of hard currency, constitute only a small part of GNP.

While Bhutan may be in listed by the UN among the least developed countries, this does not reflect the reality of life there. The economic condition of the Bhutanese cannot be compared with that of people in Africa or Asia who fall in the same category. Some 98 per cent of Bhutanese peasants own their land, there is a favourable ratio of population to cultivable area, housing is of generally good quality, and even though malnutrition exists due to poor eating habits and the unavailability of certain products, there is no famine. A middle class has been developing since the beginning of the 1980s. It is composed of government officials, businessmen and entrepreneurs. It has consumer needs that were unknown until now and the products available in the urban centres indicate a standard of life that is relatively well-to-do.

A CAUTIOUS ROAD TO DEVELOPMENT

Thanks to its small population and relatively fertile land, Bhutan has never had to face the insurmountable problems that beset some of its neighbours. Its problems are human in scale and can be worked out, a factor which contributes to the

More than 80 per cent of the population work in agriculture.

optimism and enthusiasm of those involved in the development process. King Jigme Singye Wangchuck sets an example by devoting much of his time to travelling about the country, visiting the districts and making sure that programmes are being carried out to everyone's satisfaction.

In 1961, the present King's father initiated the first five-year plan of development with Indian assistance. Top priority was given in the first two five-year plans to the building of roads and the formation of a technical and administrative framework. Once the basic infrastructure was created, natural resources could then be turned to economic account. The third and fourth plans, covering the years 1971–81, included development programmes in such varied sectors as agriculture, forestry, electricity, mines and public health.

The fifth plan (1981–86) was a turning point in government policy. It was no longer a question of simply executing projects but also of achieving economic growth in order to gain greater economic self-reliance, of making the administration more effective through decentralization, of ensuring that the population received its fair share of the progress being made, and that it was involved in carrying out the projects.

The sixth plan, (1987–1992), continues the objectives of the fifth, with supreme importance being laid on national values, which takes the form, for instance, of the 'Bhutanization' of the school curriculum. Traditional etiquette, the development of the national language and the cultural heritage are receiving particular attention. Concern about ecology is widespread among Bhutanese leaders. As this book goes to press, the eighth five-year plan, (1997–2002), is being ratified by the King.

The Seventh Plan (1992–1997) and the Eighth Plan (1997–2002) priority was given to decentralization, the strengthening of infrastructure and social services, while encouraging development in the private sector by training programmes adapted to and in aid of small business. The Ninth Plan is underway and emphasizes on rural infra-structures and communications. As for the hydro-electric schoolor, it has become a priority, with new projects.

In 1999, Bhutan joined the world of the Internet and national television was launched. Several cable operators also provide for the reception of international channels by satellite (BBC, CNN, Chinese, Japanese and Indian channels).

The year 2001 saw an internal revolution with the introduction of income tax, starting from an income threshold of 100,000 Nu./year, which really only affected the wealthiest segment of the population. For the leaders, socio-economic

SOME STATISTICS*

Districts (*Dzongkhag*): 20
Currency: Ngultrum (Nu.)
Gross domestic product, per capita: US$ 835 (2002)
Rate of economic growth: about 5.5% per annum
Rate of population growth: 2.8%
Roads/Highways: 3,636 km (2,259 mi.)
Forest cover: 72%
Arable land: 7.7%
Rural population with access to safe drinkable water: 58%
Rural population with access to latrines: 80%

HEALTH
Life expectancy (men): 65.9 years
Life expectancy (women): 66.1 years
Birthrate (per 1,000): 39.9 (1999)
Death rate (per 1,000): 9.0 (1999)
Rate of immunization and vaccination: 90% (1999)
Rate of infant mortality (per 1,000 births): 70.7 (1999)
Rate of maternal mortality (per 1,000 births): 3.8
Number of hospitals: 28 (1999)
Number of dispensaries: 145 (1999)
Number of doctors: 101 (1999)

EDUCATION
Number of schools and institutions: 361 (April 2000)
Number of non-formal education centres: 146 (April 2000)
Number of students: 117,713 (April 2000)
Number of teachers: 3,736 (April 2000)
Rate of primary school enrolment: 72% (1999)
Rate of enrolment according to gender (general education programme):
    boys 54%; girls 46%
Adult literacy rate: 54% (1999)

* Once the 2005 Census results are available in December 2005, some of these statistics will be obsolete.

Sources: *Bhutan 2020: a Vision for Peace, Prosperity and Happiness*, Planning Commission, Royal Government of Bhutan, Thimphu, 1999; *Development toward Gross National Happiness*, Seventh round table meeting, 7–9 November 2000 Thimphu, Royal Government of Bhutan, Thimphu, 2000; *Education Department General Statistics 2000*, Thimphu; *Statistical Yearbooks of Bhutan*, Central Statistical Organization, Ministry of Planning, Thimphu.

development must not contribute to the degradation of the way of life or traditional values. Each project is therefore examined carefully and can be slowed down or even stopped if it upsets beliefs or the environment. This is Bhutan's way of following a path of measured development, which is hailed as the 'Gross National Happiness' (GNH) concept. It has 'Four Pillars'—good governance, sustainable development, environment conservation and preservation of culture.

The foremost donor of aid, in the form of both technical and financial assistance, is India. From the inception of the five-year plans, India has played a major role in Bhutan's development, especially in the construction and upkeep of roads, communications, hydroelectricity and the furthering of technical and administrative skills.

Bhutan also receives aid in various forms from the UN, particularly through UNDP (United Nations Development Programme) which opened an office in Thimphu in 1979) and other UN organizations such as UNICEF, FAO, WFP, WHO, UNESCO, IFAD and Volunteers. The European Community started a programme of agricultural assistance in 1985. Switzerland, in particular, has developed special ties with Bhutan.

Switzerland carries out Education and Renewable Resources projects through its cooperation organization, Helvetas. Several governmental organizations, from various countries (Austria, Canada, Denmark, Great Britain, Germany, Japan, Netherlands, Norway) are active, through, among other means, volunteers and consultants, in the priority sectors of agricultural cultivation, livestock rearing, forests, health and education, as well as hydro-electricity (Austria).

The main challenges faced by the country today are rapid urbanization and lack of low-cost housing, too high a birthrate, too many university-level students but not enough technicians and professionals in the manual trades, where there is difficulty employing young people trained essentially for administrative jobs.

ARTS AND ARCHITECTURE

Like any other Himalayan regions, Bhutan was influenced for centuries by Tibetan art but because of varied ecological and socio-economic reasons has developed its own art forms and themes.

Bhutanese art has three main characteristics: it is anonymous, it is religious and, as a result, it has no aesthetic function by itself. A Bhutanese does not view a painting or a sculpture as a work of art but as a religious work. Paintings and sculptures are consecrated through a special ceremony whereby they come to personify the deities. In general, the term 'image' is preferred to the word 'statue', which has no spiritual connotation. When a Bhutanese commissions a painting or statue, he looks on this as a pious act which will earn him merit, and thus his name is sometimes inscribed on the work to commemorate his act. This attitude, fundamentally different from that of the modern West, explains why new paintings are often donated to temples, covering up old ones. The criterion is faith, not art *per se*.

An artist was traditionally a monk who gained merit by doing this work, but his name was never mentioned since he was expected to scorn all vanity. The disciples of a master often prepared the work while only the final, delicate touches were executed by the master himself.

The rules of iconography are firmly established and must be scrupulously respected. Each deity has a colour and special attributes that cannot be changed without altering the meaning and the religious function. The artist, therefore, cannot express himself except in small details or in the painting of minor scenes. (*See* the Glossary for a list of deities, page 295.)

However, in 2000, the Voluntary Artists Studio (VAST) was established to train children in western-style art and educate about social and environmental problems through art (www.vast-bhutan.org).

PAINTING

Traditional mineral and vegetable pigments are still widely used but they are becoming more expensive than chemical paints. Paintings can be grouped into three categories: paintings on statues, murals, and *thangkas* (paintings on banners).

Clay statues are totally painted. Metal statues—incorrectly called bronzes—only have the face painted, enhanced by delicate strokes to point up the moustache or eyes.

The fresco technique is not known. The surface of a wall to be painted is dressed with a layer of earth which is allowed to dry and is then sanded before being painted but the most widely spread technique, which seems to be peculiar to Bhutan, is cloth on wall: The paintings are made on cloth in workshops and then applied to the walls. The very finely woven cloth is applied to the surface of the layer of earth with such care that it is virtually impossible to detect it unless it becomes damaged and starts to peel off the wall. A special paste made of flour and ground pepper is also applied to prevent inschools from eating the cloth.

There are a large number of *thangkas* in Bhutan. As they are not hung permanently in the temples but are kept rolled up in boxes and only displayed during important ceremonies, their colours stay remarkably fresh.

The technique of the *thangka* involves fixing a piece of damp cotton cloth on to a wooden or bamboo frame. A mixture of lime and glue is applied to the cloth which is then sandpapered. A grid of geometric lines is then drawn on it to serve as the framework and measuring gauge for the composition. Sometimes the artist simply prints the cloth with a wooden block that has the design already carved on it, or else he uses a stencil. In the latter case, the cloth is covered with a paper cartoon that has the lines of the desired drawing pierced with small holes. The artist traces over the lines with charcoal, leaving the design laid out in dots on the cloth, ready to be painted.

Most *thangkas* are painted in different colours, but some have the background completely gilded with the drawing executed in fine red and black lines. Other *thangkas* reserved for certain wrathful deities use a black background with a drawing of red and gold lines. When the *thangka* is finished, it is mounted with a brocade border of different colours which have symbolic meanings. Finally, two pieces of wood are sewn to the upper and lower edges for hanging.

Two other techniques, unrelated to painting, are used in making *thangkas*: embroidery and appliqué. Appliqué is primarily used to make the very large *thangkas* that are hung on the outside walls of fortresses during religious festivals.

Although painting styles have changed over the centuries, it is difficult to trace the history of Bhutanese painting. The main reason is that most datable mural paintings in temples have been repainted many times by pious donors.

Tamshing, in Bumthang, is one of the few temples that has kept its original paintings from the beginning of the 16th century (see page 206). A central deity occupies almost the whole field, while the sides are divided into little compartments containing minor deities belonging to the same cycle as the central figure. The

CHORTENS AND MANDALAS

A *chorten* (*stupa* in Sanskrit) is a 'receptacle for offerings' and in the Himalayan world it symbolizes Buddha's Mind and is sacred. As a sign of respect, a *chorten* should always be walked around in a clockwise direction, which also gains merit for believers.

According to Buddhist tradition, the first *chortens* were built in India and contained Buddha's relics, which had been divided up after his death. They then became places of worship.

In all regions of the Himalayas, thousands of *chortens* are still built by the faithful. *Chortens* are built in memory of great religious figures, to obtain merit for a deceased person, or to subjugate demons.

A *chorten* is composed of five parts which symbolize the five elements: the base stands for the earth; the dome for water; the 13 parasols for fire; the moon and sun for air; and the flame on the pinnacle for ether (a rarefied element believed to fill the upper regions of space). The 13 parasols also symbolize the 13 degrees that must be ascended in order to attain Enlightenment.

Chortens are generally compact, closed structures, but some are made in the form of gateways and others contain chapels (such as Dungtse Lhakhang in the Paro valley and the Memorial Chorten in Thimphu). There are three styles of *chorten* in Bhutan: the Nepalese style, the Tibetan style and the Bhutanese style (see also page 87).

Building a *chorten* involves a number of rituals and ceremonies. The most important is installing the 'tree of life'—a piece of a tree inscribed with prayers—and placing statues, books or other precious objects in the interior of the structure, and, finally, the consecration. To break open a *chorten* is a dreadful crime.

A *mandala* (*khyil khor* in Dzongkha) is a mystic, cosmic diagram. In the centre of the *mandala* is a divinity with whom the meditating practitioner seeks to merge after traversing various stages incorporated in the *mandala*. Each divinity has a different *mandala* and certain monks specialize in making them.

The most usual two-dimensional *mandalas* are on cotton *thangkas* and are composed of circles and squares; or they are made with coloured powders for certain rituals. Three-dimensional *mandalas* also exist, many made of gilded copper and placed on altars.

(Following pages) *Monks painting a* mandala—*a cosmic diagram said to clarify the various stages through which a devotee must travel before reaching enlightenment.*

commanding proportions of the latter, the general composition, the clothing of the minor figures and the patterns of the jewellery all show the Indian influence of the Pala-Sena dynasties of Bengal (8th–12th centuries). This style also strongly influenced early Tibetan and Central Asian art through the intermediary of Nepal.

Although Chinese influence was reflected in Tibetan art in the 15th century, there is no Bhutanese example surviving from that time. Therefore, it is difficult to draw any firm conclusions since many pieces of artistic evidence from this period have been covered over with new paintings from a later date. Chinese influence by way of Tibetan art does show up in certain paintings, but much later—for instance, at Taktshang and Tango (both end of the 17th century) and Phajoding (mid-18th century). Whether murals or *thangkas*, the style of painting displaying a central deity surrounded by minor figures survives today.

From the beginning of the 18th century, Chinese influences are well indexed. Artists started to use the whole wall or the whole surface of cloth to produce asymmetrical compositions, several figures or scenes occupying the space without having a principal figure in the centre. The style became more flowery, the use of gold paint more frequent, and landscapes were treated in the Chinese manner. The names of personages are often written under their images, which helps in dating the paintings.

SCULPTURE

There is hardly any stone or rock sculpture in Bhutan except for letters carved in bas-relief on stone walls or occasionally on rocks. On the other hand, since slate is an abundant resource, slate flagstones are finely engraved with pictures of deities and religious characters. The most beautiful are found in Simtokha *dzong*, and since each one carries an inscription identifying the figure represented, they are extremely valuable in the study of Bhutanese iconography.

Clay images can be seen everywhere and are completely painted. Their size varies from the tiny images that are placed inside portable chapels or personal reliquaries to gigantic statues two or three metres (six to ten feet) tall.

A block of fine clay is worked around a core of wood wrapped in pieces of cloth that are inscribed with prayers. This core is the *sogshing*, which is the image's 'tree of life' and which is also found in metal images and *chortens*. Small votive tablets of clay mixed with the ashes of the dead are placed in sacred spots. They are moulded first and later painted or whitewashed.

Metal images are made of a copper alloy. Images in silver or gold are rare. The *cire perdue*, or 'lost wax', technique, which was introduced to Tibet and Bhutan by Newari craftsmen from the Kathmandu valley, is widely used in making small-sized images.

Large images and chortens of metal are first hammered out of metal sheets, then worked into shape by being embossed and engraved. The different parts are then assembled with rivets. Most metal images and chortens are gilded, and some are ornamented with coral and turquoise offered by generous donors. The face and jewellery of a deity are sometimes inlaid with silver, and the face and hair are often painted.

From the 18th century onwards, altars and *chortens* were frequently covered with sheets of delicately worked, gilded copper. Statues then become much more ornate, often encrusted with semi-precious stones and mounted on bases in the form of double rows of lotus petals.

The pages of the religious books are held between two wooden boards, and the front cover may be carved with deities in high relief or covered with embossed sheets of copper.

It is hard to talk about different styles of sculpture as no systematic study has been made. Newari influence (itself derived from Indian art) appears in the huge statues that are surrounded by a nimbus of mythical animals such as *garudas* (griffins), *nagas* (water-snakes) and *makaras* (a kind of crocodile) on a ground of foliage. The nimbus reflects the typical structure of Newari doors. The best examples are found in Simtokha *dzong* and in Hedi Monastery in the upper Paro valley.

ARCHITECTURE

Bhutan's architectural forms are quite diverse. *Chortens*, stone walls, temples, monasteries, fortresses, mansions and houses make up a unique architectural landscape.

CHORTENS

A *chorten*, which represents Buddha's Mind, is erected in memory of an eminent lama or to ward off evil spirits from places normally considered dangerous, such as crossroads, bridges and mountain passes. There are three types of Bhutanese *chorten*: large *chortens* of whitewashed stone modelled after the *chorten* of Bodnath in Nepal; smaller stone *chortens* very much in the Tibetan style, found especially in central and eastern Bhutan and often protected by a wooden superstructure; and square-shaped *chortens* with the roof composed of four slopes and the upper part

(Following pages) *Two traditional paintings:* (top left) *'Man leading a yak'*, (Bottom left) *'Mongol leading the tiger'*, (right) *Torments of the eight hot hells* (Semtokha Dzong).

just below the roof decorated by a wide red stripe—these are mostly found in Western Bhutan and are similar to some of the *chortens* of the Derge area (Kham in Eastern Tibet).

Like statues, *chortens* are consecrated. They contain a 'tree of life' inscribed with prayers. Statues, religious books, fragrant herbs and even weapons are placed inside them.

Two *chortens* may be linked together by a stone wall, a '*mani* wall' named after the mantra of the bodhisattva Avalokiteshvara which is most often inscribed on the stones. One also sees the mantras of two other great bodhisattvas, Vajrapani and Manjushri. The stone walls are relatively few in number and fairly short in Bhutan, a circumstance perhaps explained by the topography, which does not lend itself to lengthy constructions.

Bhutanese architecture is a remarkable adaptation of Tibetan architecture to different ecological conditions. As in Tibet, the walls of fortresses slope inwards and are whitewashed, with the windows becoming larger in the upper storeys. However, in Bhutan, the need to cope with heavy precipitation and the availability of wood have given its architecture a flavour all its own.

Wood is widely used. The assembling of windows and doors is so complicated that the work is done at ground level and the finished elements fitted into the upper walls later. Windows are characterised by frames and by complicated lintels that carry symbolic meaning in all of their parts. Lintels and window frames are painted with floral or geometric designs.

The roofs of houses are pitched above a flat floor. The beams are assembled by the dovean rail technique and covered with shingles held in place with heavy stones. These pitched roofs are completely original in style and help give an impression of lightness to the whole building. This is clearly an innovative adaptation—made necessary by rain and snow—of the flat Tibetan roof. Traditionally, all wooden elements were joined by tenon and mortise but nails have also come into use in the past 40 years. Buildings are often destroyed by fire and reconstructed just as they were before. In the 1990s, having a small pagoda-shaped top crowning the roof became fashionable among the well-to-do.

LHAKHANG

Lhakhang (temples) are fairly small buildings of simple design which are likely to comprise one storey around a small enclosed courtyard. They differ from ordinary houses by the red band painted on the upper part of their walls and an ornament of gilded copper on the roof. Inside, the walls are completely covered with paintings, and the interior space is sometimes divided by pillars into an antechamber and the sanctuary proper. These buildings seem to have been the first forms of religious architecture and some of them are centuries old. *Lhakhang* are maintained by a caretaker who may be a member of the owner's family if it is private, or be assigned by the state clergy if it is state property. There are usually several lhakhangs in one monastery or fortress.

GONPAS

Gonpas (monasteries) can be divided into two types: one that we will call the 'cluster' type and the other the '*dzong*' type.

The 'cluster' type is probably the older. It consists of a core formed by one or two temples with various dwelling structures grouped around it. Examples of this type are Dzongdrakha in the Paro valley, Phajoding in the Thimphu valley, and Tharpaling in the Bumthang valley.

The '*dzong*' type is built like a fortress with a central tower enclosing the temples and surrounded by exterior walls against which are built monks' cells and service rooms. The most impressive examples of this type are the monasteries of Gangtey, near Pele La, Tango in the upper Thimphu valley, Talo near Punakha and Drametse in Eastern Bhutan. Cheri Monastery, built in the upper Thimphu valley in 1619–20, has characteristics of both styles. The central building is a *dzong* and around it are clustered houses for meditation and retreat.

DZONGS

Bhutanese fortresses are known as *dzong*s and were constructed at strategic points for political reasons. They contain both regional Drukpa monastic communities and the administrative offices of the district government. The solidity and elegance of the sloping walls, combined with richly detailed woodwork and the ethereal character of the pitched roof, make the *dzong* one of the most beautiful architectural forms of Asia. The basic pattern of a *dzong* consists of a central tower, *utse*, built in the middle of a courtyard, while monks' cells and administrative offices back up against the walls that surround it. Gasa, Trashigang and Dagana *dzong*s are good examples. However, certain *dzong*s, such as Punakha, Wangduephodrang and Thimphu, have two separate courtyards delimited by the central tower, one encompassed by administrative buildings and the other by buildings belonging to the clergy.

(Left) *Courtyard of* dzong *above Thimphu.* (Right) *Young monk in the doorway of the* dzong *above Thimphu.* (Bottom) *The National Museum, housed in the Ta* dzong *is above the Paro* dzong.

Courtyards and buildings are sometimes constructed on different levels following the slope of the terrain. Paro, Jakar and Trongsa *dzongs* are built in this way. Trongsa is the most complex of all, with a maze of courtyards, buildings and passages on different levels.

VERNACULAR ARCHITECTURE

Vernacular architecture reflects many features of religious or fortress architecture. Lordly mansions seem to have appeared during the period at the end of the 19th century when the country began to enjoy relative peace and the lords of Bumthang acquired great political power. The construction of these residences continued during the reigns of the first and second kings. Their basic layout was, in fact, very similar to that of a fortress: the lord and his family lived in a central building surrounded by an enclosed courtyard with service buildings backed up against its walls. However, the architecture of these residences was less severe than that of *dzongs*, which were built for defence. There was considerably more decoration on the woodwork, and windows opened even from the exterior walls. The upper floor of the central building was always turned into a private chapel. This room was decorated with painted murals and contained numerous statues as well as the religious books needed for rituals. The most noted examples of this type of architecture are Wangduchoeling, Domkhar, Prakhat and Ogyenchoeling in the Bumthang region, Kunga Rabten, Enchoeling and Samdrupchoeling to the south of Trongsa, and Gangtey in the Paro valley.

All *dzongs*, lordly residences and important temples are built of stone, while village houses are constructed of different materials depending on their locations. In western Bhutan, *adobe* (rammed earth) is the commonest building material, whereas in the centre and east, stone is preferred. In eastern Bhutan, woven bamboo mats were also used for building, and often served as roofing for small houses on stilts.

Throughout Bhutan, rural houses have the same characteristics: they are rectangular, with one or two storeys. The upper floors are constructed almost universally as an open wooden framework with bamboo lathing filling the spaces, covered by white plaster. Although in former times the wooden framework and the plaster were left as they were, the tendency nowadays is to paint them and decorate them with various designs.

Windows traditionally had no permanent protective screening; sometimes bamboo screens were put up to shut out bad weather without excluding light, but today glass is used in the more populated areas. At night, windows are closed from the inside by sliding shutters.

The roof is the same as for other buildings, and the space between the flat roof and the two-sided sloping roof is used for drying vegetables or meat and for storing hay. In towns, this space is closed off with bamboo mats.

In farmhouses, formerly never whitewashed, the ground floor is dimly lit by narrow windows and used for the farm animals and as a storeroom. The upper floors are reached by a ladder with steps hollowed out from a tree trunk. If there is a middle floor, it can be used for storage or to provide rooms for servants and visiting relatives. The top floor, which receives light from many windows, is where the family lives. It is divided into small rooms which do not have specialized uses except for the latrines (if they exist), the kitchen and the little private chapel, which sometimes doubles as a bedroom for guests and lamas.

Furniture is rudimentary: a few small low tables, mattresses which are rolled up by day along with the bedcovers, some rugs, shelves for the dishes, metal or wooden trunks for keeping clothes in, a wooden altar in the chapel, and one or two looms for weaving.

The house gives on to a courtyard (sometimes covered), forming a terrace where all sorts of daily activities take place. This type of farm is found throughout the country, with regional variations and nowadays they are likely to be whitewashed and painted with auspicious designs.

The beauty of its proportions and decorations make a countryside Bhutanese house one of the loveliest examples of vernacular architecture.

In towns, the houses are similarly laid out but the ground floor has windows and contains the kitchen, the storeroom and the servants' rooms. It can also be transformed into a small shop. The kitchen and the bathroom are sometimes located in a small annex attached to the rear of the house. Unfortunately cement apartment buildings are creeping in everywhere, even if they pay a token to Bhutanese architecture by being painted.

CRAFTS

From the point of view of quality of artistic production, in Bhutan the dichotomy between art and craft disappears in many fields. This Western classification, more and more obsolete, does not exist for the Bhutanese in any case, as they group any of these forms of production within the "Thirteen Arts", *Zorig chusum*: *zo* means "maker"; *rig* "science" and *chusum* "thirteen". Probably codified at the end of the 17th century during the reign of the 4th temporal head of Bhutan, Tenzin Rabgye (1680–1694), this list comprises: woodworking, stone-working, sculpture, painting, working in clay, casting and metalwork, wood-turning, forging metal, jewellery, basketry in bamboo and rattan, paper-making, embroidery and weaving.

The fact that Bhutanese crafts are relatively expensive and not made solely for the tourist trade can be explained by social and economic factors. A lot of Bhutanese still live in semi-isolation and produce for themselves any objects and clothing that they need.

Apart from the silversmiths, goldsmiths and painters, the craftsmen are the villagers who make things in their spare time; it is the villagers' surplus production that is sold, their everyday items, their fabrics in their traditional dimensions. This never fails to surprise visitors who have heard tell of the beauty and variety of the fabrics and who believe they will be able to find pieces of cloth in the colours they want. With the development of the tourist market, other products have appeared.

Most products, particularly fabrics, are relatively expensive compared to those of other Asian countries. This is because demand exceeds supply, there is a shortage of available labour, and a new upper social class with cash came into existence at the beginning of the 1980s. In addition, there is little mechanization. Every step of production is performed by hand, from dyeing threads or hacking down bamboo in the forest to weaving or braiding the final product. The time spent in producing handicrafts is considerable and can involve as much as a year for certain textiles.

A final factor contributing to high prices is that there is no competition, which explains why there is so little bargaining. People know how much an item costs because the price is fixed by local demand and things cost the same for everybody, tourists and local people alike, so visitors never feel cheated. On the other hand, they don't have the satisfaction of driving a good bargain. Some fabrics can cost US$2,000, while others can be found for as little as US$20! Not all prices are so high, bamboo products in particular are very reasonable, but in general they are more expensive than elsewhere in Asia.

Each region has its specialities: raw silk comes from eastern Bhutan, brocade from Lhuentse (Kurtoe), woollen cloths from Bumthang, bamboo wares from Khyeng, woodwork from Trashi Yangtse, gold- and silverwork from Thimphu, and yak-hair products from the north or the Black Mountains.

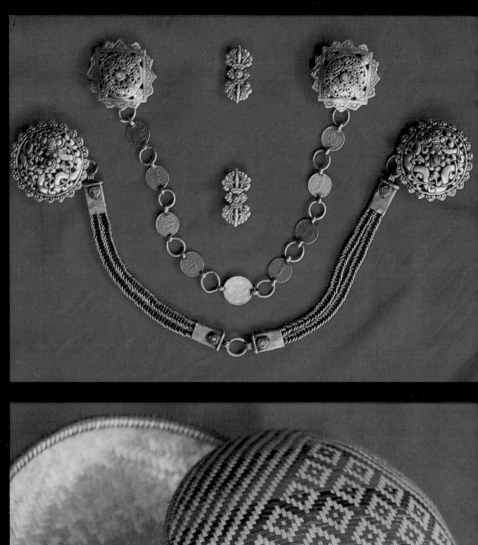

FABRICS

Fabrics are woven at home by women, mostly from central and eastern Bhutan who are famous for their skills; each region produces its own specialities.

There are four kinds of loom: a horizontal frame with pedals, a fixed vertical frame with backstrap, a card loom (used only for making belts), and a fixed horizontal frame with backstrap. The latter is used only by the women of Laya, in northern Bhutan.

The fibres used are cotton, wool, silk (raw and refined), yak hair and nettle fibre (which is still used to make very strong bags but was formerly used for making clothes as well). Yak hair is used by the semi-nomads of northern Bhutan for weaving tents, waterproof coats and clothing. Dyes are usually vegetable or mineral and are made by the weaver herself. Chemical dyes also exist and are easily recognizable by their vivid colours.

Every fabric has a name which describes its particular combination of fibre, colour and pattern. Thus, check woollen material is called *mathra*, *serthra* or *tsangthra* depending on its colour. Women's dresses with a white background covered with brocade designs of silk are called *kushutara*, and those with a blue background are called *onsham*. Material with a yellow background and green and red stripes with additional warp patterns is *mensimathra*.

Material is either striped (horizontal for women, vertical for men in wool, cotton or silk) or check (unisex, largely woollen). Extra designs are obtained by the brocade technique (supplementary weft threads) or by adding warp threads. All patterns have a symbolic meaning: the tree, the *swastika*, the wheel, the diamond-thunderbolt (*vajra*) etc.

Raw silk (*bura*) is often imported from Assam. The silkworm is the *Philosoma cynthia* and not the *Bombyx mori* that produces Chinese silk. For religious reasons, the Bhutanese do not kill the silkworms in their cocoons, so they let them escape and in doing so let the thread break before it is unrolled. This, and the different species of worm, explain why the silk looks and feels much rougher than Chinese or silk. However imported Chinese silk is used for the most expensive and finest fabrics. A visit to the Textile Museum in Thimphu is highly recommended.

JEWELLERY

Jewellery, gold and silverwork is made by a special class of craftsmen. They make objects in silver that are often covered with a fine layer of gold, and they make jewellery in both silver and gold. The silver is beaten, then embossed or engraved with good luck symbols.

(Top) *Samples of komas, the silver brooches which fasten the women's kiras.*
(Bottom) *Traditional hand-woven basket.*

The favourite Bhutanese stones are coral and agate etched with white lines, called zi. These two stones bring high prices, higher even than gold, particularly the zi which the Bhutanese (and Tibetans) believe are found in the earth just as they are. In fact, the zi are agates that were etched by man centuries ago, but the technique is said to have been lost. The necklaces of zi and enormous coral beads which women wear on festival days are not for sale as they are family heirlooms. Today, the price of a zi on the domestic market can reach 2,500 to 3,000 euros and the export of these stones is strictly prohibited.

WOOD

Wooden sculptures are usually made of pine or walnut. Most wooden utensils are made in the Trashi Yangtse region. Woodwork, wooden bowls and receptacles—mainly from this region of eastern Bhutan—are turned on foot-powered treadle lathes. Bowls lined with silver are used only for butter-tea or alcohol. Wooden receptacles are used as serving dishes for food and also as plates by the heads of the household.

Some bowls and all receptacles are lacquered black or red with a substance that is extracted from the tree *Rhus succedanea*. This is the same substance that the Japanese use for lacquer, but in Bhutan the finishes are less sophisticated.

BAMBOO AND RATTAN

Bamboo and rattan wares are mostly made by peasants in the ancient region of Khyeng (*see* page 217). Some objects are made of bamboo or rattan cut into thin strips, braided and sometimes coloured to form geometric designs. Other objects are made of much bigger lathes sewn together with bamboo cord. These make totally sealed, waterproof receptacles such as the tall, cylindrical churns for butter and butter-tea, and smaller boxes for spices, salt or cheese. Still other kinds of bamboo are used for making bows and arrows.

PAPER

Bhutanese paper is made entirely by hand from special barks, used alone or, more often, mixed together in order to obtain the best qualities. For paper-making methods, *see* page 293–294.

RELIGION

Bhutan is the only country in the world to have adopted Mahayana Buddhism in its Tantric form as its official religion. Certain valleys of Bhutan were converted to Tantric Buddhism in the eighth century; a second conversion took place from the 12th century, encompassing slowing the whole country.

TANTRIC BUDDHISM

This form of the religion emerged as the last phase in the long evolution of Buddhism. In the West it is also known as the Diamond Vehicle (*Vajrayana*). The word 'Tantrism' comes from *Tantra*, the name of a body of esoteric texts which appeared roughly between the third and the tenth century. These are divided into four groups that proceed from the simplest to the most complex: *tantras* of action, *tantras* of behaviour, *tantras* of yoga, and finally *tantras* 'without any superiors'. In other earlier forms of Buddhism, the *Tantras* of course do not exist.

Tantric Buddhism disappeared from India, where it had begun, at the time of Muslim invasions early in the 13th century. But continued to exist only in Tibet, Ladakh, Sikkim Mongolia, northern Nepal, Bhutan, China and Japan.

THE BASIC IDEAS

Tantric Buddhist concepts have been explained in many scholarly books and, rather than trying to give a detailed explanation here, we will be simply place the religion in its Bhutanese context.

Tantric Buddhism is based on the same fundamental beliefs as other forms of Buddhism: that the consequences of actions in previous lives, or *karma*, force all beings to reincarnate. All human effort should aim towards enlightenment, which means release from the cycle of incarnations into the state of *Nirvana*, annihilation of the suffering which accompanies all existence. This state of non-suffering leads to the idea of the Absolute, or the Void, a state in which there is no distinction between a subject and the object of its thoughts. Indeed, the sensory world of 'things' has only a phenomenological existence and possesses no true reality except on the plane of Relative Truth. The phenomena have no intrinsic being despite the illusion of reality that they project and do not exist on the plane of Absolute Truth.

Nevertheless, Mahayana Buddhism, and therefore Tantric Buddhism, recognises a pantheon of symbolic deities and *bodhisattvas*, or 'Buddhas-to-be'. These enlightened beings have attained the option of *Nirvana* but they voluntarily decline it and reincarnate in the world of humans in order to help others.

Tantric Buddhism has developed distinctive characteristics. The Buddha's words are contained not only in the scriptures, or *Sutras*, and the texts which lay down rules of monastic discipline (*Vinaya*), but also in the *Tantras*, esoteric writings whose meaning can only be understood through the explanations of a religious master, or lama—a source of great power for the latter.

Different approaches can be used to attain the Void. These include: sublimation, not suppression, of the passions in order to make use of them; a complex system of symbols in which all the deities are seen to represent thought forms with no intrinsic reality; and rituals and religious practices, which are given prominence. These include the reciting of mantras, verbal formulae with precise objectives; prostrations; and the creation of *mandalas*, cosmic diagrams which the faithful use as an aid to meditation (*see* page 83).

The importance of oral transmission by a religious master.

Throughout Tibet and adjacent regions including Bhutan, Tantric Buddhism evolved in a singular way which is known in the West as Tibetan Buddhism or Lamaism. It assimilated certain elements of a pre-Buddhist, shamanic religion, notably the worship of mountains, lakes and indigenous deities which often appear warlike. This syncretism is particularly evident in religious ceremonies and popular beliefs.

A human being is believed to possess four ethereal entities, three of which derive from the pre-Buddhist religion and the last from Buddhism. They are the *la*, which is a kind of soul, the *sog*, or life principle, the *tshe*, or life span (these three disappear at the time of death), and the *namshe*, the conscious principle which transmigrates when the human body dies.

The terrifying divinities are merely emanations from peaceful deities, which assume a wrathful form to subdue evil spirits hostile to Buddhism; they only frighten the ignorant, who do not recognize their true nature. Guru Rinpoche is supposed to have said that 'those who cannot be subdued by peaceful means must be dealt with by terrifying means.'

The nudity of most of these deities implies that the conventions of this world have no importance on higher planes. The various arms of the divinities hold attributes that are symbolic in nature, and the persons being crushed by the fearsome deities are either spirits hostile to Buddhism or primordial negative concepts such as ignorance, jealousy and anger.

Numerous divinities are seen in sexual union with their female counterparts. In Tantric Buddhism, the male principle represents knowledge or the means of attaining an objective whereas the female principle represents wisdom. Without wisdom, knowledge leads nowhere. Similarly, without knowledge, wisdom is useless for attaining the sublime state of Enlightenment in which the world of relative truth is extinguished. The union of knowledge and wisdom permits the attainment of this state.

RITUALS

Rituals, on the one hand, help to neutralize negative conditions and to optimize positive conditions, and, on the other hand, to attain a state in which one can bring well-being to all living things. There are three categories of rituals: those performed with precise actions in view, those addressed to divinities existing outside the four groups of Tantras, and those addressed to the tutelary deities of the Tantra groups.

The first category has four subdivisions denoting the type of action to be accomplished. These are rituals of: peaceful action (to bring rain or to cure physical and mental illnesses); prosperity (to increase financial or mental riches); submission (to subdue one's own spirit); violent action (to overcome hostile forces).

A ritual always begins with an invitation to the deity, followed by a confession of transgressions and negative actions. Next come offerings and prayers aimed at obtaining what one desires. The ritual ends with an invocation to the deity to make it withdraw into the appropriate symbolic prop which might be a statue, a painting or a *mandala*.

RITUAL OBJECTS

Certain ritual objects are the attributes of particular deities and these are also used during religious ceremonies. The most important is the 'diamond-thunderbolt', *dorje* (in Sanskrit called *vajra*, the root of the term *Vajrayana* or 'Diamond Vehicle' which is another name for Tantric Buddhism). The diamond-thunderbolt looks like a small dumb-bell. Four or eight prongs branch off from the middle of the central axis and join again at the extremities. Diamond and thunderbolt both represent purity and indestructibility; hence the Buddha-Spirit, too. The diamond-thunderbolt also symbolizes the knowledge necessary for attaining Enlightenment and therefore the male element. It is often used in rituals in combination with a bell, (*drilbu*), which stands for wisdom and therefore the female element.

The ritual dagger, *phurpa* (in Sanskrit *kila*), was used for Tantric rituals in India as early as the seventh and eighth centuries and it embodies the deity Phurpa. It has a triangular blade and its hilt is shaped like the head of an animal or deity. It is

Unveiling Ceremony, Punakha's thondroel, *March 1993.*

used primarily for sacrificing demons and thus liberating them from the evil sheath
of their bodies, allowing their spirits to obtain a better rebirth. The *phurpa* is also
used for rituals of purification and the protection of places.

T*ormas* are specific to Tibetan Buddhism. They are sacrificial cakes made of rice
or wheat dough and butter, moulded in different shapes and colours. Each deity
and each ritual has its own special *torma* and every ceremony is an occasion for
making these 'cakes', which are then placed on the altar. *Tormas* replace the human
or animal offerings that were made in the pre-Buddhist religion.

Constructions of coloured threads, *doe*, that one sometimes sees placed beside
the road or at crossroads, are offered to harmful spirits to serve as their palaces.
This palace is a substitute, or a ransom, offered to prevent such a spirit from laying
siege to a human being or an animal, causing illness or death.

Seven bowls are placed upon altars and filled with water each morning. They
represent the seven offerings which must be made to Buddha and the deities: food,
drink, water for washing, flowers and incense to please the senses, a butter-lamp
for light and perfume.

A young monk studying a holy text.

RELIGIOUS SCHOOLS

The importance accorded to the utterances of a spiritual master, and therefore to his commentaries on religious texts, has given rise to multiple religious schools which nonetheless subscribe to the same basic doctrinal principles. They differ, however, in their interpretation of the doctrine, in the importance they give to intellectual knowledge as against religious practice, in their attachment to particular texts rather than others, and in the way they perform rituals.

The religious schools that exist in Bhutan today are the official Drukpa, ("those of the thunder-dragon"), a branch of the major Kagyupa ("Followers of the Oral Transmission") school, and the Nyingmapa, or 'Elders', which was founded by Guru Rinpoche (*see* page 61).

The period called the "second diffusion of Buddhism", which extends from the end of the tenth century to the end of the 12th century, saw the emergence of the three major schools of Tantric Buddhism in Tibet: the Kadampa, the Sakyapa and the Kagyupa, the latter subdividing into numerous branches. The Drukpa school traces its origin to the Phagmogrupa, one of the four major branches of the Kagyupa school.

The Drukpa school was founded in Tibet by the religious master Tsangpa Gyare Yeshe Dorje (1161–1211) and spread to Bhutan during the early 13th century. Tradition has it that, shortly before his death, Tsangpa Gyare prophesised to the nephew who was going to succeed him that a young man would arrive from eastern Tibet. Once this man had received all of the Drukpa teachings, he should be sent to convert western Bhutan. The young man was Phajo Drugom Shigpo who, in 1222, introduced the Drukpa teachings in western Bhutan from where they spread. However, it was the arrival of Shabdrung Ngawang Namgyal that brought it to its political and religious peak at the time of the unification of Bhutan, producing the country that exists today (see page 67). The Drukpa school is headed by a Head Abbot, the *Je Khenpo* who is the most important religious authority.

THE RELIGION IN PRACTICE

The religion as it is practised at the popular level consists of profound worship of the Buddha, Guru Rinpoche and all the deities of the Tantric pantheon, along with the indigenous gods. This worship extends also to religious masters and monks.

Certain spiritual masters are reincarnations of high lamas, *Trulkus*, tho are addressed by the title of *Rinpoche*, or 'Great Precious One' (*see* page 63). The idea of the *trulku* or 'Body of Appearance' originates in the Mahayana Buddhist theory of the Three Bodies of the Buddha: the Body of Essence, the Body of Enjoyment and the Body of Appearance. However, Tibetan Tantric Buddhism is the only branch of Buddhism that declares that the Buddha's Body of Appearance could be a precisely identified human being. Rituals are performed on all occasions: birth, marriage, death, official functions, household ceremonies, departure for a trip, illness, to name a few. Ritual or religious ceremony is referred to in Bhutan by different words: *rimro* or *chogu* are the Dzongkha terms; the word *puja* is often used conversationally in English—this Sanskrit word means the same as *rimro* or *chogu*, but it also refers to Hindu rituals in southern Bhutan.

Bhutanese piety takes many forms: daily prayers before the household altar; offerings of butter-lamps; visits to high lamas and to temples or monasteries on auspicious dates in the Buddhist calendar; gifts in kind or money to monks, lamas or religious institutions; the gift of a child to the monastic community; the worship of relics; contributions of all sorts towards the construction or repair of religious monuments, banners or statues; sponsorship of readings from the holy scriptures; pilgrimages to holy places; participation in *wang* (a collective blessing), or *lung* (a collective initiation by a great master into one special text or a whole cycle of texts); putting up prayer flags; reciting prayers with a rosary or prayer wheel; taking part in religious festivals.

The Bhutanese generally do not question their religion. They are Buddhists by birth and they adopt the customs followed in their own families. Their duty is to offer material assistance to monks and others who are dedicated to the religious life, and to gain merit in a future lifetime by performing pious acts. The duty of monks, in return, is to give laymen spiritual support and help in performing acts of piety correctly. Except for the middleclass brought up since the 1970s that feels the desire to understand its religion at an intellectual level, the great majority of the population, shows no immediate need for explanation or rationalization of their religion.

(Following pages) *Skull and fairy masks used during the religious dances.*

Festivals, Dance and Music

Secular Festivals

National Day commemorates the establishment of the monarchy on 17 December 1907. HM the King's Birthday (11 November) and Coronation Day (2 June) are two other important secular festivals. National Day and the King's Birthday are celebrated in all districts with parades and dances performed by schoolchildren.

In addition, 'New Years' are celebrated at various times in different regions. Although the official lunar New Year (*Gyalpo Losar*), which corresponds to the new moon of February–March, is a holiday, no public celebrations other than archery contests take place.

The other 'New Years' are times for merry-making among friends and relatives and, among the Drukpas, a time for archery tournaments. The Nepalese New Year is celebrated in the south of the country at the new moon in April; *Lomba* takes place in Paro and Ha on the last day of the tenth lunar month and the first two days of the 11th lunar month (end of November or beginning of December) which corresponds with the old agricultural New Year (*Sonam Losar*); and New Year in the eastern regions (*Nyinlo*) corresponds with the winter solstice at the beginning of January.

At these festivities, ceremonies dedicated to certain indigenous deities are performed and the people gather to eat, drink, dance and play archery.

Religious Festivals

Religious festivals are very numerous and have different names according to their types, the best known being the *tshechus*, which are festivals in honour of Guru Rinpoche, commemorating his great deeds. These great deeds are all believed to have taken place on the tenth of the month, which is the meaning of the word *tshechu*, even though all *tshechus* do not take place on tenth days. All the district *dzong*s and a large number of villages, especially in the east, have an annual *tshechu* which attracts peasants from the surrounding countryside. The complete librettos of the Paro, Thimphu, and Wangduephodrang *tshechus* were translated by this author under the name of Trashi Wangmo and are available from the DoT.

Tshechus are celebrated for several days, between three and five according to the location, and are the occasion for dances that are clearly defined in religious content. They can be performed by monks, laymen or *gomchens*, and the repertory is the same practically everywhere. Certain *tshechus* end with the worship of a huge appliqué *thangka* representing Guru Rinpoche and his Eight Manifestations. Such a *thangka* is called a *thongdrel*, which means that simply by viewing it, people can be delivered from the cycle of reincarnations. Some festivals also have a *wang*, a collective verbal blessing given by a high lama. Coloured threads are then distributed and people tie them around their necks as witness to the blessing. Sometimes the *wang* is called *mewang*, meaning 'blessing by fire', as the participants jump over a fire which burns away their impurities accumulated during the year.

In a few important *dzongs*—Thimphu, Punakha, Paro, Trongsa, Wangduephodrang —two large festivals take place each year: a *dromchoe*, which generally includes dances and is dedicated to Yeshe Gompo (Mahakala) or Palden Lhamo, the two main protective deities of the Drukpas, and a *tshechu* dedicated to Guru Rinpoche. The *Dromchoe* at Punakha takes place in the first month of the lunar year and ends with a *Serda*, a magnificent procession which re-enacts an episode of the war against the Tibetans in the 17th century. (*See* the Punakha *Thondroel*, page 198)

Atsaras are clowns whose expressive masks and postures are an indispensable element in any religious festival: they confront the monks, toss out salacious jokes, and distract the crowd with their antics when the religious dances begin to grow tedious. Believed to represent the *acaryas*, religious masters of India, they are the only people permitted to mock religion in a society where sacred matters are treated with the highest respect. For a few days these popular entertainers are allowed the freedom to express a formulaic challenge within an established framework that does not, however, upset the social and religious order.

Some religious festivals include only a few dances and consist mostly of readings from a particular text. On these occasions, villagers assemble in the temple and participate in the prayers while at the same time drinking strong alcoholic beverages. Each village takes pride in its annual religious festival, whether it includes dances or simply prayers, and any villager who has gone to live in the city is expected to come back home for it. He/she will then sponsor a large part of the festival.

Festivals related to Bon beliefs are still practised in many parts of the country and are linked to fertility and prosperity. For the Bhutanese, religious festivals offer an opportunity to become immersed in the meaning of their religion and to gain much merit. They are also occasions for seeing people, and for being seen; for social exchanges, and for flaunting success. People bring out their finest clothes, their most beautiful jewels; they take out picnics rich with meat and abundant alcohol. Men and women joke and flirt. An atmosphere of convivial, slightly ribald good humour prevails.

(Following pages) *The dance of the 'Drum beaters from Drametse'
during the first day of the Paro festival.*

RELIGIOUS DANCES

The numerous religious dances are called *cham*. Dancers, either monks or lay practiti oners, wear spectacular costumes made of yellow silk or rich brocade, often decorated with ornaments of carved bone. For certain dances they wear masks which may represent animals, fearsome deities, skulls, manifestations of Guru Rinpoche or just plain human beings. The masks are so heavy that dancers protect themselves from injury by binding their heads in strips of cloth which support the mask. The dancers then see out through the opening of the mouth.

Dances can be grouped into three broad categories: didactic dances which are dramas with a moral (the Dance of the Princes and Princesses, the Dance of the Stag and the Hunting Dogs, the Dance of the Judgement of the Dead); dances that purify and protect a place from harmful spirits (the Dance of the Masters of the Cremation Grounds, the Dance of the Stag, the Dance of the Fearsome deities, the Dance of the Black Hats, the Dance of the Ging and the Tsholing, the dances of the Ging with sticks and the Ging with swords); and dances that proclaim the victory of Buddhism and the glory of Guru Rinpoche (all dances with drums, the Dance of the Heroes, the Dance of Celestial Beings, the Dance of the Eight Manifestations of Guru Rinpoche).

The most famous dances are the following:

The Dance of the Black Hats (Shanag) A spectacular dance in which dancers representing Tantrists with supernatural powers take possession of the dancing area to drive out evil spirits and purify the ground with their footsteps. This dance also tells the story of the assassination of the anti-Buddhist Tibetan king, Langdarma, in the year AD 842 by a monk, Pelkyi Dorje, who had hidden his bow and arrows in the voluminous sleeves of his garment. Beating drums as they dance, the 'Black Hat' dancers proclaim their victory over the evil spirits.

The Dance of the Drummers from Drametse (Drametse Ngacham) This is the best-known dance of all, composed in the 16th century at Drametse Monastery in eastern Bhutan by a saint who had a vision of Guru Rinpoche's heaven. Twelve men wearing yellow skirts and animal masks beat drums as they dance; they represent Guru Rinpoche's entourage and they are celebrating the victory of religion.

The Dance of the Masters of the Cremation Grounds (Durdag) This dance requires some measure of understanding of Tantric symbolism. Skeletons guard the eight cremation grounds which are situated on the edges of the cosmic diagram where Tantric deities dwell. Their mission is to protect the cosmic diagram from harmful influences and spirits.

The Dance of the Fearsome Deities (*Tungam*) Dancers dressed in brocade and wearing masks of wrathful deities represent the entourage of one aspect of Guru Rinpoche, Guru Dorje Droloe, who leads the dance. Armed with ritual daggers (*phurpa*), the dancers execute and redeem an evil spirit by liberating its conscious principle from its body.

The Lute Dance (*Dranyen Cham*) This dance celebrates the founding and spread of the Drukpa school.

Religious Song (*Choeshe*) Very similar to the preceding dance and performed in the same costume, this dance and the song which accompanies it commemorate the beginning of a pilgrimage to Mount Tsari in Tibet by the founder of the Drukpa school, Tsangpa Gyare.

The Dance of the Four Stags (*Shacham*) This dance commemorates the vanquishing of the God of the Wind by Guru Rinpoche who commandeers the god's stag as his own mount.

The Dance of the Judgement of the Dead (*Raksha Marcham*) This dance is one of the most interesting of the *Tshechu* and it is extremely didactic. It is divided into two parts.

First comes a long dance by the Rakshas who are aides to the Lord of the Dead. They wear yellow skirts and animal masks. Then the Lord of the Dead—Shinje Choekyi Gyelpo—enters together with his attendants, the white god and the black demon who live with all beings and bear witness to their actions. The Lord of the Dead is a wrathful representation of Avalokiteshvara, the deity of compassion. Next begins the judgement proper. The first to enter is a sinner dressed all in black with a black mask, holding a basket containing a piece of meat that symbolizes his sins. The Lord of the Dead listens to his tale, then has his actions weighed on a scale. The good actions are symbolized by white pebbles, the bad ones by black pebbles. The white god tries to save the sinner by emphasising his good actions, whereas the black demon describes the man's wicked actions in detail. In the end, the sinner is sent to hell to the great joy of the black demon who accompanies him on the road to hell, symbolized by a length of black cloth.

A general dance ensues and then a virtuous man enters. As a sign of his piety, he is dressed in white, with a white face, and he holds a prayer flag. The same judgement scene as before unfolds and the virtuous man is sent to paradise on a

(Following pages) (Left) *At Paro Tsechu, a black hat dancer expels evil spirits with his supernatural powers.*
(Right) *A 'black hat' dancer performs outside a dzong during a religious festival.*

road which is symbolized by a length of white cloth. The black demon tries to seize him at the last moment but the white god saves him and he is welcomed by celestial beings.

The Dance of the Princes and Princesses (Pholey Moley) This is certainly one of the Bhutanese public's best-loved dances and it is also a little lewd!

The written story of King Norzang concerns the king's love for his favourite queen, Yidrogma, which provokes the jealousy of the other queens. The latter arrange things so that the king goes off to war, and they then force Yidrogma to flee to her father in fear of her life. But when the king returns from battle he soon understands the stratagems of the other queens and begs Yidrogma to come back and live with him, which she finally consents to do.

The popular version of the original story is quite different: two princes go off to war, leaving their wives in the charge of a couple of old servants. As soon as the princes are out of sight, the princesses and the maidservant start romping with the *atsaras*. When the princes return they are furious and cut off the noses of their wives as punishment. The old servant also cuts off his wife's nose. Then the princes allow themselves to weaken and they call for a doctor to sew back the noses. Although the doctor gladly sews back the noses of the beautiful princesses, he is far less enthusiastic about sewing on that of the maidservant, who smells awful. In the end all's well that ends well and everyone is reconciled.

The Dance of the Stag and the Hunting Dogs (Shawa Shachhi) This dance depicts the conversion to Buddhism of a hunter named Gonpo Dorje by the great saint Milarepa (1040–1123). More like a theatrical play than any of the other dances, it is very long and is usually performed in two parts, each of which concludes one day of *tshechu*.

The story goes that while the saint Milarepa was meditating in a cave, he heard shouting and barking. He came out of his retreat and saw a stag covered with sweat and trembling with fear. Milarepa calmed it by singing a religious hymn and took it under his protection. Soon afterwards two dogs appeared which had been chasing the stag, and Milarepa won them over with one of his songs. The hunter arrived unexpectedly, looking for his dogs, and when he saw them lying down with the stag at Milarepa's feet, he flew into a rage and shot a poisoned arrow at the saint. The saint used his superhuman powers to snap the hunter's bow, while the arrow, instead of hitting him, returned to the astonished hunter. Milarepa then intoned a song that succeeded in convincing the hunter to give up hunting and take up Buddhism.

The first part of this dance has a comic tone, starting with the hunter's servant who jokes with the *atsaras*. The hunter, crowned with leaves and carrying his bow, then arrives with his two dogs. He performs non-Buddhist rituals aimed at bringing him good luck on the hunt, while his servant and the *atsaras* clown around him.

The second part is more dignified and religious. Milarepa appears clad all in white except for his characteristic red hat. He holds a pilgrim's staff in his hand and with his songs he converts first the dogs and then the hunter. The conversion is symbolized by a rope over which the hunter and the dogs must jump.

The Dance of the Ging and the Tsholing (Ging dang Tsholing) It is said that this dance was performed for the first time in Samye Monastery in Tibet, in the eighth century, by Guru Rinpoche himself. The Tsholing, terrifying deities who are seen as protectors of the religion, purify the ground of demonic influences. The Ging, who make up Guru Rinpoche's retinue, then chase away the Tsholing in order to take possession of the area and proclaim victory for the religion by beating drums. With their drumstick, they hit people on the head to drive out impurities, and the public whistles to keep demons far away.

The Dance of the Eight Manifestations of Guru Rinpoche (Guru Tshen Gye) The Eight Aspects under which Guru Rinpoche manifested himself on various occasions appear in a procession with the principal aspect of Guru Rinpoche shaded by a parasol. Certain other aspects are accompanied by their retinues and small celestial beings. In order of appearance they are:

Dorje Droloe, 'Liberated Diamond-Thunderbolt', who wears a terrifying dark red mask and a garland of skulls around his body holds a diamond-thunderbolt (*dorje*) and a ritual dagger (*phurpa*). He earned this name after vanquishing evil spirits who were creating obstacles to Buddhism at Taktshang in Paro and Singye *dzong* in Kurtoe. Dorje Droloe is followed by his entourage of fearsome deities.

Tshokye Dorje, 'Diamond-Thunderbolt Born from a Lake', who is dressed in blue brocade and wears a peaceful blue mask, carries in his hands a diamond-thunderbolt and a small bell. His name derives from his miraculous birth in a blue lotus on Lake Dhanakosha.

Loden Chogse, 'He Who Wishes to Acquire Supreme Knowledge', who wears a robe of red brocade and a white mask with a knot of hair and a crown, holds in his hands a little drum and a bowl. He got this name after he had listened to the teachings of the *Vajrayana* and mastered the sciences inculcated by the Indian masters; tutelary deities then appeared to him.

(Following pages) (Left) *A young monk taking a rest from his part as a fairy during a festival.* (Right) *Guru Rinpoche surrounded by his entourage during the dance of his 'Eight Manifestations'.*

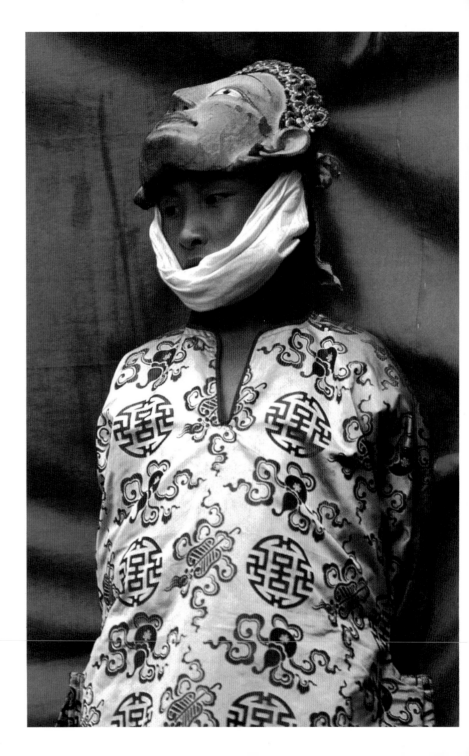

Padmasambhava, 'Born of the Lotus', clad in a monk's robe of dark red and yellow, wears a white mask with a pointed red hat, a so-called pundit's hat. He got his name after he used his supernatural powers to transform the wood-pile (on which the king of Zahor wanted to burn him alive) into a lake.

Guru Rinpoche, 'Most Precious Master', is the chief aspect, yet he is not listed as one of the Eight Aspects. He wears a human mask of gilded copper crowned by his characteristic hat and is attended by two monks while a third shades him with a parasol.

Shakya Sengye, 'Lion of the Shakya Family', clad in a red and yellow monk's robe, wears a mask resembling Buddha's face with a hairstyle of tight blue curls, holds a begging bowl in his hands. He was called by this name when, after having renounced his kingdom, he went to meditate and study in the cave of Maratika in Nepal with the master Prabahati.

Pema Gyelpo, 'Lotus-King', who wears a robe of red brocade and a pinkish-orange mask with a beard, holds in his hands a mirror and a small drum. He got this name when he returned to his native kingdom of Ogyen (Oddhyana); at that moment the chiefs of the country wanted to burn him but could not succeed in doing so. Seeing this as a sign of the spiritual realization of Guru Rinpoche, they converted to Buddhism and offered him the Kingdom.

Nyima Oezer, 'Sunbeam', who is dressed in yellow brocade, wears a yellow mask with a beard of blue hair and holds a trident in his hand. He got this name when, as he was preaching in the cremation grounds, he conquered evil spirits and made them promise to protect the Buddhist doctrine ever afterwards.

Sengye Drathok, 'He with the Voice of a Lion', is clad in blue brocade; his blue mask crowned with five skulls is terrifying. He was called by this name after the power of his words vanquished 500 heretical masters who had tried to destroy the doctrine of Buddhism.

The principal aspect of Guru Rinpoche is seated, whereas each of the other aspects, with the exception of Padmasambhava, dances before going to join the principal aspect. Then a public blessing takes place and the fervour of the people is fully demonstrated: the faithful press forward to receive a thread of blessing, not from a monk who represents Guru Rinpoche but from Guru Rinpoche himself, incarnated as a human being. The dance area is transformed into a heaven, and celestial beings adorned with bone ornaments come to dance and sing the praises of Guru Rinpoche. The dance concludes with a final procession and the exit of all the aspects of Guru Rinpoche. It is the culmination of a *tshechu* and the end.

RELIGIOUS MUSIC

Like the dances, religious music reflects a strong Tibetan influence. The instruments are long trumps (*dungchen*), oboe (*gyaling*), a double-sided drum (*nga*) held in a frame and beaten with a curved drumstick, different types of cymbals (*rolmo*), a trumpet made from a femur (*kangling*), and a conch shell. In addition there is the *damaru*, a small, double-faced, hand-held drum that is beaten with hard pellets attached by strings, and the small bell (*drilbu*). Music gives rhythm to the dances and religious ceremonies, and it punctuates the singing or recitation of the texts. The sound of the long trumps indicates the end of a dance.

SECULAR DANCES AND MUSIC

These dances are performed by both sexes, either separately or together, and can be divided into two groups: dances from southern Bhutan which are influenced by Nepalese culture, and those of the rest of the country which are influenced by Tibetan culture. Generally, dancers accompany themselves by singing; musical instruments being used only on the most official occasions. A flute, drums and, more recently, a harmonium and guitar make up the orchestra for the music of southern Bhutan. In the north, the orchestra is a flute (*lim*), a six-stringed lute (*dranyen*), a two-stringed violin played with a bow (*piwang*), and more rarely, a trapezoidal tabletop zither played with two hammers. The musical scale is pentatonic.

While "Nepali" dances from the southern borderland usually have a lively rhythm, dances in the rest of the country have a much slower rhythm which often picks up speed as the dance progresses, the steps sliding and tapping.

Many of the songs, even folksongs, have a religious base. There also exist mystical songs—composed by saints, prayers and biographies of saints sung by wandering monks, and the great epic cycle of King Gesar (*drung*). All these are in classical Tibetan. Songs associated with daily life, on the other hand, are in the vernacular languages and are much freer, even allowing a certain amount of improvisation. Songs ring out at times such as rice-planting, ploughing and harvesting, when women pound earth for building the walls of a house, or when they weave with the rhythm of the shuttles, when a carpenter fits his timbers or a herdsman drives his animals to pasture, when a village makes merry at a wedding or when muleteers set off along precipitous paths. Today, young people are abandoning, to some degree, traditional music in favour of Bhutanese pop music, called *rigsar*, which blends Western, Indian and Tibetan melodies. These songs are very popular and, even if they are not to the taste of everyone, allow young people to express their feelings in *Dzongkha*. As such, these songs contribute very effectively to the spreading of the national language.

The central tower of Paro dzong.

THREE FREQUENTLY SEEN RELIGIOUS SERIES

In Bhutan you will see three sequences of objects that might be called, for want of a better term, a 'religious series'.

The Eight Auspicious Signs (Trashi Tagye)

The Treasure Vase symbolizes the contents of the Buddhist doctrine, treasures that will overcome all desire on the part of its believers.

The Endless Knot is a symbol of love.

The Victorious Banner proclaims the victory of Buddhism and the victory of virtue over sin.

The Wheel of Law, as it moves, symbolizes that the Buddhist doctrine is alive and dynamic.

The Golden Parasol offers protection against the sun; in the same way, the Buddhist doctrine protects a person's spirit.

The Golden Fish keep their eyes wide open in spite of the water, and they have knowledge of obstacles and objectives; similarly, the Buddhist doctrine permits the faithful to take correct actions in the world.

The White Conch symbolizes the propagation of the Buddhist doctrine.

The Lotus symbolizes non-attachment; as the lotus does not remain caught in the mud, so the non-attached spirit does not remain caught in the life of this world.

The Seven Treasures of the Universal Buddhist Monarch (Gyelsi Nadun)

The Flaming Wheel allows the Monarch to travel wherever he wishes at great speed and thus vanquish his enemies.

The Precious Jewel is made of lapis lazuli and dispels the gloom of night. It fulfils the wishes of the Monarch and his subjects.

The Precious Queen is adorned with all the virtues and is a perfect companion for the Monarch.

The **Precious Minister** is strong, brave, and takes good care of the Kingdom while remaining perfectly loyal to the Monarch.

The **Precious Elephant** is as strong as a thousand elephants and an irreplaceable helper in battle.

The **Precious Horse** can fly in the sky and enables the Monarch to circle the world three times in a day.

The **Precious General** possesses great physical and mental strength, and does not wantonly harm others but only fights to save his Monarch.

The Eight Kinds of Chortens (Chorten Degye)

The Eight Chortens commemorate eight different events in Buddha's life and each has a slightly different design from the others.

Desheg Chorten To celebrate the birth of his son at Lumbini, Buddha's father ordered a *chorten* to be built.

Changchub Chorten To commemorate Buddha's Enlightenment at Bodhgaya, the king of the region ordered a *chorten* to be built.

Choekhor Chorten To commemorate Buddha's first sermon in the Deer Park at Sarnath near Benares, his five disciples had a *chorten* built named after the Wheel of Religion.

Chotrul Chorten To celebrate Buddha's victory over the non-Buddhist masters at Sravasti, the king of the region ordered a *chorten* to be built named after miracles.

Lhabab Chorten To celebrate Buddha's return to earth after he had ascended to the Heaven of the Thirty-Three Gods to preach the doctrine to his mother, the king of the region ordered a *chorten* to be built named after the descent from the godly heaven.

Yendum Chorten To celebrate Buddha's victory at Rajagriya over his wicked cousin who had sown discord among the monks, the king of the region ordered a *chorten* to be built named after reconciliation.

Namgyal Chorten To commemorate Buddha's voluntary prolongation of his life at Vaisali, the gods built a *chorten* named after victory over death.

Nyende Chorten To commemorate Buddha's Nirvana at Kusinagara, the people of this country built a *chorten* named after his passing away.

THE IMPORTANT STAGES OF LIFE

Birth

The birth of a child, whether boy or girl, is always welcome. The mother receives no visitors except for family during the first three days after the birth. A *lhasang*, or purification ceremony, is then performed in the house, after which visitors may present themselves. The customary gifts in a village are eggs, rice or maize in diverse forms, while in a town they are children's clothes and nappies (diapers). A little money is always given to the newborn to bring good luck. The mother is given a rich diet and encouraged particularly to drink a hot alcoholic beverage made with *ara*, butter and eggs that will help her breast feed. This beverage is also served to visitors and the atmosphere is very jolly.

Naming the Child

The child is not named immediately; if possible, it is named by an eminent religious personage or the lama-astrologer whom the parents visit. The child's horoscope, *kyetsi*, is then established. It gives the date of birth by the Bhutanese lunar calendar and the list of rituals to be performed each year, or in the event of problems. The birth also has now to be registered with the government.

Marriage

No special ceremony takes place at puberty and the next important stage is marriage. The marriage can be a completely informal affair or it can be a complicated ceremony, depending on the status of the families and the way the young people came to know one another. It can be a marriage of love or an arranged marriage; in the latter case, both the young people are consulted by their families about the choice of a partner, who usually belongs to the family of friends so they are already acquainted with each other. This kind of arranged marriage is unlike those in some parts of Asia where the future spouses are total strangers. Moreover, there is always the possibility of refusing. Even in a marriage of love, the partners want their parents to approve of their choice. If the families disapprove, the young couple either comply with

their parents' wishes, or they run away together, presenting their parents with a *fait accompli*.

A marriage between two youngsters of affluent families is a social occasion. At an auspicious hour prescribed by the astrologer, the bridegroom and his friends go to fetch the bride at her home and bring her and her friends back to his house. Two members of the family stand in front of the door holding a bowl of milk and a bowl of water, symbolizing prosperity for the new couple's life.

The *marchang* ceremony is performed next and then the couple sits down near the monks who intone the marriage ritual. The religious ceremony does not carry the same weight as the sacrament of Christian weddings. The couple then exchange cups of alcohol and are declared man and wife. The families, followed by friends, cover them with white scarves and the gifts pile up, especially fabrics that are always presented in quantities of three, five or seven. A copious meal (with plenty to drink) and dancing end the day.

Among members of the population who are less well-off, young people simply start living together, thus declaring themselves married in the eyes of society. Very often the marriage is not even announced verbally; it is just a fact. Nowadays, the legal registration of a marriage is encouraged by the government but it is not always done outside the towns.

Traditionally, separation is frequent; if it is the woman who seeks the divorce, her new companion has to pay a fine to the former husband. The new laws give 25% of the income or salary to the partner.

Promotions

A promotion up the social ladder is blessed in much the same way as a marriage by monks who perform a ritual in the home of the person being promoted. He/she sits on a raised seat and receives the traditional gifts of cloth or money accompanied by a white scarf from visitors.

Funerals

A funeral is by far the most spiritually important and costly ceremony because of all the expenses it entails. Death does not mean the end but simply the passing into another life, so everything must be done to

A village headman celebrates at the Punakha Tsechu.

make it happen in the most favourable manner. As rapidly as possible after death has occurred, monks, lamas or *gomchens* must be called to perform the ritual to help the conscious principle to exit from its carnal envelope, and to read the *Book of the Dead*. This reading guides the dead person through all the stages that his conscious principle must pass through, and it explains the visions that he will see. This intermediate state between death and the conscious principle's reincarnation in another body is called the *bardo*.

The rituals are complex and can last up to 49 days without interruption if a family is very well off. Most often the rituals last for seven days with more on the 14th, 21st and 49th days. Those that take place between the 21st and the 49th days have to be performed in a temple and not in the house. After the 49th day, a ceremony intended to purify the atmosphere and bring prosperity to the living takes place in the house of the deceased.

From the moment of death, the deceased is placed in a curled-up position on a catafalque covered with a multicoloured cloth, which, for most of the time, is placed outside the house. Visitors who come to offer condolences to the family place a gift of money and a white scarf on the catafalque. Meals are served to the deceased throughout the period following death and until all rituals are finished.

The cremation of the body takes place on a day decided by the astrologer but at least three days after the death. If the deceased comes from an affluent background or is a monk or lama, the body is placed in a special clay construction which acts as a funeral pyre. Otherwise it is wrapped in a white shroud and simply placed on the funeral pyre. When the fire is lit, relatives and friends throw white scarves and money into the blaze while praying for a good reincarnation for the deceased. During the next three years, an important ritual should take place on the anniversary of the death, the most extensive being the one performed after the third year, marking the true end of funeral observances.

After the cremation, the ashes are usually scattered in the river or mixed with clay to become votive tablets. Then, depending on the piety and affluence of the family, prayer flags and chortens are raised to bring merit to the deceased. Small children are not cremated but are exposed to vultures or thrown into the river.

PLACES TO VISIT

The following chapters introduce the main centres of interest in Bhutan, from the west to the east. While the interior of temples, monasteries and *dzong* are, for most of them and to date (mid 2005), still closed to visits by foreigners, a short description will be given. In some special cases, permission can be granted by the National Commission for Cultural Affairs (NCCA, which is under the Home and Culture Mininistry).

Although the interiors of some temples, monasteries and *dzong*s are forbidden to foreign travellers at the present time, short descriptions of all these sites will nonetheless be given.

WESTERN BHUTAN
THE PARO VALLEY

The first thing you will notice in the Paro valley is the transparent purity of the air and the absence of noise.

As you disembark at the Paro airport and breathe your first wisp of Bhutanese silence, you will notice that Bhutan is unlike other places; and Paro is a perfect entry to this other world. The Paro valley has kept its bucolic nature in spite of the airport and the existence of development projects. Fields, brown or green depending on the season, cover most of the valley floor, while hamlets and isolated farms dot the landscape. The houses of the Paro valley are considered to be among the most beautiful in the country; they are the only ones with rows of windows on three levels, and the prosperity of the valley is evident from their size.

Closed off except for a narrow, arid gorge at Chhuzom or Chuzomsa ('the confluence'), the valley opens up little by little, reaching its widest point before the airport. Then it divides in two near the *dzong* and Paro village: one valley called Dopchari runs northwards for about 15 kilometres (nine miles), while the main valley with the paved road continues northwest. The road terminates at Drukyel *dzong*, 16 kilometres (ten miles) from Paro. The end of the valley appears to be blocked by the *dzong* but in fact it continues, growing steadily narrower, for about a dozen more kilometres (about seven and a half miles).

The Paro valley is enchanting. The road is lined by willow trees following a mountain stream; the gaily decorated houses have shingled roofs; peasants lead horses adorned with bright woollen pompoms; sturdy young women work in the

rice fields with their skirts tucked up to their knees, easing their hard labour by singing or joking with passers-by. A walk on foot across the valley is without doubt the best way to appreciate its beauty. Carts pulled by mules, a shop sunk to the back of a house and new bridges juxtapose together, giving the valley its soul.

Paro is believed to be one of the first valleys to have received the influence of Buddhism, and two temples bear witness to the glorious introduction of the religion: Kyichu and Taktshang.

KYICHU LHAKHANG

Kyichu Lhakhang is composed of twin temples which are somewhat set back on the left of the road to Taktshang and Drukyel *dzong*. Built on a terrace and surrounded by a low wall, the two temples are visible from the road through a cluster of prayer flags.

According to Bhutanese tradition, the first temple at Kyichu was built by the Buddhist Tibetan king, Songtsen Gampo, in the seventh century. The story goes that a giant demoness lay across the whole area of Tibet and the Himalayas and was preventing the spread of Buddhism. To subdue her, King Songtsen Gampo decided to build 108 temples which would be placed on all the points of her body. Of these 108 temples, 12 were built in accordance with precise plans. In about the year AD 638 the temple of the Jokhang in Lhasa was built over the very heart of the demoness. Kyichu Lhakhang was built on her left foot and belongs to a group of four temples categorised as 'subjugating regions beyond the frontiers'. This initial construction put the Paro valley on the Buddhist map.

The history of Kyichu Lhakhang remains unclear until the beginning of the 13th century, at which time it is known that it was under the administration of the Lhapa school. It can be assumed that the temple came under the protection of the Drukpas at the end of the 13th century when the Drukpas defeated the Lhapas.

In 1839, the temple was restored on the orders of the 25th Je Khenpo, Sherab Gyeltsen, who also donated the superb statue of Avalokiteshvara with a thousand hands and a thousand eyes, which is located in the sanctuary.

In 1968, H M Ashi Kesang, the Queen Mother of Bhutan, arranged for a second temple to be built alongside the first one, in the same style.

Opposite the entrance of the small courtyard that leads to the two temples, a small building provides a place for devotees to offer butter lamps. The walls are decorated with paintings of the Guardians of the Four Directions, a water deity, and

Taktshang, 'the Tiger's nest', in Paro valley marks the place where Padmasambhava meditated.

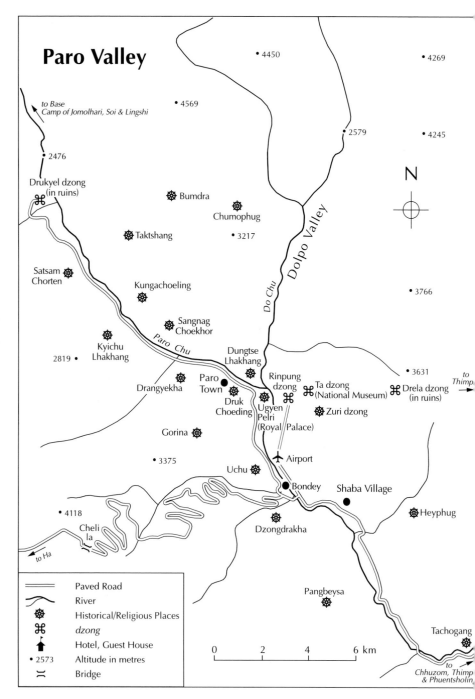

Paro Valley

to Base
Camp of Jomolhari, Soi & Lingshi

• 4450
• 4569
• 4269
• 2579
• 4245

• 2476

Drukyel dzong
(in ruins)

⚘ Bumdra

⚘ Chumophug

⚘ Taktshang
• 3217

Satsam ⚘
Chorten

⚘ Kungachoeling

• 3766

⚘ Sangnag
Choekhor

⚘ Kyichu
Lhakhang

Paro Chu

Dungtse
Lhakhang ⚘

Do Chu

Dolpo Valley

2819 •

• 3631

to
Thimp.

⚘ Drangyekha

Paro
Town ●

Rinpung
dzong ⌘

⌘ Ta dzong
(National Museum)

⌘ Drela dzong
(in ruins)

Druk
Choeding ⚘

Ugyen
Pelri
(Royal Palace)

⚘ Zuri dzong

⚘ Gorina

Airport ✈

• 3375

Uchu ⚘

● Bondey

Shaba Village ●

• 4118

Cheli
la

⚘ Heyphug

to Ha

⚘ Dzongdrakha

Pangbeysa ⚘

Legend

═══	Paved Road
∿	River
⚘	Historical/Religious Places
⌘	dzong
⬆	Hotel, Guest House
• 2573	Altitude in metres
≍	Bridge

0   2   4   6 km

Tachogang ⚘

to
Chhuzom, Thimp
& Phuentsholing

© Airphoto International Ltd.

Genyen Dorje Dradul, a local mountain-deity turned Protector of Buddhism, mounted on a red horse. An orange tree grows in the little courtyard. The ancient temple stands opposite the entrance with the modern temple on the right.

The Ancient Temple is deeply venerated for its antiquity and for the role it has played. Turquoise and coral that have been donated by the faithful are set into the floor at the place where prostrations are performed. The paintings covering the walls on all sides of the sanctuary show the Twelve Acts of Buddha and his Previous Lives.

On the left side of the window is a painting of three personages: at the top is Guru Rinpoche, below him is Shabdrung Ngawang Namgyal with the First *Desi* of Bhutan; at the bottom is the 25th *Je Khenpo*, Sherab Gyeltsen, who restored the temple in 1839. To the right of the window is a painting of Buddha and the Sixteen Arhats, the first persons to attain the state of Buddhahood. At the corner of the wall above is the long life and mountain goddess Tsheringma, mounted on a white lion, while below is the Protector of Buddhism, Genyen Dorje Dradul, riding a red horse.

Many statues attest to the reverence in which this temple is held, and nearly all of them are statues of Avalokiteshvara in his form with a thousand hands and a thousand eyes. There is also a statue of the Tibetan king, Songtsen Gampo and a statue of Amitayus, sitting in a posture of meditation with a vase of long life in his hands.

The sanctuary is closed, but it is possible to catch a glimpse of magnificient statues of the Eight Bodhisattvas and most especially of one of the holiest statues of Bhutan, the statue of the Jowo, Buddha as a prince at the age of eight, which is similar to the one in the Jokhang Temple in Lhasa.

The recent temple is dedicated to Guru Rinpoche and the teachings (called the *Kagye*) that he gave to his disciples for subjugating harmful forces, and which constitute a part of the essential teachings of the *Nyingmapa* school. The temple contains a large and spectacular statue of Guru Rinpoche as well as a statue of the great master Dilgo Khyentse Rinpoche (1910–1991).

THE WAY TO TAKTSHANG LHAKHANG

Beyond Kyichu Lhakhang, the road continues downward into the valley and after about five kilometres (three miles) you will see the Taktshang Lhakhang complex on the right, at 2,950 metres (9,678 feet) above sea level. In April 1998 Taktshang burnt down but the government rebuilt it and it was consecrated at the end of March 2005. The buildings cling to the black rock, overhanging the valley below by 800 metres (over 2,600 feet). The fact that the access path to the complex of temples called Taktshang Pelphug is scarcely visible makes its location all the more impressive.

Taktshang (2,950/3,200 metres) is one of the most venerated places of pilgrimage in the Himalayan world and, within it, there are thirteen holy places. However, most people only go to the one called Taktshang Pelphug, where Guru Rinpoche meditated.

The (car) road now crosses the river, and the path rises gently through a forest and comes to a hamlet where the car has to be left and the walk starts.

For people unaccustomed to the altitude it takes about two hours at an average walking speed to reach the temples. As on all walks in the mountains, sweaters or jackets are essential, just as it is wise to take a water bottle and some food.

The path crosses a meadow on the other side of which the real climb begins, up through a forest of oak and rhododendron. You come to the first level ground at a place where there is a cluster of prayer flags. On the right, a short route about 100 metres (328 feet) long leads to the Taktshang tea house, a log cabin that can be seen through the trees from the prayer flags. The view over the temples from this tea house is extraordinary, and the effort of climbing up to it is amply rewarded. Take note, as well, of the archery field near the tea house.

After a refreshing drink, the climb continues, but it is still very steep. The forest now takes on a ghostly appearance because some of the trees have become diseased and Spanish moss hangs like tattered shrouds from the branches. The path passes the edge of a field below a house; this is the only flat part of the walk, and is, alas, short. You arrive now at the second group of prayer flags and you notice that you are, in fact, much higher than the main Taktshang complex; one overlooks the complex and the view is breathtaking.

The descent begins along the wall of the precipice and for a few dozen metres, the walk can be rather worrying, although the path is always perfectly laid out. There is no rock-climbing to be done at all. The path then widens, but continues to descend, down to a bridge that connects two rock clusters. Now it is Taktshang that overlooks the visitor. A small house wedged in a crevice of the rock serves as a place of meditation. Right next to it runs a holy spring, which would have been created miraculously when Yeshe Tshogyel, one of Guru Rinpoche's wives, threw her rosary against the rock. This place, always in shadow, is damp and very cold, and it is not uncommon to find, even in June, bits of ice. From there, a long flight of steps along the rock wall leads, by a final steep climb, to the entrance door of the Taktshang Pelphug complex that was burnt down.

A final staircase inside the entrance leads up to a landing. The narrowness of the place makes the whole ground plan somewhat complicated, but the three main temples are all situated in the same building.

An old woman turns a prayer wheel and wish for a good rebirth (Kyichu Lhakhang).

TAKTSHANG PELPHUG

Taktshang, the 'Tiger's nest', gets its name from the story of its foundation. According to tradition in the eighth century, Guru Rinpoche came to Taktshang in a miraculous manner, flying on the back of a tigress from Khenpajong in the region of Kurtoe. According to Bhutanese tradition, the tigress was a form taken by one of the Master's consorts for the occasion. Guru Rinpoche meditated for three months in a cave at Taktshang and converted the Paro valley to Buddhism. In his terrifying form of Dorje Droloe, Guru Rinpoche used the religious cycle of the *Kagye* to subjugate the Eight Categories of Evil Spirits during his stay there.

Guru Rinpoche then returned to Tibet and transmitted the teachings of the *Kagye* cycle to his disciples, particularly to Langchen Pelkyi Singye who, in his turn, came to Taktshang to meditate in the year 853, following in the footsteps of his master. He gave his name of Pelphug to the cave, "Pelkyi's cave". He then went on to Nepal where he died. His body was brought back miraculously to Taktshang by the grace of the deity Dorje Legpa and is now sealed inside the chorten standing in the room on the left at the top of the entrance stairway. The chorten was restored in 1982–83 and again in 2004.

Many Tibetan saints came to meditate in this intensely spiritual place, notably Milarepa (1040–1123), Phadampa Sangye (died 1117), the famous Tibetan yogini Machig Labdoenma (1055–1145 or 1153) and Thangton Gyelpo (1385–1464).

The first sanctuary to be built at Taktshang Pelphug probably dates back to the 14th century. Sonam Gyeltshen, a Nyingmapa lama of the Kathogpa branch, came from Tibet and constructed the first sanctuary. The paintings, which can still be dimly discerned on the rock above the principal building seem to bear witness to this earlier structure which no longer exists today.

Taktshang remained under the authority of Kathogpa lamas up until the 17th century, but in 1645 the whole site was offered to Shabdrung Ngawang Namgyal when he visited the locality with his Nyingmapa master, Rinzing Nyingpo. The Shabdrung immediately expressed his desire to put up a new building, but at that time he was involved in the construction of the Paro *dzong* and he died before he was able to carry out his aim. It was the Fourth *Desi*, Tenzin Rabgye, who fulfilled the Shabdrung's wish and arranged in 1692 the buildings that could be seen until 1998.

The edifice was apparently restored in 1861–85 at the time of the 34th *Je Khenpo*, Sheldrup Oezer. Before the 1998 fire, the most recent restorations took place in 1982–83 and 1992. Three important temples were located in the building on the right-hand side of the entrance stairway, the foremost of which contained the cave where Guru Rinpoche and Langchen Pelkyi Singye meditated. To reach it, you had to go down several steps; the view from the temple is vertiginous since it perches 800 metres (over 2,600 feet) above the Paro valley.

In April 1998 Taktshang burnt down. The paintings and some of the statues were lost, but the government has photographic records of most of these, as well as the buildings. This catastrophe caused a terrible shock that was felt beyond the borders of Bhutan. Since then, the government and the people of Bhutan, with considerable effort, have been rebuilding Taktshang. The reconstruction work is spectacular, given the difficulty of the physical situation.

A room just on the left of the main entrance contains the chorten where are kept the remains of Langchen Pelkyi Senge, one of the disciples of Guru Rinpoche.

The most important spot of Taksang is the cave itself, which is protected by a embossed copper door and opens to public only once a year in the 5th Bhutanese month. The antechamber houses a large clay statue of Guru Dorje Droloe and paintings of different cycles of teachings associated with Guru Rinpoche adorn the walls. Above this temple, is another magnificent temple where the main statue is of 'Guru Rinpoche who spoke by itself'; it is also lavishly decorated by cycles of teachings associated with Guru Rinpoche and by historical religious people.

One of the most visited temples is the new temple of Amitayus (Tshepame), the Buddha of Long Life. It houses huge statues of Amitayus, Guru Dorje Droloe, and Guru Rinpoche.

There are three other complexes above that of Taktshang Pelphug: Taktshang Ugyen Tsemo, built initially in 1408 and then rebuilt after a fire in 1958; Taktshang Oezergang, built in 1646; and Taktshang Zandropelri, built in 1853. These are also places of pilgrimage that are highly venerated and visited, but difficult to access.

Facing Taktshang, off the main road at Satsam Chorten, is the new monastery of the lineage of the great Dilgo Khyentse Rinpoche, whose current reincarnation was born in 1993. The *chorten* of the previous Dilgo Khyentse Rinpoche (1910–1991), whose cremation took place here in 1991, stands in the middle of a garden in a spot conducive to meditation.

DRUKYEL DZONG

If you continue to the end of the paved road you will come to Drukyel *dzong*. In fine weather, the towering peak of **Mount Jomolhari**, 7,314 metres (24,000 feet) high, appears as a backdrop. This mountain, which marks the frontier with Tibet, is sacred, as are all the mountains in Bhutan, and it is the dwelling place of the

Goddess Jomo. It was first climbed in 1937, but the expedition made it clear that it had not actually set foot on the summit. Jomolhari has never been climbed since and it is now a 'protected peak'.

Drukyel *dzong*, with a delightful village nestling at its foot, is built on a rocky spur that blocks the Paro valley and protected it from invasions from the north. The *dzong* was built in 1647 by Shabdrung Ngawang Namgyal to commemorate his victory over the Tibetans in 1644. Drukyel *dzong* means 'fortress of the victorious Drukpas'.

The *dzong* was enlarged in 1651 by the Shabdrung's half-brother, Tenzin Drugda, who was the Paro Penlop at the time. The remains of protected passages can still be seen, where the occupants could go to fetch water from a cistern, safe from enemy arrows.

In 1951, a butter-lamp fell over and started a terrible fire. Only the walls remained and Drukyel *dzong* became no more than a dramatic silhouette falling into ruins. In 1985, in order to save the *dzong* from total ruin, a shingled roof was put on, giving it the same appearance as in the first photograph of it, published in 1914 in *the National Geographic*. Skirting the *dzong*, a road heads towards the end of the valley and points towards the base camp of Jomolhari, three days' further walk. A short incline leads up to the *dzong*, but the visit will only bring a sigh of nostalgia as you consider the glorious past of this sentinel.

One of the targets for the local archery field is located very close to the path leading to the *dzong*. It is not particularly noticeable and, given the distance between the two targets, you may not be aware when an archery tournament is taking place so keep a sharp look-out.

DUNGTSE LHAKHANG

This temple is remarkable primarily because it is in the form of a *chorten*, one of the very few which exist in Bhutan. It is situated on the edge of a hill that thrusts forward between the principal Paro valley and the Dopchari valley, across the bridge of Paro village, on the road to the National Museum.

Dungtse Lhakhang was built in 1421 by the famous Tibetan lama, Thangton Gyelpo (1385–1464), also known by the name of Chagzampa, 'the builder of iron bridges' or Drubthob, 'the Realized One'. Thangton Gyelpo had come to Bhutan to search for iron ore and built eight bridges there before he returned to Tibet. In Paro, a demoness was terrorizing the valley and this very hill turned out to be her head.

A thangka representing the Buddha of Medicine.

BHUTANESE MEDICINE

One of the ancient names for Bhutan was 'the Land of Medicinal Herbs', for Bhutan exported many herbs to Tibet.

Bhutanese medicine has been influenced by traditional Indian Ayurvedic medicine from which it borrowed the theory of Three Humours (bile, phlegm and wind), and by Chinese medicine which taught the reading of pulses. Like both of these, it has a rich pharmacopoeia with preparations based on vegetable, animal and mineral substances.

Bhutanese medicine is similar to the traditional medicine formerly practised in Tibet, where Bhutanese doctors used to receive their training.

The origin of this medicine goes back to the seventh, and particularly the eighth, century when the first Indian and Chinese works were translated into Tibetan. The first great Tibetan doctor, Yuthog the Elder, lived during that period and one of his descendants, Yuthog the Younger, was equally famous in the 11th century.

There are about 300 medical treatises in Tibetan, of which the most important are the *Quadruple Treatise: Gyuzhi* and the *Vaidurya Ngonpo*. All teachings in the 'science of treatment' (*Sorig*) go back, according to Buddhist tradition, to the Medicine Buddha (*Menlha*). Medical science went through a remarkable development in the 17th century when the first medical school was founded in Lhasa and the *Quadruple Treatise* was revised by the Regent, Sangye Gyatso, into the form that we know today.

Diagnosis begins with an examination of the 12 pulses, the tongue and urine, and questions to the patient. Illnesses develop with the increase, decrease or destabilization of the humours caused by bad food, the weather, evil spirits, the weight of previous actions, *karma*, or way of life. Remedies, in general, consist of a diet that varies with the nature of the illness, and medicines, which may be aided by acupuncture and moxibustion.

Physical treatment is accompanied by religious treatments aimed at subjugating evil spirits and ameliorating bad *karma*.

Traditional medicine has always been regarded as important in Bhutan, and a dispensary which doubles as a training centre was opened at Dechenchoeling in 1967. In 1979, a traditional medical hospital with a laboratory for making medicines was opened in Thimphu, subsidized by the World Health Organization. This hospital can be visited (*see* page 246). Four dispensaries were also set up in the rest of the country. In 1988, a project for cataloguing plants and establishing a training centre for doctors was begun with the help of an Italian non-governmental organization. This project today is being continued by the European Union.

Thangton Gyelpo built a temple in the form of a *chorten* to overpower her, as *chortens* often play the part of a nail which immobilizes a demon at the same time as proclaiming the victory of Buddhism.

In 1841, the 25th *Je Khenpo*, Sherab Gyeltsen (reigned 1836–39), decided to restore the temple and all the villages contributed to the effort. The names of the donors are inscribed on the tree-trunks which form the columns of the ground floor. The paintings were redone at this period.

Dungtse Lhakhang possesses one of the most interesting collections of paintings in Bhutan or even in the Himalayan world. Bring a torch (flashlight) for the visit, (if one is allowed access) as the lighting inside can be dim. Be careful, as the temple stairs are really just ladders! The paintings are remarkable as much for the artistic quality of the work as for the quantity of deities who are depicted and arranged according to a very precise religious order. The collection provides a priceless example of an iconography of one religious school, the Drukpa Kagyupas, at a given time. The number of images is so great that it is impossible to give a detailed description of the whole temple. It will have to suffice here to point out the most important images and the guiding principle behind the arrangement of the paintings.

This temple is conceived as a *mandala* (*see* page 83) with the different storeys corresponding to different levels of initiation, leading progressively upwards towards the heart of the *mandala*. The ground floor contains the Five Buddhas of Meditation, also different forms of Avalokiteshvara, Guru Rinpoche, various historical figures including Thangton Gyelpo—the founder of the temple, as well as various forms of Kubera/Vaisravana and some protective deities. The second storey, corresponding to a higher degree of initiation, shows the forms of Mahakala displayed on the outer wall. On the interior wall can be seen visions of the *Bardo*, the intermediary state that exists between death and another rebirth.

The images on the third floor belong to the highest Tantric cycles. The great deities of these cycles are represented on the exterior wall: Guyasamaja, Vajrabhairava, Cakrasamvara, Hevajra, Kalacakra, Vajravarahi, Hayagriva, Mahamaya. On the inside wall are depicted the Eighty-Four Indian Saints, the Mahasiddhas, who, although their occupations did not dispose them to a religious life, were the first to receive the Tantric teachings, which enabled them to attain the state of Buddhahood in their lifetime. Also shown are the Tibetan saints who obtained these teachings from the Mahasiddhas and who are at the origin of the Kagyupa school: Marpa, Milarepa, Gampopa. At their side is Tsangpa Gyare, who founded the Drukpa Kagyupa school in the 12th century. Particularly worth noting on this floor, is a magnificent statue of Milarepa, the 12th-century Tibetan poet-saint.

Local market in Paro.

Prayer wheel in Paro.

View of Paro old bridge from Paro dzong.

THE NATIONAL MUSEUM (TA DZONG)

The National Museum is located just above Paro *dzong*, but the paved road passes first in front of Dungtse Lhakhang and then climbs for five more kilometres (three miles) up the hill to reach the museum. The museum is in fact housed in Paro *dzong's* ancient watchtower, the Ta *dzong*. This tower was built around 1651—the date is uncertain—by Tenzin Drugda, the half-brother of Shabdrung Ngawang Namgyal, while he was the *Penlop* of Paro.

It was in this tower that Ugyen Wangchuck, the future 1st King of Bhutan, was imprisoned in 1872 when he came to put down a revolt. By the 1950s, the Ta *dzong* had fallen into a badly dilapidated condition. In 1965, the 3rd King, Jigme Dorje Wangchuck, conceived the idea of restoring the Ta *dzong* as a place to house the National Museum, which was inaugurated in 1968.

The museum is open from Tuesday to Saturday 9 am to 4 pm; on Sundays 11 am to 4 pm. It is closed on Mondays. It can be very cold in the galleries. The museum is considered to be a temple because of the number of religious objects it contains, and this is why you must proceed in a clockwise direction. A guardian will point out the way.

Iron chains lie on the parapets by the footbridge leading to the museum. These chains, which have all been collected from different parts of Bhutan, are the remains of the iron bridges constructed by Thangton Gyelpo in the 15th century (*see* pages 160–1).

THE COLLECTION

The National Museum not only contains works of art but also handcrafts related to daily life, stuffed animals, costumes, armour and even stamps. You can thus get an idea of the cultural and ecological richness of Bhutan in a very short time. Moreover, the massive exterior architecture and the beautiful interior decoration are worth seeing in themselves.

The **first gallery** after you enter contains a collection of costumes and traditional fabrics, as well as masks, hats, splendid harnesses and saddles of chased silver, and ancient books, and a presentation of Bhutan at the beginning of its history.

A small staircase on the left leads up to a **gallery of *thangkas***; this is constructed as a balcony overhanging the first gallery. The *thangkas* are of great artistic interest and offer a good introduction to the complexities of Bhutanese iconography. There is a magnificent *thangka* embroidered in a way rarely used in Bhutan. It was imported from China through Tibet. Also to be seen is an impressive piece of appliqué cloth which demonstrates the skill acquired by the Bhutanese in this particular technique. Equally interesting are the giant constructions of threads which are palaces for evil spirits. There are good examples of *tormas* here too (*see* page 103).

In the centre of this gallery, a staircase leads to the **stamp gallery** located at the top of the building. All the famous Bhutanese stamps are on display here: three-dimensional stamps, disc-stamps, stamps made of silk, stamps of the coronation in relief, not to mention the triangular stamp with the yeti. On this floor is a chapel with a 'tree of lineage' showing the great lineages: to the east, the main statue represents the primordial Buddha Vajradhara (Dorjechang); to the south, the *Kagyupa* master of the 12th century, Dagpo Lhaje (Gampopa); to the west, Guru Pemajune (Guru Rinpoche/Padmasambhava); to the north, the Indian master, Jowo Atisa (11th century). This tree of life, consecrated in 1968, is a superb example of the art of sculpture clay. (Shoes must be removed before entering this room.)

You will also visit the **hall containing statues and engraved slates** found directly below the chapel.

Descending the staircase again to the level of the *thangka* gallery, you will find a **room of statues and engraved slates** directly underneath the chapel. The exceptionally fine statues and slates are displayed individually in alcoves that are enclosed in the same trilobed framework as the windows of houses. Leaving this room you can then complete the tour of the *thangka* gallery. Be sure to notice the beautiful ritual objects and musical instruments that are kept behind glass.

The windows of the **gallery of silversmithing and armour** overlook Paro *dzong* and provide a superb view of this architectural ensemble and the valley, as well as Ogyen Pelri palace, built in 1930.

Shown in these showcases are the windows of the silverwork and armour gallery offer a superb view of the entire architectural structure of Paro *dzong*. In the showcases against the left-hand wall are exhibits of armour, helmets and shields made of bamboo and rhinoceros hide as well as lances and bows. Beyond the door that leads to the 3rd King's large collection of guns (about 180) there is a spectacular display of lacquered wooden receptacles. On the shelves to the right, boxes for betel nut, portable reliquaries, ancient clasps and pins for dresses are all examples of skilful Bhutanese silverwork. Necklaces made of enormous coral beads and etched agate show which stones are the most favoured by Bhutanese women. An ancient seven-stringed lute, a *dranyen*, has delicate decorations; it is just to the right of the door leading to a gallery of copper and silver utensils.

(Following pages) *The western dzong of Paro and its beautiful, roofed, cantilever bridge.*

This **circular gallery**, on the same floor, displays objects made of copper and silver such as jugs for water or milk and particularly huge teapots with massive outlines and magnificent decorations.

The **animal gallery** on the floor below contains an exhibition of Bhutan's most famous animals: takin, Himalayan bear with its white collar, blue sheep, musk deer, snow leopard, trophies of the *mithun*—the mighty indigenous buffalo, amazing hombill and spectacular Bhutanese butterflies. The circular gallery contains traditional receptacles and utensils made of wood. On the floor below, you can look at utilitarian objects made of bamboo and clay, and alcohol containers made of horn decorated with chased silver. The bamboo work is nearly all made in the Khyeng region of south central Bhutan and the articles are used as part of daily life.

At the exit level are **display of gigantic metal pots** that were used to cook food for monastic communities or men-at-arms. On either side of a little sanctuary to the water deity, there are two small rooms that were formerly used as prisons but where only a few muskets and matchlocks hang today.

From the Museum you can go down to the *dzong* by way of a short, very steep path. There is also a motorable road leading there.

PARO DZONG

The full name of Paro *dzong* is Rinpung *dzong*, which means 'the fortress of the heap of jewels'.

In the 15th century, two brothers named Gyelchok and Gyelzom lived in the Paro valley; they were descendants of Phajo Drugom Shigpo, the founder of the Drukpa Kagyupa school in Bhutan. While Gyelzom established himself at Gantakha Monastery, his brother Gyelchok went off to Tibet to study theology with the great masters of that time. When he came back to Paro, he cut a very sorry figure after all the years he had spent studying without earning any money. His brother, Gyelzom, refused to receive him, telling him that there were no beggars in their family.

Gyelchok went away to live beside the river at Humrelkha, a place which took its name from the guardian deity of Paro, Humrel Gompo. There he constructed a little building that would later become the Paro *dzong*. Gyelchok's descendants are well known through Bhutanese history as the 'Lords of Humrel' and they controlled a large part of the valley.

In 1645, the Lords of Humrel gave their little fort to Shabdrung Ngawang Namgyal, thus recognizing his religious and political authority. The Shabdrung immediately began construction of a much more commanding fortress and the *dzong* was consecrated in 1646. In October 1915, the *dzong* burnt almost to the ground but it was immediately rebuilt to the same design by the Paro *Penlop*, Dawa Penjor, with money raised by a special tax levied throughout Bhutan. In 2005 the *dzong* was given a new roof.

Today the *dzong* is the administrative seat of the district of Paro and it also contains a state monastic community of about 200 members. It is approached by a gently sloping flagstone road and a beautiful wooden bridge roofed with shingles and abutted by two guard houses.

INSIDE PARO DZONG

The **first courtyard** of the *dzong* is lined with administrative offices. The entrance is guarded by two traditional effigies standing on either side of the gate: a Mongol holding a tiger on a leash and a man holding a black yak.

The **central tower** of the *dzong*, the *utse*, is one of the most beautiful in Bhutan with its superb woodwork. The central tower includes a temple dedicated to the line of Drukpa Kagyupa lamas, a temple of Hayagriva, another one dedicated to the great Tantric deities, a temple of the Eight Kinds of Chortens and a temple of the Taras.

Beneath the gallery that runs along the courtyard are classical paintings of the Mongol holding his chained tiger, the Old Man of Long Life and the Four Friends. The latter are characters in a fable that recounts how a bird, a rabbit, a monkey and an elephant combined their efforts to grow a fruit tree and enjoy its fruit. The bird brought the seed, the rabbit watered it and the monkey supplied natural fertilizer while the elephant provided shade and protected it from harm. This fable,with its moral of co-operation and unity among different kinds of beings, is very popular and is represented in many places.

The Old Man of Long Life, originally a Chinese Taoist theme, has become, in Buddhism, the example of the longevity that can be achieved by careful practice of the religion. Immortality is symbolized by the stream, the mountains and the trees. The deer refers to the First Sermon which Buddha preached in the Deer Park. This representation also emphasizes that men and animals can live in harmony within nature if they will respect certain rules of conduct. The paintings of deer and birds are noteworthy for their artistic quality and the rareness of their composition.

(Following pages) (Top left) *Young monks watching dances;* (Bottom left) *monks with oboes and an incense burner;* (Top right) *monk dancer at rest;* (Bottom left) *the 'master of discipline' with his heavy whip;* (Bottom right) *an elaborate silver incense burner.*

A flight of stone steps leads to a **second courtyard** on a lower level which belongs to the clergy. On the left side of the courtyard is a large hall, **the Kunre**, where the monks study and eat. Here the main statue is of the Buddha in his Jowo form. Paintings of Guru Rinpoche, the Buddhas of the Three Ages, Shabdrung Ngawang Namgyal and other divinities cover its walls.

In the gallery that gives access to the Kunre can be seen extraordinary cosmic *mandalas*, representing the universe as seen by two different philosophic streams. The significance of these images in Buddhist cosmology is as great as the beauty of these works of art.

The two *mandalas* on the left portray the cosmos as seen through the teachings of the *Kalacakra*, 'the Wheel of Time', a Tantra that was taught in the tenth century. The first *mandala* shows the cosmos seen from above, divided into four concentric circles, each representing an element: air (yellow); fire (red); water (blue); earth (dark blue). Four continents are laid out at the edge of the ocean and the earth, each with two sub-continents of its own. Next come 18 slender concentric circles which represent the combination of earth-ocean-mountain six times. In the central part, the Mount Sumeru represents the pillar of the world. The 12 brightly coloured circles represent the 12 months of the year. The next *mandala* repeats the same theme, but here Mount Sumeru is seen in perspective; another difference is that the earth element and the 12 months are omitted.

The *mandala* on the right is painted according to the cosmology of the *Abhidharmakosha*, a text written in the fifth century by the Indian scholar Vasubandhu. In the centre rises Mount Sumeru with its different levels where the gods dwell. Mount Sumeru is surrounded by seven ranges of golden mountains. The continents, each with a different shape and its two subsidiary continents, float on the ocean. The various colours of the ocean are caused by reflection of the minerals which make up the composition of Mount Sumeru: white conch, blue turquoise, red coral and yellow gold. A chain of iron mountains closes the universe which, in both cases, is flat and not round.

In the gallery on the right side of the courtyard are painted different episodes from the life of Milarepa. The room on that side is the monks' assembly hall. The paintings on the walls show the former lives of the Buddha.

PARO TOWN

The road which goes from the *dzong's* bridge to the village of Paro is lined by large square *chortens*. On the right, the royal palace of Ugyen Pelri is barely discernible. It was built in around 1930 by the *Penlop* of Paro, Tshering Penjor. On the left of the lane is the local archery field.

On arriving at Paro town, the **temple of Druk Choeding** lies by the road, slightly to the left; it was built in 1525 by Ngawang Choegyel, the great-great-grandfather of Shabdrung Ngawang Namgyal. The latter lived there when he arrived in the Paro valley in 1616.

Paro town was only constructed in 1985 and in 2005 it is undergoing unprecedented development. As so often in Bhutan, there was in the past no village near the *dzong*, and what might mildly be called an urban centre is a recent creation. Houses built in traditional style and painted with coloured designs line the main street. Small shops occupy the ground levels and provide the basic necessities that one would expect to find in a mountain village: pots and pans, hardware, flour, butter, oil, sugar, salt, lentils and a few tinned goods. With its main street straight and windswept, its caravan drivers leading their horses, its occasional idlers leaning against the store-fronts, Paro strangely resembles a village of the old American West.

There are some handicrafts shops, the best being Chencho Handicrafts and 'Made in Bhutan' which also sells photos and books, as well as an art gallery, the Vajrayana, opened by a Bhutanese artist.

Just above the town, a beautiful residence catches the eye. It is the Gangtey Palace, privately owned today and converted to a hotel, it has an excellent view of the *dzong*. It was built at the end of the last century to be the home of the Paro *Penlops*. Women were not permitted to stay overnight in the *dzong*, so the families of the *Penlops* were housed outside.

PARO HOTELS AND RESTAURANTS

Two small and popular restaurants have opened on the upper floor of houses in the main street: the Sonam Trophel and The Travellers.

A number of hotels have been built recently but the top end ones are the classic **Olathang Hotel** (tel. 975-8-271304) nested in a pine forest on a slope overlooking the village; next by is the **Palri Hotel**; the **Gangtey Palace Resort** truly a 'heritage' hotel with a lot of charm. It was the mansion of the Governor of Paro and still keeps its ancient architectural features. It also commands a magnificent view on the *dzong* and the valley; Next to Kyichu Lhakhang, the **Kyichu Resort** (tel. 975-8-271468) , a complex of cottages. Further away from the town, the cosy **Eye of the Tiger Hotel** has been constructed opposite Taktshang as well as the imposing **Yangphel Hotel** in Satsam, which has a conference hall. Nearby the **Rinchenling** also has conference facilities. The **Zhiwaling**, a new luxury hotel, also has conference facilities.

(Following pages) *Prayer flags, a stone* chorten *and a cluster of homes is typical of a western Bhutanese village.*

Since 2004, Paro boasts two luxury hotels but they are not bland five-star hotels. They each have their characteristics. The **Uma**, belonging to the Como group (tel. 975-8-271597; www.uma.como.bz), is a high end resort which has been established in a quiet pine forest above the Paro *dzong*. It is simply but tastefully decorated with Bhutanese motifs and the Bhutanese staff is really efficient and friendly. The main building which is in the shape of a Bhutanese fortress has a restaurant, bar, library-cum internet facilities, a spa with different massages à la carte and a recreation space: yoga classes, fitness centre, swimming-pool, jacuzzi, hot stone bath and steam bath. The rooms in the main building as well as villas built in Bhutanese style are very comfortable with great bathrooms and telephone, TVs and DVDS. One of Uma's strong points is its closeness to the airport (10 minutes drive) when flights are so early in the morning .

At the end of Paro Valley, below Drukyel *dzong*, the exclusive Aman group has opened a luxury hotel that caters essentially to people "addicted to the Aman experience around the world". The **Amankora-Paro** (tel. 975-8-272333; www.amanresorts.com) has a great view of Mt Jomolhari when the weather is clear and are certainly luxurious for Bhutan but the CGI roofs are unfortunate. The hotel stresses on quietness—the rooms have no TV or telephone—and relaxation with its spa. The resort is comfortable and staffed by diligent people but one might regret that the whole atmosphere and decoration, with its trendy minimalism and muted colours, are rather more Japanese or South-East Asian than local. It is Bhutan revisited by Western fantasy. In both hotels, the food cooked by foreign chefs emphasizes on health values and can be defined as 'fusion cuisine'.

In Paro, the winter cold pulls the temperatures down and while the hotels are moderately heated, walking outside can be a chilling experience, even at the Aman or the Uma.

The Paro airport is impressive and was inaugurated in April 1999. In addition to the first-floor restaurant, there is a bank counter, a postal counter, a national and international telephone counter, two souvenir and book shops, and a duty-free shop. Although the airport was supposed to be heated in the winter, it is not, except in the coffee-shop and the VIP pavillion. Therefore it is better to dress for the cold, especially for the early morning flights. Allow a good half-hour on the road to reach the airport from the centre of Paro and an hour and a half from Thimphu.

TACHOGANG LHAKHANG

Tachogang Lhakhang, 'temple of the hill of the excellent horse', rises in austere surroundings on the left bank of the river, a few kilometres before Chhuzom at the confluence of the Paro and Thimphu rivers. This private temple was founded by

A PITCHED BATTLE

*E*arly one morning the sound of a very sweet-toned gong warned us that the spring ceremony of blessing the rice-fields was about to begin. A long, picturesque procession of men and women, led by the Donyer, came winding down the hillside until the first rice-field, into which water had been running all the day before, was reached. The field below was still dry, and, turning in there, they all sat down and had some light refreshment. Suddenly, the men sprang up, throwing off their outer garments; this was the signal for the women to rush to the inundated field and to commence throwing clouds of earth and splashes of muddy water on the men below as they tried to climb up. Then followed a wild and mad, though always good-humoured, struggle between the men and women in the water, the men doing their utmost to take possession of the watery field, the women equally determined to keep them out. The Donyer, the leader of the men, suffered severely, though the courtesies of war were strictly observed, and if one of the assailants fell his opponents helped him up and gave him a breathing-space to recover before a fresh onset was made. But gradually the women drove the men slowly down the whole length of the field, the last stand being made by a very stout and powerful official, who, clinging to an overhanging rock, with his back to his foes, used his feet to scoop up such quantities of water and mud that no one was able to come near him. However, all the other men having been driven off, he and the Donyer were allowed at last to crawl up on the path, and the combat for that year was over. This was looked on as a very propitious ending, as the women's victory portends during the coming season fertility of the soil and increase amongst the flocks, so they dispersed to their various homes rejoicing.

J Claude White
Sikhim & Bhutan Twenty-One Years
on the North-East Frontier, 1887–1908

TERMS OF ADDRESS

The male members of the royal family are called *Dasho* and the female members are called *Ashi*.

A Minister is called *Lyonpo* (pronounced 'Lonpo'); a vice-minister and all high ranking officials including judges are called *Dasho*.

A common man with a certain amount of education and all teachers are called *Lopen*, but current convention styles the director of a department as *Dasho* out of respect, even if he has not received the red scarf; however, it would be incorrect to address him as *Dasho* in any official correspondence.

A monk is called *Gelong*, *Lopen* or *Lam* according to this rank.

Wives of officials and married women are called *Aum* (pronounced 'Am').

One can address a villager as *Lopen* in order to be polite or if he is educated; otherwise simply *Apa* or *Ap* followed by his first name.

To call a child you do not know, use *Aloo* for a boy and *Bum* or *Bumo* for a girl. A married woman is addressed as *Am* or *Ama*. If people are old enough to be grandparents, they may be respectfully called *Agye* (for male) and *Angye* (for female).

In all cases these terms of address may be followed by the first name or the entire name of the person, but never directly by the last name unless told so.

CEREMONIAL SCARVES

The large scarves (*kabne*) that men wear—for official occasions or to go to a *dzong*—indicate a person's rank.

A white scarf with fringes is for commoners. A white scarf with fringes and a red band running lengthwise down the middle, with one, two or three red stripes across it, is worn by an assistant district administrator (*Dzongrab, Dungpa*). A white scarf with fringes and two broad, red, vertical borders is called a *khamar* and is worn by village chiefs, the *gups*.

A red scarf without fringes is worn by a *Dasho*. This title means 'the best'. It is not hereditary but is conferred by the King on people of his choice as a reward for service.

A dark blue scarf shows that a person is a Representative of the People, a member of the Royal Advisory Council.

An orange scarf without fringes is worn by Deputy Ministers; Ministers wear the same scarf, but with part of it folded on the left shoulder. Since 2005, Judges wear green scarves.

The King wears a saffron yellow scarf, as does the *Je Khenpo*, the head abbot of the country.

All high-ranking officials wear a sword. Certain scarves are conferred by the King, while those of lesser rank are given by the Minister of Home Affairs. The personnel of the Royal Body Guard, the Armed Forces and the Police wear narrow scarves of stiff material.

Women of all ranks wear a red striped scarf with fringes on their left shoulder, folded in three lengthwise and then doubled over. This scarf is properly called a *rachu* but the term *kabne* is often applied to it.

the Tibetan saint, Thangton Gyelpo (1385–1464), who also built Dungtse Lhakhang. While he was meditating here, Thangton Gyelpo had a vision of the excellent horse Balaha-an emanation of Avalokiteshvara. He decided thereupon to build a temple at this spot in addition to one of his famous iron bridges later carried away by floods in 1969. A traditional style bridge with iron chains is being built in 2005.

The exact date of the temple's construction is not certain, but it was probably around the year 1420. Monkeys can sometimes be seen running through the fields that surround the building.

CHHUZOM

Chhuzom is a junction where the roads from Ha, Paro, Thimphu and Phuentsholing meet. On the left bank of the Paro River, at the place where it meets the Thimphu River (Wang chu/Raidak), three *chortens* have been constructed. They protect the site from the influence of any evil spirits. Built at different times, they reflect the three styles of architecture commonly found in Bhutan: Nepalese, Tibetan and Bhutanese. The Bhutanese style chorten was built at the beginning of the 1980s.

THE HA VALLEY (OR HAA)

The district of Ha opened to tourism in 2004. The road from Chhuzom passes by the Dobji *dzong* and the small Bitekha *dzong* before reaching the Ha valley (2,700 metres), the heart of the high altitude largely forested Ha district close to the Chumbi (Gromo) valley in Tibet (China). Buckwheat and barley are the main crops and there is a lot of yak herds and cattle, part of the latter still migrate along the Amo chhu river to the souther region of Samtse in winter. In the south of the district, at lower altitude, crops of cardamom and oranges are grown mainly for export.

Ha has two famous temples, the Lhakhang Karpo and the Lhakhang Nagpo which are part, according to the Bhutanese tradition, of the temples built in the 7th century by the Tibetan King Songtsen Gampo who emanated as a pigeon.

The Wangchuklo *dzong* built in 1915 is close to the Indian army training team cantonment. A small town has sprouted with its usual shops and government offices. The 9-hole golf course is quite a curiosity. There is a small new guesthouse, the Risum guesthouse, near the IMTRAT hospital.

Ha is being promoted as a trekking destination for people interested in botany and good vistas on the mountains.

The 26 kilometre road to Chelila (4000 metres), which leads directly into the Paro valley, goes through forests and then provides good views on Ha. If the weather is clear, there are beautiful vistas from the prayer-flags at the pass on the Mt Jomolhari and Jichu Drakye in Bhutan as well as the Mt Kangchenchunga in Sikkim.

THE PARO–THIMPHU ROAD

The road to Thimphu follows the valley of the Thimphu River through a rather arid and rocky landscape. A few houses here and there cling to the slopes. The valley widens somewhat near the village of Khasadrapchu where the side valley of Gidakom opens into it.

After Khasadrapchu, the valley turns again into a gorge before it widens out for a second time at Namseling, about a dozen kilometres (seven miles) from Thimphu. Namseling is a very lovely spot with a forest of conifers covering a gentle slope and a large village surrounded by rice fields below the road. After Namseling, villages close to Thimphu begin to appear and a large new chorten is being built.

The new expressway cut through the paddy fields, leading to Thimphu in 15 minutes. This wider, faster road on the right bank of the river will be finished by the end of 2005 and will lessen the traffic on the old narrow road.

The state veterinary farm of Wangchutaba and the botanical garden of Serbithang are above the old road five minutes drive away. Two large images of the Guardians of the East and the North sit at a bend in the road. The way then passes through a camp of the Dantak, an Indian organization that takes care of the upkeep of portions of the roads. The city of Thimphu now comes into view in a cross-valley that runs north-south. After the road crosses a bridge and bears off towards the north, you can see Semtokha *dzong* on the left. The Royal Institute of Manangement (RIM) opened on November 11, 1996, sprawls on the floor of the valley beneath Semtokha *dzong*. The institute specializes in management and information technology training for Bhutan's public and private employees. It also houses the chancery of the Royal University of Bhutan established by Royal Charter in 2003.

The old road now passes through Lungtenphug, the Bhutanese army HQ, and is very congested. The wider, faster road be under construction on the right bank of the river, will lessen the traffic on this narrow road. The new low-cost housing units of Changjiji are built just before Thimphu where ten years ago there were paddy-fields.

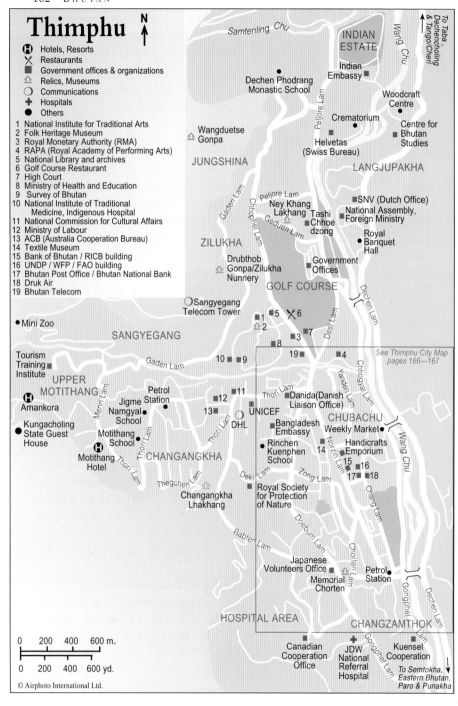

Thimphu

N ↑

- Ⓗ Hotels, Resorts
- ✕ Restaurants
- ▦ Government offices & organizations
- ⚖ Relics, Museums
- ○ Communications
- ✚ Hospitals
- ● Others

1 National Institute for Traditional Arts
2 Folk Heritage Museum
3 Royal Monetary Authority (RMA)
4 RAPA (Royal Academy of Performing Arts)
5 National Library and archives
6 Golf Course Restaurant
7 High Court
8 Ministry of Health and Education
9 Survey of Bhutan
10 National Institute of Traditional
    Medicine, Indigenous Hospital
11 National Commission for Cultural Affairs
12 Ministry of Labour
13 ACB (Australia Cooperation Bureau)
14 Textile Museum
15 Bank of Bhutan / RICB building
16 UNDP / WFP / FAO building
17 Bhutan Post Office / Bhutan National Bank
18 Druk Air
19 Bhutan Telecom

To Taba,
Dechencholing
& Tango/Cheri

Samtenling Chu

Wang Chu

INDIAN
ESTATE

Dechen Phodrang
Monastic School

Indian
Embassy

Woodcraft
Centre

Wangduetse
Gonpa

JUNGSHINA

Crematorium

Helvetas
(Swiss Bureau)

Centre for
Bhutan
Studies

Peljore Lam

LANGJUPAKHA

Peljore Lam

Gaden Lam

Chhophel Lam

Geduen Lam

Ney Khang
Lakhang

Tashi
Chhoe
dzong

SNV (Dutch Office)

National Assembly,
Foreign Ministry

ZILUKHA

Drubthob
Gonpa/Zilukha
Nunnery

Royal
Banquet
Hall

Government
Offices

GOLF COURSE

Dechen Lam

Sangyegang
Telecom Tower

1
2
5
6

3
7

8

Desi Lam

Mini Zoo

SANGYEGANG

19
4

See Thimphu City Map
pages 166—167

Tourism
Training
Institute

Gaden Lam

10 9

UPPER
MOTITHANG

Amankora

Kungacholing
State Guest
House

Menri Lam

Petrol
Station

Jigme
Namgyal
School

Motithang
School

Motithang
Hotel

Thori Lam

CHANGANGKHA

Thegchen Lam

11

12

13

DHL

UNICEF

Thori Lam

Danida(Danish
Liaison Office)

Bangladesh
Embassy

Rinchen
Kuenphen
School

Royal Society
for Protection
of Nature

Changangkha
Lhakhang

Deki Lam

Chhogyal Lam

Yanden Lam

CHUBACHU

Weekly Market

Handicrafts
Emporium

14

15 16
17 18

Norzin Lam

Zong Lam

Wang Chu

Chang Lam

Rabten Lam

Doebum Lam

Japanese
Volunteers Office

Memorial
Chorten

Chorten Lam

Petrol
Station

Gongphel Lam

Dechen Lam

HOSPITAL AREA

CHANGZAMTHOK

| 0 | 200 | 400 | 600 m. |

| 0 | 200 | 400 | 600 yd. |

© Airphoto International Ltd.

Canadian
Cooperation
Office

JDW
National
Referral
Hospital

Kuensel
Cooperation

To Semtokha,
Eastern Bhutan,
Paro & Punakha

The distance from Paro Airport to Thimphu is 50 kilometres, Drukgyel *dzong*—Thimphu 70 kilometres; Paro town—Thimphu 55 kilometres. The altitude is 2,350 metres (7,700 feet) at the Thimphu bridge, 2,450 metres (about 8,000 feet) at Motithang.

THIMPHU

The entry into Thimphu is over a large and ugly concrete bridge. The bridge is named **Lungten Zampa**, which means 'the bridge of the prophecy'. In accordance with a prophecy, Phajo Drugom Shigpo, the founder of the Drukpa school in Bhutan, and his future wife, a young country girl, spent their first night in a cavern beneath this bridge. Their sons would contribute to the spread of the Drukpa school in Western Bhutan.

On the right of the bridge is the bus terminal.

Note, as you pass beyond the bridge and the first roundabout, that even the petrol station on the right was built in traditional style. By royal decree, all buildings in Bhutan must keep the traditional style and this helps to give a distinctive character to the new urban centres. The petrol pump can still be operated by hand in case the electricity is cut off; its electrification only dates from 1986.

The traffic policemen, standing on wooden pedestals, direct the traffic with highly elegant gestures and salute officials as their cars pass by. It is very rare for them to castigate a motorist who disregards the law or visitors who become so fascinated by their dance-like movements that they forget what the gestures are telling them to do.

Thimphu has a population of more than 50,000, composed of the state clergy, the Kingdom's royal family, government officials and civil servants as well a growing middle class. Some families are still engaged in agricultural activities and most of them sell their goods in the weekend market. Although it is historical place for the Bhutanese, by international standards, Thimphu's emergence as a capital city is fairly recent and the cost of living is quite high compare to similar size cities in South Asia.

Thimphu was established as the permanent capital in 1952–1953, but at that time it was hardly more than a *dzong* surrounded by some huts. The houses of the peasants were scattered throughout the valley in hamlets whose names still exist as districts in modern Thimphu: Kawajangsa, Changzamthok, Hejo, Zilukha, Motithang, Changangkha, Changlimithang, Langchupakha, Taba to name but a few. Dechenchoeling Palace, seven kilometres (nearly four and a half miles) north of the city, was built in 1952–53.

It was only in the late 1960s and early 1970s that Thimphu began to take on the aspect that we see today. The 1980s saw the beginning of the real-estate boom fuelled by private initiative and the 1990s witness that boom mushroom with many new businesses, hotels, restaurants and even dance clubs and pools halls. Automobile traffic having increased increased wildly in the last 10 years, a sign of prosperity which has its bad sides. Bhutan today has about 28,000 vehicles and the Thimphu region alone has about 17,000 vehicles of which more than 80 percent ply in the capital's estimated 100 kilometres of roads. An attempt to control the traffic and the parking in town with fees is under way. There is too infrequent public transport, as well as many taxi vans whose unruly road behaviour causes much damage. In 2005, Thimphu was gripped in a road-building frenzy.

Unlike many Asian modern cities, Thimphu has kept a national character in its architecture although concrete apartment and shopping complexes are cropping up everywhere. Street names are a recent innovation, so it might be better to ask a passerby the place you are looking for rather than the name of the street. The centre is compact and it is very difficult to get lost, but government offices are sometimes not easy to find. It is wise to buy the good Thimphu city map. (see pages 166–7)

Stores change very quickly, both in name and commercial activity. Don't be surprised if stores or restaurants no longer exist at the time of your visit. Small shops are worth a visit and the shopkeeper will not be offended by a visitor who only wants to look around.

Night-life in Thimphu is relatively limited, but is growing fast. People still tend go to bed early and official evenings end about 10.30 pm. On the other hand, dinners with friends are common and for a minority, private card or *mah jong* parties can last all night! For the young crowd, several nightclubs and pool-rooms exist. The trendiest place is the **Om bar** where upper-class Bhutanese and expatriates go after dinner for a cozy drink and chat. But one can also go to the **Buzz lounge**, dance away at **Space 34**, and sing karaoke or play pool at **4 Degrees** or the **Zone**.

THE CENTRE OF THIMPHU

Thimphu is unlike any other world capital. The city is rather quiet and huge traffic jams which are familiar in other Asian capitals do not exist. The best way to explore Thimphu is to go off on foot. In the town centre, above the main roundabout the Swiss Bakery has almost achieved historical monument status. Originally run by a Swiss-become-Bhutanese, the Swiss Bakery serves as a tea room and you can get a quick snack there at any time. Their baguettes and wholemeal bread are good. However the best cakes and biscuits are made on order by Choying, a lady working from her home (tel. 975-2-322363).

Another place for excellent home-made cakes, French style lunches and coffee is the **Art Café** just next to the Swiss Bakery. It is a great spot to observe the trendy crowd and the expats. Nearby is the comfortable **Peling (Pedling) Hotel**.

A walk up and down the high street will always be enlightening. From the rough farmers that come into the city to trade supplies, to Bhutanese businessmen, to the ubiquitous monks, there will always be a colourful gathering passing by.

The main street in Thimphu, **Norzim Lam**, is lined with shops of all descriptions. For part of its length, just south of main roundabout, it is split, with the clock tower square and its new amphitheater on the lower part. From the petrol pump to the main roundabout, the upper side of the street is entirely allocated to small business and small hotel-restaurants.

Tucked above Chorten Lam, the street that runs up in front of the Swiss Bakery, the **Yeedzin guest-house** (tel. 975-2-325702) is a family-owned hotel, and offers among the best quality/price in Thimphu; its cleanliness is exemplary, and the staff are charming and efficient. It is the first choice of regular visitors to Bhutan and has now a small cafe-bar, the **In Fusion**.

On the lower side of the street, at the bend, right below the main roundabout, is a small restaurant with a *terrasse* and parasols! The **Mid-Point** serves excellent South Indian specialities, *dosa* in particular, as well as other simple dishes. This is a friendly and popular place.

On the right, a small street, Gatoen Lam, gently slopes down to the stadium. Going down this street, on the left, you find the small **Benez** restaurant, which is inexpensive and has a bar. Just after it, a multi-storey building houses a health club, a Thai restaurant which has good spicy food, and the **Bhutan Kitchen**, a restaurant serving Bhutanese delicacies. Souvenir stores and a tailor occupy the ground-floor. You then arrive at the sports field and a flight of stairs leads to the squash and tennis courts. Beyond the sports field, near the river, is the administrative building of Thimphu district and the site of the market.

The buildings along Chang Lam street above the sports field, house, among others, the very good **Wangchuk Hotel** with a friendly staff and the Druktrin Handicrafts, and electronic shops.

Chang Lam Plaza is a new (2004) multi-storied building with a photo shop, the Kuensel shop, handicrafts shops, a Druk air office, and cafes such as **Khamsa** on the last floor which serves several kinds of coffee, waffles and crepes and **Yummy's**, on the ground floor which has a short multi-cuisine menu.

Also a multi-storied complex, Jojo building has various shops: **Namgyal** on the groundfloor sell fleece and outdoor garments at unbeatable prices, Internet places,

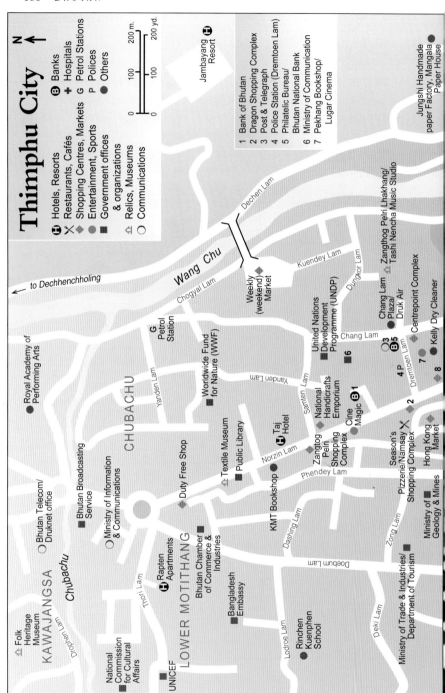

Thimphu City

- 🄷 Hotels, Resorts
- ✕ Restaurants, Cafés
- ◆ Shopping Centres, Markets
- ● Entertainment, Sports
- ■ Government offices & organizations
- ⛩ Relics, Museums
- ○ Communications

- 🄱 Banks
- ✚ Hospitals
- G Petrol Stations
- P Polices
- ● Others

1 Bank of Bhutan
2 Dragon Shopping Complex
3 Post & Telegraph
4 Police Station (Dremtoen Lam)
5 Philatelic Bureau/
  Bhutan National Bank
6 Ministry of Communication
7 Pekhang Bookshop/
  Lugar Cinema

0 · 100 · 200 m.
0 · 100 · 200 yd.

N ←

to Dechhenchholing →

Wang Chu

Dechen Lam
Chogyal Lam
Kuendey Lam
Dungkor Lam

Jambayang Resort 🄷

Jungshi Handmade paper Factory, Mangala Paper House ●

Royal Academy of Performing Arts ●

CHUBACHU

G Petrol Station

Worldwide Fund for Nature (WWF) ■

Yanden Lam

Weekly (weekend) Market

United Nations Development Programme (UNDP) ■

Chang Lam
Chang Lam Plaza
Druk Air ✕
Zangthog Pelri Lhakhang/
Tashi Nencha Music Studio ⛩
Centrepoint Complex ■
Kelly Dry Cleaner ●

Samten Lam
Dremtoen Lam

6 ■
4 P
7
8
⌀3
🄱5

National Handicrafts Emporium
🄱1

Cine Magic ●
2

Bhutan Broadcasting Service ■

Ministry of Information & Communications ○

Duty Free Shop ◆

⛩ Textile Museum
Public Library ■

Taj Hotel 🄷
🄷

Zangtog Pelri Shopping Complex

Season's
Pizzerie/Namsay ✕
Shopping Complex

Hong Kong Market ◆

Norzin Lam
Phendey Lam

KMT Bookshop ●

Dashing Lam

Doebum Lam
Zong Lam

Ministry of Geology & Mines ■

CHUBACHU

Folk Heritage Museum ⛩

KAWAJANGSA

Chubachu

National Commission for Cultural Affairs ■

UNICEF ■

Bhutan Telecom/ Druknet office ○

Rapten Apartments 🄷

LOWER MOTITHANG

Bhutan Chamber of Commerce & Industries ■

Thori Lam

Drophen Lam

Bangladesh Embassy ■

Rinchen Kuenphen School ●

Lodroe Lam
Deki Lam

Ministry of Trade & Industries/ Department of Tourism ■

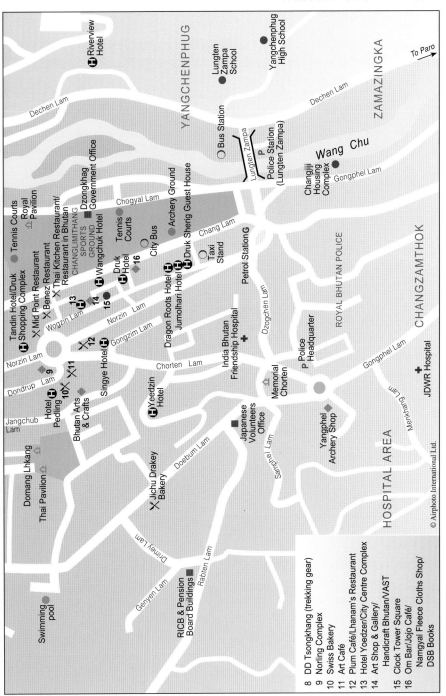

Riverview Hotel

To Paro

YANGCHENPHUG

ZAMAZINGKA

Lungten Zampa School

Yangchenphug High School

Dechen Lam

Bus Station

Police Station (Lungten Zampa)

Wang Chu

Gongphel Lam

Changjiji Housing Complex

Dechen Lam

Tennis Courts

Royal Pavilion

Tandin Hotel/Druk Shopping Complex

Mid Point Restaurant

Benez Restaurant

Thai Kitchen Restaurant/ Restaurant in Bhutan

Dzongkhag Government Office

CHANGLIMITHANG SPORTS GROUND

Wangchuk Hotel

Chogyal Lam

Archery Ground

Druk Sherig Guest House

Tennis Courts

Druk Hotel

City Bus

16

Taxi Stand

Chang Lam

Petrol Station G

Wogzin Lam

13

14

15

Norzin Lam

Dragon Roots Hotel

Jumolhari Hotel

India Bhutan Friendship Hospital

Dzogchen Lam

ROYAL BHUTAN POLICE

Police Headquarter

CHANGZAMTHOK

Gongphel Lam

JDWR Hospital

Menkhang Lam

Norzin Lam

12

Gongzim Lam

Singye Hotel

Chorten Lam

Memorial Chorten

Dondrup Lam

9

X 11

Hotel Pedling

10

Bhutan Arts & Crafts

Yeedzin Hotel

Japanese Volunteers Office

Yangphel Archery Shop

HOSPITAL AREA

Jangchub Lam

Domang Lhkang

Thai Pavilion

Doebum Lam

Samphel Lam

Jichu Drakey Bakery

Swimming pool

Drimey Lam

Genyen Lam

Rabten Lam

RICB & Pension Board Buildings

© Airphoto International Ltd.

8   DD Tsongkhang (trekking gear)
9   Norling Complex
10 Swiss Bakery
11 Art Café
12 Plum Café/Lhanam's Restaurant
13 Hotel Yoedzer/City Centre Complex
14 Art Shop & Gallery/
    Handicraft Bhutan/VAST
15 Clock Tower Square
16 Om Bar/Jojo Café/
    Namgyal Fleece Cloths Shop/
    DSB Books

the cozy Om bar, the Space 34 night club, the DSB bookshop and a small store selling dried fruit and lemon grass oil.

The city buses and the taxis have their terminus at the end of the Chang Lam opposite the Yarkay building.

Two very comfortable hotels are located on the lower side of the main street, just past the clock tower: the **Druk** (tel. 975-2-322966), at the lower corner of the Clock tower square, and the **Jumolhari** (tel. 975-2-322747; www.hoteljumolhari.com). They both have very good restaurants that serve excellent Indian dishes, including tandoori, as well as Chinese and Western specialities. Here one finds the high civil servants and everyone that Thimphu considers important, like visiting diplomats and development experts. The Druk Hotel also has a beauty salon, sauna and a gym club.

The **Druk Sherig Guesthouse**, a little further down the main street, is a simple but comfortable hotel. Another hotel, the **Dragon Roots** was completed in late 2004 next to the Jomolhari and in 2005, the **Hotel Senge**, opened on the main street.

Several shops open onto that square, where a clock, decorated with dragons, was erected and which in 2005 was being converted into an open-air theatre. There is a friendly optician of Austrian origin, well-stocked stationery shops, the art gallery with an adjacent café, which has home-made cakes, and a crafts shop. Nearby the Tashi Supermarket has a good choice of hygiene and beauty products (including Garnier, l'Oréal, Revlon), as well as food products that include mineral water and beer, cheese, as well as excellent dried mushrooms (*shitake*).

A choice of toiletries and groceries from Bangkok are in fact available in many of the downtown shops. The famous shop No.7 has moved location and is now a great supermarket named Lhatshog and located in the residential area of Motithang.

Let us now go back up to the main roundabout where the elegant policeman presides. Tucked away on the first floor of a building is **Plum's**, a restaurant popular with civil servants.

From here the main street, running towards the north, is no longer split. A number of shops open onto the left side of the street: the Norling music store, with a restaurant of the same name on the first floor, a pharmacy, the Druk Medical Store, the Norling jewellery store, and Tshering Drolkar's store, selling carpets and Bhutanese items.

In the new (2005) building in front of the old cinema-hall there is a Chinese restaurant and a trekking gear shop. Continuing up the main street, almost opposite the Handicrafts Emporium, one finds a handicraft shop, the large KMT bookshop which also has a lot of new religious items, the Sharchopa grocery store, where the delicious Bumthang cheese is available and round the corner, the milk booth where the Gogona cheese can be purchased. Then one finds the Public Library, the sales counter of the National Library, the Textile Museum, and the government duty-free store as well as small grocery shops.

The **Textile Museum**, under the patronage of Her Majesty the Queen Ashi Sangay Choden, was inaugurated in June 2001. A place for the exhibition of this unique and traditional art, it pays hommage to the weavers of Bhutan and their skilfulness. Eventually, it will be a centre for conservation, restoration and documentation of Bhutanese textiles.

On the right side of the main street, a little after the central main roundabout, stands the large building that houses the simple but very decent, **Tandrin Hotel**, and the Druk Shopping Complex. On the ground floor is a string of stores selling items mostly imported from Thailand and Nepal, a large store selling fabric, including silk, two crafts shop, **Kezang Handicrafts** and **Kurtoe Handicrafts** which are very well stocked with small souvenirs, and a stamp counter. The cinema shows mainly Indian and Bhutanese films, and, tucked in on its groundfloor, is a good little bookshop—**Pekhang**—which also sells cards, Indian and English newspapers, magazines and stationery.

Further up the main street, on the right side, you pass the new building, covered in marble of the Royal Insurance Corporation of Bhutan (RICB). It is now rented to the Bhutan Power Board. Then one comes across the Bank of Bhutan (BoB), the crafts store run by the government (Handicrafts Emporium) and the Druk Air office. A large luxury hotel (a partnership between the Tashi Group of Companies and the (Indian) **Taj** group) is being built in what was an asparagus field.

Drentoen Lam, a small street off the main street, to the right, just after the cinema, leads to the large Post office building, where the Philatelic office, but also the Bhutan National Bank (BNB) is located. Opposite the post-office, there is Lungta, a handicrafts shop which sell a lot of expensive items from Nepal but also nice CDs.

The small shopping centre of Centrepoint has music shops, a tailor and a very good simple restaurant with friendly owners on the first floor. Further along are the ministry of Communications and the UN building, which houses the UNDP, WFP, FAO and UNV.

Doebum Lam which runs parallel to the main Norzim Lam is basically a residential street, but a sports complex with a swimming-pool and a basketball court, the Chamber of Commerce, the Department of Tourism, and the Ministry of Trade as well as the Jichudrake bakery are located there. This street rejoins the main street, Norzim Lam, further north, near the second roundabout near the Ministry of Works and Housing located in the old "Bhutan hotel".

(Top) *Entrance to Memorial Chorten, Thimphu.*
(Middle) *Chilli seller at Thimphu market.*
(Left) *Typical shops in main street of Thimphu.*
(Bottom) *Paro* dzong *which is built on the hillside overlooking Paro.*

Inexpensive public telephone counters, or phone booths, are found pretty well everywhere. To make an international call, look for the ISD lozenge-yellow sign. Internet places are also cropping up but the connection can be slow and frustrating.

THE MEMORIAL CHORTEN AREA

From the main roundabout Chorten Lam leads, as its name indicates to the Memorial Chorten about 200 metres (656 feet) up the street after passing **Hotel 89** and the **Indian military hospital** on the left.

The Memorial Chorten is an impressive monument with its golden spires shining in the sun, its bells tinkling in the wind and an endless procession of elderly people circling around it.

The Memorial Chorten was built in 1974 in memory of the 3rd King, H M Jigme Dorje Wangchuck, who died in 1972. There are no mortal remains of the King inside the Memorial Chorten and only a photograph draped in ceremonial scarves on the ground floor serves as a discreet reminder that the Memorial Chorten was built to fulfil one of his wishes. The late King had, in fact, decided to put into tangible form the three traditional pillars of Buddhism; the Word, Body and Mind of Buddha. He had the Commentaries of Buddha, the Tanjur, transcribed in letters of gold to represent the Word of Buddha and had 1,000 statues made to represent the Body of Buddha, but he died before completing the Mind of Buddha which was to be represented by a Chorten. His mother, the Royal Grandmother Ashi Phuntsho Chogron, put up the monument on his behalf and in his memory.

The Memorial Chorten is approached through a small garden with a gate decorated both outside and inside with three slate carvings. On the exterior are representations of Buddhism's three protective bodhisattvas: Avalokiteshvara, the symbol of compassion; Manjushri, the symbol of knowledge; and Vajrapani, the symbol of power. On the interior slates are engraved the image of Shabdrung Ngawang Namgyal, the historical Buddha and Guru Rinpoche. Over to the left, enormous prayer wheels are kept turning by the faithful.

The Memorial Chorten was conceived by Dungse Rinpoche, the son of the great master, Dudjom Rinpoche (1904–87), according to the Nyingmapa tradition, and it has the special distinction of being a *chorten*-chapel. On the east side of the Chorten, and visible from the outside, is a large image of the historical Buddha.

The ceilings of the small porches that grace all four sides of the Memorial Chorten are painted on the south with the *mandala* of the Buddha Ratnasambhava, on the west with that of Hayagriva, on the north with the *mandala* of Phurpa, and on the east with that of Vajrasattva. The Chorten is entered by a door on the north side. The number, size and forms of the clay statues may surprise you. Remember that peaceful deities assume these wrathful forms expressly to overcome the evil spirits that attack the Buddhist doctrine.

The ground floor is consecrated to the cycle of teachings of the deity *Phurpa*, the next floor to the Kagye cycle, the teachings for subduing eight kinds of harmful spirits, and the top floor to the cycle of teachings of the Lama Gondu. Together these form the three esoteric teachings of the Nyingmapa school. All three are revealed texts that were hidden by Guru Rinpoche in order that they be rediscovered at propitious moments by lamas called *tertons*, the 'discoverers of religious treasures'. This particular cycle of the Phurpa was rediscovered by the first Dudjom Rinpoche, Trakthung Dudjom Lingpa, in the 19th century. The text of the Kagye was discovered by Nyangrel Nyima Oezer in the 12th century and that of the Lama Gondu by Sangye Lingpa in the 14th century.

The top floor walls are covered with painting representing the different protective deities of the Nyingmapa school, and the visions which appear in the bardo, the intermediary state after death. An exterior gallery above the top floor makes it possible to circle the Chorten at the level of its spires from where there is a splendid view over the city.

The Memorial Chorten is an excellent introduction to Tantric Buddhism in all its complexity but you should try to visit the site in the company of someone who understands its significance. This advice holds for all Tantric Buddhist temples, of course, but most especially for the Memorial Chorten where the teachings are esoteric and can be easily misinterpreted.

From the Memorial Chorten, continuing straight along the street called Gonphel Lam, you arrive at the hospital: the Jigme Dorje Wangchuck Referral Hospital (JDWRH).

CHANGLIMITHANG AREA AND THE WEEKLY MARKET

If, from the Memorial Chorten, you head down the hill along the wide winding street, whose real name is Dzogchen Lam but which everybody calls 'Python Road', you arrive at the petrol pump and then Lungten Zampa bridge, which is at the entrance to the city.

On the other side of the river, the Dechen Lam forms a delightful promenade right along the river until the *dzong*. Several schools, the Bhutanese paper Jungzhi factory with its shop and two hotels are located there. The Jampelyang, up on the side of the hill, is a nice small hotel with a superb view of Thimphu. **The Riverview** is a large, imposing hotel frequented by high-ranking civil servants, diplomats and distinguished guests. Its rooms offer a beautiful view of the river, but its general architecture is rather unbecoming.

The sports ground is called Changlimithang. A decisive battle in Bhutanese history was fought here in 1885, and it gave virtual control of the whole country to the future 1st King, Ugyen Wangchuck. Football, cricket matches, and archery competitions take place on the sports ground. North of the sports ground, a squash court, billiard parlour and a banquet hall surrounded by forsythia make an attractive boundary to the tennis courts.

The low building is the administrative and judiciary seat for the district of Thimphu. Just in front of it, a big square chorten indicates the spot where, formerly, people had to dismount from their steeds before approaching the *dzong*. Some 200 metres (656 feet) further on to the north is the square where the market is held on Friday, Saturdays and on Sunday mornings. These are the only days when Thimphu's residents can buy fresh fruit and vegetables. The market is therefore the most important shopping event of the week and should not be missed.

For years the market took place directly on the ground, in the open air, and merchants sometimes had to spend the night in the pouring rain. In 1986, platforms were built and, in 1989, covered market halls were erected over the platforms and a building for meat was constructed on the north side of the market. In 2005 more stalls were being built to accomodate the growing number of sellers.

The weekly market certainly offers the best opportunity to see agricultural products and watch people. In winter, now that communications are easier, Bhutanese from remote provinces come to sell products such as yak butter, strings of cheese cubes, fermented cheese, bowls made of turned wood and, of course, fabrics. The products that are sold change with the seasons and movements of people, the only imperative being that hot peppers (chillis/*hema*), both fresh and ground, must be available all year round!

There is no bargaining and the same price is charged for everybody. Religious men say prayers in front of their portable chapels, buyers examine betel leaves or blow into trumpets, the smell of dried fish and herbs for ritual fumigation mix with that of the little cheeses, farmers who barely know how to count sell their rice or the products they have picked in the forest with full trust in their clients, while a passer-by accidentally knocks people with a leg of beef that he carries on his shoulder. Nowadays, cheap souvenirs from Nepal are more prominent while traditional Bhutanese handicrafts get lesser. Also, behind the open market, several shops sell Chinese and Bangladeshi goods. A nice walkway has been built between the Choegyal Lam and the river and a new bridge in traditional style was being constructed in 2005.

(Following pages) *Monks in procession passing Tashichoedzong in Thimphu.*

THE DZONG AREA

Continuing north along the river after the marketplace, you arrive via the traditional road—Choegyal Lam—at Tashichoedzong, Thimphu *dzong* and the seat of government and the centre of all religious affairs in the Kingdom. However, the road normally used to get there is by way of Desi Lam which starts at the end of Norzim Lam, the main street.

Near the second roundabout on Norzim Lam are the last of the shops, including a traditional boot maker which makes boots on order. Since the *dzong* is below the level of the road, nothing can be seen of it but its red roofs. Desi Lam, on the right, leads straight to it, passing the white, shingle-roofed edifice of the High Court of Justice on the left and skirting the golf course where a few animals may still be seen grazing. The golf course has a restaurant. Lamp-posts in Bhutanese style line the majestic avenue. The small buildings in front of the *dzong* are government offices which have been built to relieve the pressure of space within the *dzong* resulting from the development and expansion of the administration.

TASHICHOEDZONG

Thimphu's *dzong*, named Tashichoedzong, delights the eye with its balanced proportions and air of majesty. Its history is very old, dating back to the 13th century, but the original *dzong* was not built on this flat land, which offers no strategic advantages.

Gyelwa Lhanangpa, the religious man who founded the Lhapa school, a branch of the Drigung Kagyupa school, built a *dzong* in the Thimphu valley in 1216 which was named Do Ngon *dzong*, 'Fortress of the Blue Stone'. The location of this fortress was excellent. It was situated on a spur to the northeast of the present *dzong* where one can see a white building that houses the monastic school of Dechen Phodrang.

A few years later, Gyelwa Lhanangpa took offence at the religious influence of Phajo Drugom Shigpo of the Drukpa Kagyupa school, and in the struggle that ensued the fortress was badly damaged.

It is not clear what role it played or to which religious group it belonged during the following centuries, but the *dzong* became the property of Shabdrung Ngawang Namgyal towards the end of the 1630s after he triumphed over the Five Groups of Lamas, which were headed by the Lhapas. In 1641, the construction of the new *dzong* was finished at the same spot and the Shabdrung named it Tashichoedzong, 'The Fortress of the Auspicious Religion'. The fortress became the summer residence of the Shabdrung and the state clergy, while Punakha *dzong* became their winter home.

The *dzong* suffered serious damage from fire in 1772. Zhidar, the Desi at that period, and Yonten Thaye, the *Je Khenpo*, then decided to rebuild it at the bottom of the valley, in the place where it now stands. After this reconstruction, the *dzong* caught fire once again in 1869 and was restored in 1870 when Jigme Namgyal, the father of the future 1st King, was the *Desi* of Bhutan. Further repairs had to be undertaken after the earthquake of 1897 and the Lhakhang Sarp was built in 1907 by the then Thimphu *dzongpon* Kunzang Trinley.

After the 3rd King, H M Jigme Dorje Wangchuck, had made Thimphu his permanent capital, he started to enlarge Tashichoedzong in 1962 so that it could serve as the seat of government. The new *dzong*, which was constructed by traditional methods, was consecrated in June 1969.

INSIDE THE DZONG

The official gate of the *dzong* is on the east side. The high-relief sculptures in the first entranceway represent the Guardians of the Four Directions. They are bracketed on the left by the *bodhisattva* Vajrapani, who is coloured black and shown brandishing a diamond-thunderbolt, and on the right by the great Drukpa tutelary deity Hayagriva, who is red with a horse's head in his headdress. To the right of Hayagriva is Bhutan's most popular saint, the 'divine madman' Drukpa Kunley (1455–1529), holding a bow and arrow and accompanied by his dog. At the end, on his right, is the easily recognized fable of the Four Friends (*see* page 145). The unadorned gate for the public is further down and there is a security-check.

The courtyard where you will emerge leaves an indelible impression. The majesty of the architecture, the beautiful proportions and the lavish decoration are enough to take your breath away.

On this side of the central tower, in which temples are located, is the **courtyard of the state clergy**. In the middle of this courtyard, the **Lhakhang Sarp's** (new temple) façade is decorated with mythical animals. An image of Guru Rinpoche 'Victorious in the Three Worlds' is the main statue on the upper floor. The coffered ceiling is covered with superb mandalas.

A large building with a porch occupies the north side of the courtyard. Large paintings of cosmic *mandalas* and a magnificent Wheel of Life decorate the porch on the ground floor. The *mandalas* represent the universe in the same way as those at Paro, but the artistic rendering is somewhat different. Inside, the ground floor houses a large assembly hall for the monks where the principal statue represents the historical Buddha. The Royal Grandmother Ashi Phuntsho Choegron (1911–2003) had this three-storey statue made as well as murals depicting the 12 stages of Buddha Sakyamuni's life in the room above; it is the former **Chamber of the National Assembly.** The National Assembly Hall is now situated in the Convention Centre on the other side of the river. Paintings inside the former national assembly hall are of the highest quality and illustrate different episodes from the life of Buddha, while on the ceiling is a great *mandala* depicting the Buddha and the Sixteen Arhats. The King's throne, intricately carved, stands in the middle of the Chamber. The Chamber serves as a hall for special occasion such as the investiture of the Crown Prince as Chhoetse Penlop in October 2004. At other time, it is a workshop for the tailors of the government and the clergy. It is then possible to admire their skilled work in applique and embroidery.

On the other side of the central tower is the courtyard of the central administration and all around it are the ministries and the Royal Chamber.

THE VALLEY NORTH OF THE DZONG

The door on the north side of the *dzong* gives access to a traditional cantilevered bridge with a shingled roof. A little further along is the cremation site. Opposite the bridge, the convention centre, built in the same style as a *dzong*, is the seat of the Planning department and the Foreign Ministry, and also houses the National Assembly Hall. This building was inaugurated on 17 December, 1993.

Behind the *dzong* are the houses of the Royal Bodyguard, and hamlets still subsist in the middle of paddy fields as far as the Indian Embassy complex. Four kilometres (two and a half miles) further north is **Dechenchoeling Palace**, the Queen Mother's residence and, on the other side of the river, the crowded village of Taba where the Forestry Institute is located.

Pangri Zampa Temple is situated just beyond Dechenchoeling. Two imposing structures are set in the middle of a meadow, not far from the river; this was the residence of Shabdrung Ngawang Namgyal when he arrived in Bhutan in 1616. The temple was built during the first quarter of the 16th century—the exact date is not known—by Ngawang Choegyel, the great-great-grandfather of the Shabdrung and 14th hierarch of the Drukpas. A prayer wall covered with carved and painted stones, and huge cypress trees combine to give this place an almost magical charm. it is now the seat of the monastic school of astrology.

Dechenphug lhakhang in a beautiful side valley is the very venered temple of the local deity Genyen Jagpa Melen turned into the guardian deity of the Drukpa. It was originally built in the 14th century by Jamyang Kunga Sengye, the 7th hierarch of the Drukpa from Ralung in Tibet and restored by the Shabdrung Ngawang Namgyal in the 17th century. It was further restored and the site landscaped in the 1990s by UNESCO.

Beyond Dechenphug, the motor road ascends the valley for about 10 kilometres (6 miles) and after crossing the river on a a bridge at Begana, comes to Dodina (2,600 metres), a dead end at the foot of a mountain. The Dodina covered bridge leading to the monastery is new, but it is built in traditional style with cantilevers and shingles.

It takes a good half an hour walk to reach the monastery. **Cheri** was built high on the slope in 1619 by the Shabdrung Ngawang Namgyal as his first monastery in Bhutan and he established there the first monastic body. The Shabdrung received there its full monk ordination in 1633. A chorten built by Newari craftsmen in 1621 contains the relics of his father Yap Tenpe Nyima whose body had been brought from Tibet. Cheri was always a reknown meditation place and the Shabdrung spent three years in retreat while the first and third temporal ruler of Bhutan died there, also in retreat.

Tango Monastery is close by (about a 45 minutes walk uphill), on the right of the motor road, at the same level as Cheri but out of sight. Tango dates originally from the 13th century as it was the residence of Phajo Drugom Shigpo who introduced the Drukpa Kagyupa school in Bhutan. it was rebuilt in its present form in 1688 by Tenzin Rabgye, the 4th Temporal Ruler of Bhutan and 1st Tri rinpoche. It was extended by Druk Rabgye, the 8th Temporal Ruler, in the early 18th century and in the late 19th century the Shabdrung Jigme Choegyal had a golden roof installed. The monastery was restored in the mid 1990s and is now the residence of the 7th Tri Rinpoche, the young reincarnation of Tenzin Rabgye.

Built like a *dzong*, the monastery has a characteristic curved outside wall and a beautiful main tower with recesses. Behind the row of prayer-wheels, there are beautiful engraved slates. Inside the courtyard, a gallery depicts the lineage of the Drukpa kagyupa religious lineage.

Tango is an upper-education-level monastic school. From Cheri mountain, a trail leads across gorges and passes to the northern region of Lingshi (4100 metres).

A STROLL THROUGH OTHER AREAS OF THIMPHU

If, from the roundabout after the small bridge on Desi Lam, you leave the *dzong* avenue on the right and take the street Choephel Lam on the left, you pass the Bhutan Telecom (telecommunications satellite station) and then the superb Royal Monetary Authority (RMA) building.

Leaving the High Court on the right, you then come to a small red brick building which is the golf club. On the other side of the road, a high white building in the traditional style and covered with shingles catches one's attention. This is the National Library, which you can visit, and where old manuscripts and books printed with wood blocks (xylography), as well as printing blocks, are kept. You can also consult some one thousand books and magazines on Buddhism, the Himalayas and Bhutan as well as the largest book in the world (about Bhutan), produced in 2004, by the MIT, USA. A large archive complex is being built next door.

A road on the left leads to the Ministry of Health and Education, the Geographic Survey of Bhutan, and the Hospital of Indigenous Medicine. The latter can be visited on request.

The School of Traditional Arts (*Zorig chusum*) is also in this area, just above the National Library. There, boys and girls learn traditional drawing and painting techniques, and a visit is extremely interesting, not only to see how skilful the students are, but also to observe the traditional methods of teaching, which are very different from those used in the West. Note that embroidery done by women is a new trend in Bhutan as this was an art reserved for monks.Upstairs the older students paint *thangka*, sculpt in clay, work in wood and with slate, and make boots.

Next to the School of Traditional Arts, small handicrafts shops have been set up by former students. Just below, one of the oldest houses in Thimphu, was restored and transformed into the **Folk Heritage Museum**. Inaugurated in August 2001 under the patronage of Her Majesty the Queen Ashi Dorji Wangmo, the museum is meant to serve as an account of everyday rural life for the young urbanized generations and as a place for preserving objects related to this life, in case this way of life should disappear. Choeki Handicrafts, which offers nice masks, *thangkas* and wooden objects, is next to the museum.

Continuing along the Choephel road after the National Library, the golf course and the *dzong* are on the right. At a gentle slope the road climbs along the side of the mountain up to the red nunnery of Thangthong Dewachen in Zilukha. Built in 1976 by the Tibetan master Rikey Jigdrel, its other name, "Drubthob Lhakhang", derives from the fact that the Rikey Jigdrel was the reincarnation of the famous Drubthob Thangton Gyelpo (1361–1485) who built temples and iron-chain bridges. After Rikey Jigdrel died, his reincarnation was found in a Bhutanese family. Sixty nuns reside in this small complex situated just above the *dzong* and surrounded by prayer flags. From this spot the view of the *dzong* and the valley is breathtaking, especially in the afternoon.

A kilometre (a little over half a mile) further up, you arrive in the area called **Motithang**, "the meadow of pearls".

MOTITHANG

Motithang is the smart residential district of Thimphu. Its growth dates from the middle of the 1980s, although its beginnings can be linked to the construction of the Motithang Hotel in 1974, on the occasion of the coronation of HM Jigme Singye Wangchuck. At that time, the hotel was situated in a forest far from the main road. Today, the fields and fallow land that once lay between the hotel and the city have been replaced by houses surrounded by gardens. The old hotel will be converted into a hotel and tourism management institute.

A few minutes' walk above this building, there is a large enclosure with the national animals, the takins (*Budorcas taxicolor*), that look like a cross between a goat and a moose. The road that carries on leads up to the communications antenna, an isolated spot much appreciated by lovers!

The present **Motithang Hotel** (tel. 975-2-322435) now occupies a delightful little complex of houses. A secluded residential area is further up in the forest and the state guest houses, **Kungacholing** and **Lhundupling**, as well as **Amankora-Thimphu** (tel. 975-2-331333; www.amanresorts.com) are located there.

A good way to return to the city is by following Thori Lam all the way down to the top of the main street, at the level of the second roundabout. A few offices, have been set up in this area. The National Commission for Cultural Affairs and DHL are also located there as well as some grocery shops, among them the Lhatshog supermarket.

CHANGANGKHA

This district gets its name from **Changangkha temple**, which lies on top of the knoll that stands out above Thimphu and from where the view of the valley is superb. This place has a special magical atmosphere with its prayer flags floating in the wind and its feeling of riding above the hurly-burly of the city.

Changangkha Lhakhang is one of the oldest temples in the Thimphu valley, having been built in the 15th century by a descendant of Phajo Drugom Shigpo, the founder of the Drukpa school in Bhutan. The main statue here is an image of Avalokiteshvara. One of the most remarkable paintings on the wall opposite the entrance is of Tsangpa Gyare Yeshe Dorje (1161–1211), the founder of the Drukpa school in Tibet. The temple was restored in 1998–99, and the development works on the hill have been completed.

Around the knoll of Changangkha, the many Bhutanese houses with their little gardens give the neighbourhood a rural charm. A very good walk with a magnificent view runs along the foot of the knoll and avoids the main thoroughfares. It goes from Changangkha to the Memorial Chorten along Rabten Lam.

Besides the Motithang hotel restaurant, the only restaurant in this area is the Rabten in lower Motithang who reopened in 2005 and is dedicated to Bhutanese dishes.

SEMTOKHA DZONG

Semtokha *dzong* (Sinmo Dokha/Semtokha) lies six kilometres (nearly four miles) south of Thimphu where the roads from Thimphu, Paro/Phuentsholing and Punakha/Wangduephodrang cross. Its strategic position is evident since it controls all the approaches to and from Thimphu. This *dzong*, whose complete name is San Ngag Sabdon Phodrang, 'the palace of profound Tantric teachings', was the first *dzong* to be built by Shabdrung Ngawang Namgyal. Its construction started in 1629 and it was consecrated in 1631. The *dzong* was attacked by the army of the Five Groups of Lamas in 1634, but the Shabdrung's army was victorious. In 1671, the *dzong* was restored by the Third Desi, Minjur Tenpa.

In 1961, the 3rd King, Jigme Dorje Wangchuck, decided to turn the building into a centre for traditional studies for lay students who would be trained as teachers of Dzongkha. Today the Institute of Language and Cultural Studies (ILCS) has moved above the *dzong* and with 500 students became co-educational in 1989. It is now part of the Royal University of Bhutan and plans to move to a new campus south of Trongsa after 2007.

The main temple of the Semtokha *dzong* is in the **central tower**. The Guardians of the Four Directions are represented under the porch of the entranceway, along with a magnificent Wheel of Life. A widely seen design is painted on the right-hand wall—a flaming sword placed over a book and a lotus. A bird with two heads stands on each side of the sword. The lotus represents Guru Rinpoche in his form as Padmasambhava; the book, which represents knowledge, and the flaming sword, which cuts through ignorance, are the attributes of the great Tibetan king, Trisong Detsen. The two-headed yellow waterfowl symbolizes the Indian masters, Santarakshita and Kamalasila, and the two-headed green parrot represents two great translators of religious texts from Sanskrit into Tibetan. These paintings were partially restored in 1983 in memory of a Japanese lady, Mrs Sugiura, who died in Bhutan. This is explained in a Japanese and Dzongkha inscription on the left side of the wall.

The **statues in the sanctuary** inside are certainly among the most impressive and beautiful in Bhutan. They are very large and they show the extraordinary degree of skill that has been achieved in metalworking. They represent the historical Buddha and his two main disciples, Maudgalayayana and Sariputra. Along the walls stand statues of the eight principal *bodhisattvas*: Maitreya,

The guardian of the 'eastern direction' (Semtokha dzong).

Manjushri, Vajrapani, Avalokiteshvara, Samantabhadra, Kshitigarbha, Akashagarbha and Sarvanivarana Vishkambhini.

The paintings in the sanctuary represent the Sixteen *Arhats* (actually 18, as two were added to the original list, but the identifying name remains unchanged). They are of the highest quality due as much to their composition as to the rich colours and the fine lines of the drawings. Equal in excellence are the paintings in the chapel of Avalokiteshvara on the left side of the big hall. There, too, the paintings are among the finest to be seen anywhere in Bhutan. They show the Drukpa Kagyupa lamas and the first three Buddhist Kings of Tibet surrounded by the first translators of holy texts. In this chapel the statues of Avalokiteshvara and Tara, his female counterpart, are also of exceptional quality.

On the right side of the big hall, a door flanked by two figures in armour signals the entrance to the *Gonkhang*, the temple of fearsome deities.

SUGGESTED DAY WALKS AROUND THIMPHU

There are some very good day walks in the vicinity of Thimphu. It is best to take somebody along who knows the way, however, because paths are not signposted and it is easy to get lost in the maze of tracks marked out by herds of grazing animals. Also, given the altitude and the condition of the paths, it is important to be in good shape before setting out on a hike. In April and May, any of these walks will offer an opportunity to see blooming rhododendrons. (The times given below are for the average walker.)

TALA MONASTERY

If you are feeling energetic, a walk of one and a half hours above Semtokha *dzong* will take you to the mountaintop where Tala Monastery is situated at 3,050 metres (10,000 feet). The monastery was built during the 1860s by the 34th *Je Khenpo*, Sheldrup Oezer. On a clear day there is a wonderful view over the mountains north of Thimphu. You can now reach the monastery in a 4 wheel drive car and choose the option of walking down.

PHAJODING MONASTERY AND EXCURSION TO THE LAKES

One of the most enjoyable hikes goes to Phajoding Monastery, which can be seen on the mountain to the west of Thimphu. It is about a three-hour walk to the monastery from Kyebitsho, a little meadow above Motithang, which can be reached by four-wheel-drive vehicle. At the meadow it is easy to make a mistake: the correct route, half-hidden, is the one that goes down towards the stream on the right, not the one that continues straight ahead towards the far end of the meadow. Much of the walk is through forest, but approaching the monastery, situated at 3,700 metres (12,140 feet), the vegetation thins out and there is a magnificent view over the valley and the surrounding mountains.

As its name implies, the complex of Phajoding takes its name from the Drukpa saint Phajo Drugom Shigpo, who meditated here in the 13th century. The monastery itself is composed of several buildings and it contains a state monastic school. The two most important temples are the **Khangzang**, built in 1749 by the 9th *Je Khenpo*, **Shakya Rinchen**, and the **Ogmin**, built in 1789 by the l6th *Je Khenpo*, Sherab Singye.

In winter and spring there is a good chance of encountering herds of yak in the pastures above the monastery. Continuing up towards the ridge at 4,100 metres (13,450 feet), the route passes in front of Thugjedra, which is one of the places where Phajo Drugom Shigpo meditated. The present building dates from 1749 and was also constructed by the 9th *Je Khenpo*, Shakya Rinchen. It is a very steep, hour-long climb to the summit. The view is rewarding if the weather is clear.

From the ridge it takes three hours more to walk to the lakes. If you plan to visit the Jimilangtsho lakes, you should count on making a two-day excursion.

THADRA MONASTERY

This hike starts above Yanchenphug high school on the far side of the Lungten Zampa Bridge, on the slope of the mountain lying east of Thimphu. It takes two hours to walk to the pretty Thadra Monastery, at 3,270 metres (10,730 feet), which was built in 1731 by Lama Tsulag Gyatso. The monastery perches directly above the Lungtenphug military camp; you will see it high on the mountainside as you come into Thimphu on the Paro–Phuentsholing road.

TRASHIGANG NUNNERY

Another very beautiful day walk leads to the **Trashigang Nunnery**, at 3,200 metres (10,500 feet). Starting at the village of Oesepang, about 15 kilometres (nearly nine and a half miles) from Thimphu on the road to Punakha, the path goes down into the valley, crosses the river, and then climbs for about one and a half hours up to the monastery. Built in 1768 by the l2th *Desi*, Kunga Gyatso, it is made up of little houses inhabited by Drukpa nuns. You can also reach Ttrashigang nunnery from Dochula pass.

THIMPHU TO PUNAKHA BY THE OLD ROUTE

If you are brave and a botany lover, it is interesting to walk the old Sinchu La route from Thimphu to Punakha. This can be done in one day, but you need a car to fetch you back from the upper reaches of the Punakha valley at the village of Sirigang. The hike takes about ten and a half hours and covers some 40 kilometres (nearly 25 miles).

The path starts at **Phanri Zampa**, just behind Dechenchoeling. Crossing the river, it climbs for three hours through a forest filled with rhododendron to the **Sinchu La Pass**, which is marked by a small *chorten* at 3,400 metres (11,155 feet). The long descent through another forest takes about five hours and passes through several different levels of vegetation. It has no view, and since the route is not frequently used nowadays, it may be necessary to beat a path through the tunnels of greenery. The first village is **Tonshinkha** where the Indian saint, Ngagi Rinchen, is said to have drawn a thousand pictures of Buddha on a rock with one magic gesture. From there the path goes down by much gentler slopes and crosses rice flelds for a couple of hours to the village of **Sirigang**, situated on the motor road north of Punakha *dzong* at an altitude of 1,350 metres (4,430 feet).

TO THE SOUTHWEST: CHHUZOM TO PHUENTSHOLING

Before 1968, it took at least five days to reach the plain and and one had to struggle across a leech-infested jungle. The 141 kilometres (87 miles) ride from Chhuzom to Phuentsholing now takes four and a half hours by car. The road from Thimphu to Phuentsholing via Chhuzom was only finished in 1968 and important enlargement work started in 2005.

After leaving the Paro road at Chhuzom, the Phuentsholing road enters a gorge and, miraculously, it remains straight and flat for four kilometres. The road follows Thimphu's river, the Wang Chu, which takes its name from Wang, the region of Thimphu, and makes its way southward through the mountains. You need a sharp eye in order to spot **Dobji** *dzong* perched upon its rock; it used to guard the narrow gorge and has also been used as a prison but today it houses no prisoners.

After the defile comes the climb of the **Chapcha Pass**, situated at 2,900 metres (9,500 feet). From here, the entire Wang Chu gorge can be seen with the naked eye, all the way to the last range before the Plain of Bengal, a mere 50 kilometres (just over 30 miles) away as the crow flies.

Chapcha, situated on the southern face of the mountains, is made up of numerous houses scattered over the slope, and a little *dzong*, which can be reached by a 15-minute walk from the road. The people of Chapcha are considered well-off by other Bhutanese because their soil is suitable for growing potatoes and, above all, they own trucks for transporting merchandise between India and Bhutan.

After descending from the Chapcha Pass, the road runs along the side of the mountain and arrives at **Bunakha**, lying at 2,200 metres (7,220 feet) where a log cabin restaurant provides good food. The village of Bunakha, with its shingle roofs, lies below the level of the restaurant.

Some 15 minutes later, the road passes through **Chimakhoti**, a straggling new village that only came into existence with the building of the road and the construction of the Chukha hydroelectric plant. The latter is at the bottom of the gorge at the outlet of a natural lock through which the Wang Chu passes. Built with Indian aid, this plant is one of the most important in the Himalayas (336 Megawatts) and a major part of the electricity is exported to India. A bridge crosses the river at the outlet of the lock and this unofficially marks the half-way point between Thimphu and Phuentsholing. **Chukha** *dzong*, which formerly stood on the valley floor and constituted a stopping place on the trail from the south, no longer exists, but Chukha is now the name of a newly created district which extends as far as Phuentsholing.

The road now runs along the mountainside which forms the right bank of the Wang Chu and enters a zone of dense subtropical forest. There is hardly any sign of habitation on this portion of the route until it reaches Gedu, 30 kilometres (18.6 miles) further on. There is, however, a small canteen at a spot named **Taktichu** which serves a few south Indian specialities. A few kilometres beyond Taktichu on the other side of the valley, a splendid waterfall plunges 200 metres (650 feet) into the river below. The area beyond Taktichu is often foggy, which makes it look like a landscape in a Chinese painting, with great banks of mist floating in the valley. From here on it is also the domain of leeches and in the rainy season the paths alongside the road abound with them.

The way through **Gedu** is strewn with pot-holes, tree trunks, and trucks. Houses made of boards line both sides of the road. Gedu, a 1980s creation which owes its existence to the installation of a big plywood factory that has since closed, is now an important base for the construction of the Tala hydro-electric station. From Gedu, a side road goes to the Tala hydel project. Small restaurants provide a place to have something to eat or to warm up, the climate of Gedu being known for its dampness. Heavy trucks ply the road for the Tala hydro-electric project between Gedu and Phuentsholing.

Half an hour after leaving Gedu, you arrive at what can be defined as the 'balcony of the Himalayas', the last mountain chain before the Plain of Bengal. A pass, at an altitude of 2,200 metres (7,220 feet), is marked by many prayer flags. From here, in fine weather, you will have a magnificent view. The wooded spurs of the Himalayas seem to mount an onslaught as they rise towards the pass and beyond, the vast plain spreading out endlessly towards the horizon. On the right, the valley of the Torsa River bores through the mountains. It takes roughly an hour to cover the 30 kilometres (18.5 miles) of vertiginous descent through tropical jungle and the 'Sorchen Bends'. At the bottom, Phuentsholing is located on the left bank of the Torsa River at the exact point where the plain meets the mountains. In Phuentsholing, as in Samdrup Jongkhar in Bhutan's far southeast, it is strikingly obvious how the Himalayas form a mighty barrier rising like a wall from the plain.

In former times the trail did not pass through Phuentsholing but through Pasamkha, formerly also called 'Buxa Duar', which is slightly to the east of Phuentsholing.

Five kilometres (three miles) before reaching Phuentsholing, a police checkpoint is set up at a spot called **Kharbandi**. Here the Bhutanese police check over travellers' papers and permits for visiting the interior of Bhutan. Not far from the police checkpoint there is the Kharbandi Technical School and, just beyond that, Kharbandi Monastery comes into sight on the left.

On the last hillock, at an altitude of 400 metres (1,300 feet), **Kharbandi Monastery** stands above the Plain of Bengal like a sentinel. The monastery was founded in 1967 by the Royal Grandmother, Ashi Phuntsho Chogron. From the monastery garden there is a beautiful view over the plain and the town of Phuentsholing. The Eight Kinds of Chortens commemorating the life events of the historical Buddha stand in front of the temple which contains paintings of the life of Buddha and statues of Shabdrung Ngawang Namgyal, Guru Rinpoche and the historical Buddha. After a rapid descent through jungle where teak trees are easily recognizable by their huge flat leaves, the road enters Phuentsholing.

PHUENTSHOLING

Phuentsholing, a sub-district of Chukha, is a true example of a frontier town where different ethnic groups mingle: Bhutanese in national costume, suffering from the hot climate; Bengalis in light *dhotis*; Nepalese wearing their characteristic hats; and Indian businessmen carrying their briefcases. Despite an effort to give the town a Bhutanese appearance, the various buildings are more or less devoid of charm. The centre of the city is made up of wholesale and retail shops selling groceries, paper products, tyres, construction materials and plumbing fixtures. Cars, buses and trucks create a cacophony that announces the proximity of India.

A small public park allows the inhabitants to stroll in the fresh air at day's end, and a temple was built in the middle of it in 1982. Named the **Zangdopelri**, it represents the heaven of Guru Rinpoche. On the ground level there are statues of the Eight Manifestations of Guru Rinpoche arranged as a tree of life, and paintings of the life of Buddha. On the next floor are the Eight Bodhisattvas and statues of Avalokiteshvara with a thousand eyes and a thousand hands, and of Shabdrung Ngawang Namgyal. On the top floor, the main statue is of Amitabha.

The frontier post stands beside a wonderfully decorated gate which marks the entry into Bhutan. On the far side of it is the Indian town of Jaigaon, all noisy hustle and bustle.

Phuentsholing has a very comfortable hotel, the **Druk Hotel** (tel. 975-5-252426), which also has a good restaurant; but it is located next to the bus station and one shouldn't count on sleeping in each morning. For the less well-heeled, there are a number of local hotels of which the **Peljorling**, the **Central** (tel. 975-5-252172)and the **Namgyal** are the best. The **Kunga**, located just opposite the Druk, is a simple but decent hotel; its restaurant (Indian cuisine) is very good.

THE ROAD TO PUNAKHA AND WANGDUEPHODRANG

The road to Punakha and Wangduephodrang, and beyond to central and eastern Bhutan, branches off a short distance before Semtokha *dzong*. One or two kilometres (about a mile) after the crossroads, there is a very fine view back to the *dzong*.

The road climbs rapidly and the sharp bends may seem even more numerous than usual! The first hamlet is Oesepang, famous for its experimental potato and seeds farm. Apple trees grow in orchards. Five kilometres (three miles) further on, the road passes through the village of **Hongtso**, where there is a checkpoint for inspecting the travel permits of foreigners and the local buses. The houses lining

the road belong to Tibetans who have become Bhutanese citizens. In small stalls, they sell apple, oranges and cheese to the travellers.

Hongtso (2900 metres) is 19 kilometres (nearly 12 miles) from Thimphu. The ancient village of Hongtso is set on the hill up from the road, and not far from it stands the Hongtso Lhakhang which was founded in 1525 by the 14th Drukpa hierarch of Tibet, Ngawang Choegyel. It was the residence of the famous Bhutanese Lama, Lama Sonam Zangpo also called 'Meme Lam' who died in 1982.

Four kilometres (two and a half miles) beyond Hongtso, and three quarters of an hour after leaving Thimphu, the traveller arrives at the **Dochula Pass** ('*La*' actually means 'Pass', but it is common practice to refer to passes in this way), which lies at an altitude of 3,050 metres (10,000 feet). The pass is marked by quantities of prayer flags and an impressive field of 108 *chortens* called the Druk Wangyal; they were built in 2004 at the initiative of HM the Queen Ashi Dorje Wangmo as a thanksgiving for the victory of Bhutan in the military campaign of December 2003 against the Bodos and ULFAs (*see* page 71). Nearby, Ashi Dorje Wangmo is building a temple, which is expected to be completed in 2006.

Below the pass, there is a restaurant in a log cabin where you can spend the night if you want to see the sunrise over the Himalayas (in the right season!). Indeed, Dochula, or rather the lookout point 500 metres (1,640 feet) lower, offers a spectacular view over the high peaks of the eastern Himalayas. However, the peaks can be seen only from mid-October to mid-February, and it is extremely unusual to see them at any other time unless, by chance, torrential rain has cleared the atmosphere. If this happens, get there quickly, since the mist soon rises again.

The pointed peak standing opposite Dochula is Masangang, at 7,158 metres (23,484 feet), which dominates the region of Laya. Next are Tsendagang, at 6,960 metres (22,835 feet), Terigang, at 7,060 metres (23,163 feet), then Jejegangphugang, at 7,158 metres (23,484 feet), Kangphugang, at 7,170 metres (23,524 feet), Zongaphugang, at 7,060 metres (23,163 feet)—a table-mountain that dominates the isolated region of Lunana—and finally Gangkar Puensum, the highest peak in Bhutan, at 7,541 metres (24,596 feet) north of Bumthang.

The descent from Dochula into the Punakha valley and Wangduephodrang is long, as the altitude difference between the pass and the valley is 1,700 metres (5,580 feet), the valley lying at an altitude of 1,300 metres (4,265 feet). The road passes first through a temperate type of leafy forest where rhododendron and magnolia bloom in March and April, then a semi-tropical zone where orange trees, banana trees and cactuses are found in abundance.

Geometric poem dedicated to the glory of the Shabdrung Ngawang Namgyal (Punakha dzong).

It takes about two hours to cover the 65 kilometres (40 miles) between Thimphu and the Mitshina/Lobeysa village, where the roads to Punakha and Wangduephodrang fork. A few kilometres before Lobeysa, the road leads into a reforested area where the Chir pine grows, a species of pine unique to the semi-tropical regions of the Himalayas.

Below Lobeysa, the temple standing on a round hillock is called **Chime Lhakhang**. It was built in 1499 by the 14th Drukpa hierarch, Ngawang Choegyel, the site having formerly been blessed by the famous 'divine madman', Drukpa Kunley (1455–1529), who built a *chorten* there. The temple is a pilgrimage site for women who cannot have children. It was restored in 1998–99 and the walk there is very pleasant.

From Mitshina/Lobeysa a growing hamlet, where the National Institute of Agriculture (NRTI) is located, the road turns northward and runs along a dry valley for 12 kilometres (seven and a half miles) to Punakha. A few kilometres before Punakha, a small road on the left leads up to the hotels, **Zangdopelri** (tel. 975-2-584125) and the **Meri Puensum** (tel. 975-2-584236) both situated on a beautiful site. The **Amankora-Punakha** lodge (tel. 975-2-584222; www.amanresorts.com), featuring a traditional farmhouse, is also situated in this picturesque area. On your way to Punakha, you pass through **Kuruthang**, a new town, without any charm, which is growing to be the main centre of the district since Punakha itself is a site prone to flooding.

PUNAKHA

Thirty years ago, Punakha, at 1,350 metres (4,430 feet), was only a *dzong*. Then a High School was constructed and the village expanded in the mid-1980s. The small size of the place is surprising considering the primordial role that Punakha has played in the history of Bhutan and the fact that it was the country's winter capital for 300 years.

Punakha *dzong*, or Punthang Dechen Phodrang *dzong*, was built in 1637 by Shabdrung Ngawang Namgyal. However, the site had already been occupied as far back as 1328 by a saint, Ngagi Rinchen, who built a temple there which can still be seen today opposite the large *dzong* and, which is called the **Dzongchung**, meaning 'the little *dzong*'. In addition Guru Rinpoche is said to have blessed the site in the eighth century and issued a prophecy which said that 'on the front edge of the hill that looks like an elephant's trunk, a man named Namgyal would come and build a fortress.'

When the Shabdrung arrived at the confluence of the Pho and Mo rivers, he set up a camp and that very night had a dream in which he heard the prophecy of

Guru Rinpoche. He decided then and there to build a *dzong* on that spot and place there the Ranjung Karsapani, the most sacred relic that he had brought with him from his monastery at Ralung in Tibet. The **Ranjung Karsapani** was a statue of Avalokiteshvara which had appeared miraculously from a vertebra of Tsangpa Gyare, the founder of the Drukpa school in Tibet, at the time of his cremation. This relic was so sacred that the Tibetans attacked Punakha *dzong* in order to take it back but were repelled by the Bhutanese. This episode gave rise to the festival of Punakha, the *Punakha Serda*, which takes place every year at the end of the winter in the first lunar month. A great banner (*thondroel*) is hoisted at the time of the *Dromchoe* festival just before the Serda during which people reenact their victorious battle (*see* page 198).

Exactly covering a spit of land at the confluence of the two rivers, the *dzong* resembles a gigantic ship. The Shabdrung made Punakha his winter capital since it was situated at a fairly low altitude, and the government moved every year from Thimphu to Punakha until the early 1950s, when Thimphu was established as the permanent capital. The monks of the central clergy, true to ancient custom, still migrate from Thimphu and come back to spend the six coldest months in Punakha. The Shabdrung died in 1651 while he was in meditation at Punakha and his body is preserved in one of the *dzong*'s temples, the **Machen Lhakhang**.

It was in Punakha *dzong* that Ugyen Wangchuck, the 1st King of Bhutan, was crowned on 17 December 1907.

The monks' **great assembly hall** was constructed at the time of Tenzin Drugda, the Second Desi (1656–67) and half-brother of the Shabdrung, and the central tower was rebuilt at the time of Minjur Tenpa, the Third Desi (1667–80).

The *dzong* was damaged six times by fire, twice by floods and once by an earthquake. In 1985, a fire then in 1994, a flash flood due to the rupture of a glacial lake in the Lunana region caused extensive damage to the building. Since then, major consolidation works have been done and the dzongchung as well as the assembly hall have been rebuilt. In 2003, after almost ten years of work, the *dzong* was reconsecrated in a spectacular ceremony.

The first courtyard is the area of administration and a large *chorten* which was finished in 1981 stands next to a Bodhi tree (*Ficus religiosa*). The *dzong* is the administrative headquarters for Punakha district. The second courtyard is now practically non-existent since a temple to the Tantric deity Cakrasamvara was built there in 1983. The *dzong* has twenty-one temples, the largest of which is the monks' assembly hall (*Kunre*), located on the prow of the *dzong*, in the third courtyard. The sheer size of the *Kunre*, the pillars, the paintings and the clay images of Buddha and the Shabdrung stand witness to the accomplishements of Bhutanese craftsmen.

The impressive clay statues represent Guru Rinpoche, the Buddha Shakyamuni and the Shabdrung Ngawang Namgyal. Statues of Indian, Tibetan and Bhutanese masters belonging to the Drukpa Kagyupa religious school are kept in niches along the wall. The exquisite paintings represent the Twelve major deeds of the life of the Buddha (*Dzepa chunyi*).

Beyong the *dzong* to the north, the motorable road continues about thirty kilometres (nineteen miles). The countryside in this part of the valley is very beautiful: rice fields, little hamlets, rivers and sand banks are followed by a semi-tropical forest which stretches on to Tashinthang at the end of the road. From here it is a 12-hour walk through more forest to reach Gasa *dzong* which controls the route to the northern regions of Laya and Lunana.

On the road, about ten kilometres (six miles) north of Punakha, on a hillock called **Nyizergang**, on the other side of the river, HM the Queen Ashi Tshering Yandon has had a three-storey *chorten* built for the protection of the country. Known as the **Khamsum Yuelley Namgyal** *Chorten*, it was consecrated at in December 1999.

Situated in idyllic rural countryside, a half-hour's climb from the road, this is well worth a visit for its paintings, which are beautiful and present an incredibly complex iconography. The deities represented belong to a teaching cycle of the great Nyingmapa master, Dudjom Rinpoche (1904–87) and their function is to subjugate enemies and harmful influences as well as to spread peace and harmony. The statues and paintings were done under the religious supervision of the Bartsham Lama Kunzang Wangdi.

The ground floor contains images of all the manifestations of Dorje Phurpa (Vajra Kilaya). The first floor is dedicated to Khamsum Namgyal, one of the most powerful manifestations of Dorje Phurpa. Khamsum Namgyal is the esoteric form of positive forces that must subjugate the negative influences in the three worlds.

The second floor contains images of Nampar Gyalwa, another powerful manifestation of Dorje Phurpa. The dome contains an old and holy statue of the Buddha Shakyamuni, which comes from Punakha *dzong*, and was given by the Zhung Dratshang (the state monastic community), which also sends a sacristan to take care of the building.

When driving back to Punakha from the Khamsum Yuelley Namgyal *Chorten* or Tashithang, the view of Punakha *dzong* is impressive.

WANGDUEPHODRANG

Wangduephodrang, or simply 'Wangdue', is at an elevation of 1,350 metres (4,430 feet). It is 71 kilometres (44 miles) from Thimphu, a trip that takes about two and a half hours by car. Nine kilometres (six miles) straight south from Lobeysa, after passing a row of newly built Eight chortens commemorationg the great events of Buddha's life, the road arrives at the bridge check-point just below **Wangduephodrang** *dzong*. Perched on a spur at the confluence of two rivers, its position is remarkable as it completely covers the spur and commands an impressive view over both the north-south and east-west roads.

At the bridge, a motor road completed in the 1980s, leads in a four-hour drive through a gorge to the southern region of **Chirang**, a realm of orange and cardamom groves, and to Dagana, an important *dzong* for the history of Bhutan.

The original bridge of Wangduephodrang was washed away by floods in 1968. It had been built in 1685 on orders from the 4th Desi, Tenzin Rabgye, and the massive towers which served as its piers can still be seen. An elegant, modern bridge built with Swiss aid was opened at the end of 2002.

The main road now climbs the length of the spur and on the left, across the river, comes the first glimpse of the picturesque village of **Rinchengang** whose inhabitants are celebrated stonemasons. This kind of village with its houses all attached to one another is rare in Bhutan.

The new Wangdue town is being built among the rice fields a little distance away from the *dzong*.

The road passes the entrance to a military training centre and finally comes to the central square of Wangduephodrang, which is marked by an antique petrol pump. All around the square, small shops, hardly more than stalls, are lodged in temporary huts while Wangdue's urbanization plan is being put into effect. One characteristic of Wangdue is its gusty wind which blows from the south in all seasons, raising whirling clouds of dust.

The place, once very dirty, is now clean and orderly. On the right-hand side of the *dzong* is the charming house of the District Administrator, the *Dzongda*; from the parapet there is a fine view over the river valley and the village of Rinchengang.

Two stories explain the origin of the *dzong*, one religious and the other popular. The first one tells us that the protective deity Mahakala appeared to the Shabdrung and made a prediction to him, saying: 'At the top of a rocky spur where two rivers meet, at the place where a flock of ravens (the bird associated with Mahakala) will

(Following pages) *The Punakha* dzong, *capital of Bhutan for three centuries.*

THE PUNAKHA THONDROEL—*David Keen*

In March 1993, Punakha *dzong* celebrated its annual *Dromchoe*, a festival dedicated to the legendary figures of Yeshe Gonpo and Palden Lhamo.

For the residents of the lush Punakha Valley, this particular festival had enormous significance. A new *Thondroel* (a giant appliquéd *thangka*) was to be unveiled on the second day in the presence of His Majesty King Jigme Singye Wangchuck, His Holiness the *Je Khenpo* Geduen Rinchen, Their Majesties the Queens of Bhutan, the entire Royal Family and senior members of the government.

On the morning of the unveiling, decked in their finest *gos* and *kiras*, honoured guests paraded into the courtyard closely followed by hundreds of pilgrims. To the resonating echo of a gong, monks lining the top of the monastery's central tower raised the massive appliqué from the cobble-stoned floor. Slowly the *Thondroel* was revealed to a spellbound audience. When it was fully unfurled, the *Je Khenpo* and monks gave offerings and thanks to the Guru. Then, accompanied by His Majesty, they prostrated themselves, offered ceremonial scarves and lit butter-lamps before the *Thondroel*.

Measuring 83 feet by 93 feet, Punakha's *thondroel* is one of the largest ever made (*see* page 103). Composed entirely of appliqué on more than 6,000 metres of silk brocade, the *Thondroel* cost Nu2.1 million (US$70,000) and took 51 artists two years to complete.

The *Thongdrel* was created under the guidance of the *Je Khenpo* in homage to the *Shabdrung* (unifier of the country) and for the well-being of all sentient beings. Deliverance from *Samsara*, or rebirth, is assured for all those who are fortunate enough to set eyes on the *Thondroel*.

Depicting 20 of the greatest gurus and sages around the central figure of Shabdrung, the top half of the *Thondroel* is devoted to the eleven manifestations of the Shabdrung's lineage. The bottom half depicts Bhutan's spiritual leaders including the *Je Khenpo* (died 2004) dedicated the *Thondroel* to Shabdrung Ngawang Namgyal, who built the Punakha *dzong* in 1637.

Punakha *dzong*'s previous *Thondroel* was burnt in one of several fires to consume the monastery over the centuries. The new *Thondroel* is unveiled every year at the *Dromchoe*.

fly off in the four directions, there you will build a *dzong*.' In 1638 the *Shabdrung* came to the place that the prophecy described and built a fortress which he named Wangduephodrang, meaning 'the palace where the four directions are gathered under the power (of the *Shabdrung*)'.

However, the popular story has it that the *Shabdrung* arrived at the river and happened to see a little boy building a sandcastle. He asked for the boy's name. It was Wangdue, and thereupon decided to name the *dzong* Wangduephodrang, or 'Wangdue's palace'.

The *dzong* is roofed with shingles and has an oddly rustic, yet disquieting, charm about it. The first courtyard, surrounded by administrative buildings, is not a true square as its side walls make it slightly oblong. This part was built in 1683 on orders from the 4th *Desi*, Tenzin Rabgye. The second part of the *dzong* is separated from the first by a small ravine which is spanned by a short bridge. This part dates from 1638 and contains a narrow interior courtyard that ends in a flight of steps leading to the central tower. On the far side there is another courtyard, at the southern end of which is the monks' assembly hall, graced by statues of the Past, Present and Future Buddhas.

There is a small guesthouse in Wangdue, as well as some simple restaurants. Four hotels are in the vicinity. The **Dechen Cottages** (tel. 9752-4271392) are secluded high upon the Thimphu road; the **Y.T. Hotel** (tel. 9752-481331) at Lobeysa, is a real family guesthouse where one feels welcome and comfortable, and where having a coffee under the papaya tree is indeed pleasant; the **Dragon Nest** (tel. 9752-481366), well-located near the river and below the *dzong*, has a beautiful panorama and an attractive dining room; and the spectacular **Kyichu Resort** (tel. 9752-481359) is also located alongside the river, at Chuzomsa, on the road to Trongsa.

(Following pages) *The fertile and rich western valley of Wangduephodrang. On the hilltop in the background stands the temple of* Chime chakhang.

THE ROAD TO CENTRAL BHUTAN

The tarring of the central road was completed in 1985 and it brought tremendous changes for the residents of central Bhutan. The two-day trip of the 1970s from Trongsa to the capital Thimphu now takes only six hours from Trongsa and nine hours from Bumthang. However, the road is not well stabilized and heavy rains or earthquakes frequently cause collapses between May and the end of September. If this happens, the road may remain closed for several days or even weeks; road maintenance on this portion is carried out throughout the year by teams of workers who live in camps.

OVER THE BLACK MOUNTAINS: WANGDUE TO TRONGSA

The distance from Wangdue to Trongsa is 129 kilometres (80 miles) and the trip by car takes about four hours. The road to central and eastern Bhutan starts from the east side of the *dzong* and is flat for the first ten kilometres (six miles) or so, as far as a hamlet called Chuzomsa, or 'confluence'. There is a slate mine not far from here.

View near Wangdepore, the archaic name of Wangduephodrang, *1837,*
J C Armytage, from a sketch by Davis.

Just beyond Chuzomsa, a cable lift transports goods and raw materials between the valley and **Trashila**, a pass at an altitude of 2,900 metres (9,185 feet) at the top of the ridge. It gives access to the isolated valleys of Kothoka and Gogona.

The road begins its climb over the Black Mountains immediately after the bridge at Tikke. The valley is very narrow, with houses and fields perched on steep slopes. Little by little, habitations become sparser and the road starts to snake through the middle of a dense forest where monkeys can often be spotted. 40 kilometres (25 miles) from Wangdue, the featureless, recent village of Nobding stands on a plateau surrounded by forest; it is reknowned for the quality of its chillies.

Ten kilometres (six miles) beyond Nobding, the road passes a place called Drundrung Neysa where there is a small but good local restaurant. If you continue a further seven kilometres (four miles) through a forest of oak and rhododendrons, you will be taken to Pelela pass; at one point the road branches and leads off into the broad **Phobjika valley** at 3,000 metres (9,840 feet) where the Gangtey monastery is located.

PHOBJIKA VALLEY AND GANGTEY GONPA

Phobjika is one of the few glacial valleys in Bhutan and the valley floor is quite marshy in places. The other side of the pass that overlooks the valley is a realm of high-altitude dwarf bamboo (the favourite food of yaks) and rhododendron bushes.

For several years, the cultivation of potatoes has brought a certain degree of prosperity to the valley. Phobjika is also the chosen home of the rare black-necked cranes which migrate from the Tibetan plateau, avoiding the extremely cold winters. These elegant and shy birds can be observed from the end of October to the end of March. The road continues for a few more kilometres beyond the Gangtey monastery to different villages of Phobjika.

This valley is one of the most beautiful spots in Bhutan and well worth a one to two day visit. Short three to four hour nature walks through the villages and the valley are a wonderful experience.

The surprise of finding such a wide, flat valley without any trees after the hard climb through dense forest is augmented by an impression of vast space, an extremely rare experience in Bhutan where most of the valleys are tightly enclosed.

Cranes have their foraging grounds on the floor of the valley and a Crane Study Centre managed by the Royal Society for Protection of Nature has been established. The telescopes allows very good views of the birds. It is not allowed to approch the cranes and their habitat. The Crane Centre has a small non-profit shop, which sells local handicrafts.

(Following pages) *Farmer carrying his harvest.*

The **Dewachen** hotel opened in November 2004, not far from the Crane Centre. It is beautifully built at the edge of the forest with a splendid vista of the valley. This hotel has an underground generator for electricity and the best beds in Bhutan. The **Amankora-Gangtey** resort (tel. 975-2-331333; www.amanresorts.com) is here too, near the monastery.

GANGTEY MONASTERY

Gangtey Gonpa, is perched atop a small hill that rises from the valley floor. The monastery is surrounded by a large village inhabited mainly by the families of the 140 *gomchens* who are linked to the monastery. In winter these families, together with the monastery's monks, move away to Pchitokha, a warmer place and monastery. Gangtey is the only Nyingmapa monastery on the western side of the Black Mountains and is also the biggest Nyingmapa monastery in Bhutan. It is directed by the Gangtey *trulku*, the ninth reincarnation (*trulku*) to bear that name.

Gangtey was founded by Pema Trinley, the grandson of Pema Lingpa, the famous Nyingmapa saint of Bhutan. Pema Lingpa visited this area and predicted that a monastery would be established by one of his descendants near the summit (*tey*) of a mountain (*gang*). Thus, in 1613, Pema Trinley established the monastery and became the first Gangtey *trulku*. The religious tradition of Pema Lingpa is still taught there. The second *trulku*, Tenzin Legpe Dondrub (1645–1726), enhanced the size of Gangtey while keeping up good relations with the Drukpas, and rebuilt the monastery in the form of a *dzong*.

The entrance to the monastery displays a large painting of Hayagriva. The monks' dwellings are all around the courtyard, while the central tower housed five temples. The porch of the central tower contains paintings of cosmic *mandalas*, a Wheel of Life, Zangdopelri (the heaven of Guru Rinpoche), as well as a rare (in Bhutan) representation of the mythical land of Shambala inside its circle of snow-capped mountains. The monastery began major structural works in 2001 and unfortunately these paintings were not preserved. It was still under reconstruction in early 2005.

The wood craftsmen carve very nice religious motifs, which their wives sell nearby the monastery. A religious festival takes place in the 8th lunar month in the monastery courtyard. A monastic school (*Shedra*) has been established behind a ridge close to the monastery.

KHEWANG LHAKHANG

Built in the 15th century, this is a small community temple in the middle of the marshy area. A side trip to Gangtey Gonpa takes three hours from the Wangdue-Trongsa main road.

THE PELELA PASS

On the way to the Pelela Pass, the forest is made up almost entirely of rhododendron and magnolia, which can be seen in April and May. If the winter has been cold, there is also a good chance you will see herds of yaks that have not yet been taken up to the high pastures. Yaks browsing and grunting under rhododendron in full bloom is certainly a sight never to be forgotten. However, it is advisable to be cautious and not get too close to yaks as they are nervous animals and may attack you without provocation.

Just before the pass, if the weather is clear, the high range of the Himalayas can be seen, including the summit of Jomolhari, at 7,219 metres (23,685 feet), to the west.

The Pelela, at 3,300 metres (10,825 feet), is marked by a large prayer flag, and the ground is covered with high-altitude dwarf bamboos. The Pelela is traditionally considered the boundary between western and central Bhutan and in former times the jurisdiction of the Trongsa *Penlop* extended just to the pass. The landscape on the far side of the pass is completely different from that on the western side.

On the eastern side, 11 kilometres (seven miles) beyond the pass, a plateau divided into large fields appears on the right at the head of which is the large village of Rukubji. The road continues downwards and comes to the bottom of a valley at the bridge of Nikkarchu, near to which a few houses have recently been built, and it is a simple lunch stop. Nikkarchu is the starting point of a path that goes to the isolated northern region of Lunana; the walk requires four or five days and the path crosses several very high passes, among which is the fearsome Rinchenzoe at 5,400 metres (17,715 feet). The whole region, including the areas between Gangtey Gonpa and the Pelela, the part between Rukubji and Nikkarchu and other areas to the north, is the domain of yak and sheep herders and is called in Bhutan, the 'Black Mountain Bjop'.

CHENDEBJI CHORTEN

After Nikkarchu, the road enters Trongsa district where it follows the river along a narrow, enclosed valley for about ten kilometres (six miles). On the right-hand side it passes the picturesque village of Chendebji which is reached by an ancient bridge roofed with bamboo matting. A great, whitewashed stone *chorten* then appears at a bend in the road. Chendebji *Chorten* is in Nepalese style, with eyes painted at the four cardinal points. It was built during the first half of the 18th century by a lama named Shida, in order to nail into the ground a demon who had been terrorizing the inhabitants of this valley and the Ada valley just over the ridge. A long stone *mani* wall stands in front of the chorten bearing an inscription that tells the story of its founding. On the left side, a *chorten* was constructed in Bhutanese style by H M the Queen Mother in 1982.

The 2003 movie "Travellers and Magicians" directed by Dzongsar Khyentse Rinpoche was partly shot near Chendebji.

There are 42 kilometres (26 miles) between Chendebji and Trongsa. In this region until Trongsa, grows a species of cherry tree (*Prunus cerasoides*) that flowers in the autumn, at which time the whole gorge is dotted with pink trees.

The road emerges from the gorge and follows the Mangde River valley, then it turns and heads straight north to Trongsa crossing the village of Tshangkha where a new temple is being built. After Tsangkha, the landscape is dramatic and the road is hewn into the side of the rock with a sheer drop on the right. The route runs parallel to a road that is visible on the other side of the valley and leads south to Zhemgang then to Geylegphug, a trading town on the Indian border.

Trongsa *dzong* appears at the end of the valley 20 kilometres (12 miles) before reaching it. There is a splendid lookout point with a view over Trongsa at the place where the old track branches off and it is at a bend signaled by a *chorten* and a viewpoint. The old footpath led down to the bottom of the gorge, crossed the stream, then climbed very steeply up to the gate of the fortress but unfortunately is not practicable any more. The paved road was not able to follow this ancient route so it makes a detour of 14 kilometres (nine miles) into a side valley where a police check-post has been set up at the Bjizam bridge, 5 kilometres to the west of Trongsa.

Winter forest 3,200 metres high, near Gangtey Gonpa.

CENTRAL BHUTAN
TRONGSA DZONG

The landscape around Trongsa is spectacular, and for miles on end the *dzong* seems to tease you so that you wonder if you will ever reach it. Backing on to the mountain and built on several levels, the *dzong* fits narrowly on a spur that sticks out into the gorge of the Mangde River and overlooks the routes south and west. The view from the *dzong* extends for many kilometres and in former times nothing could escape the vigilance of its watchmen. Furthermore, the *dzong* is built in such a way that in the old days, no matter what direction a traveller came from, he was obliged to pass by the *dzong*. This helped to increase its stronghold as it had complete control over all east–west traffic. Above the *dzong* a watchtower, the Ta *dzong*, strengthened its defence.

Trongsa means 'the new village' and the founding of Trongsa first dates from the 16th century when it was just a temple. The Drukpa lama, Ngagi Wangchuk (1517–54), the great-grandfather of Shabdrung Ngawang Namgyal, founded the first temple at Trongsa in 1543. He was meditating nearby when he saw a light at the furthest point of the spur. He took this to be an auspicious sign and decided to build a temple. The original site is situated today at the end of the *dzong*, at the 'Temple of Chortens'.

In 1647, the Shabdrung began his great work of expansion and unification and, realizing all the advantages that could be gained from Trongsa's position, he constructed the first *dzong* at the place where his ancestor had erected the temple. The *dzong* was called Choekhor Rabtentse *dzong*. In 1652, Minjur Tenpa, the future 3rd of Bhutan who at that time was *Penlop* of Trongsa, had the *dzong* enlarged. It was changed still further in 1715 when the *Penlop* Druk Dendrup built the Chenrezig (Avalokiteshvara) Lhakhang and in 1771 when the whole complex including the Maitreya (Jampa) temple was added. In 1765 the Trongsa *Penlop*, Zhidar, established the Trongsa monastic community with about 50 monks and in 1853, the 10th Trongsa *Penlop*, Jigme Namgyal, father of the 1st King, built the Demchog (Cakrasamvara) Lhakhang in the central section of the *dzong*.

Following the earthquake of 1897, the *dzong* has been repaired several times, in particular by the 1st King, Ugyen Wangchuck. In 1927 the 2nd King Jigme Wangchuck renovated the Chenrezig Lhakhang. It was extensively restored with Austrian aid from 1999 and reconsecrated in October 2004.

Chorten, with typical slate roof and prayer flags in western Bhutan.

INSIDE TRONGSA DZONG

At an altitude of 2,200 metres (7,220 feet) the *dzong* is a masterpiece of architecture, a maze of courtyards, passageways and corridors containing, in addition, 25 temples. The most important ones are those dedicated to the great Tantric deities Yamantaka, Hevajra, Cakrasamvara and Kalacakra. Other temples include the **Maitreya** (Jampa) temple, constructed in 1771, which contains a large clay statue of the Buddha of the Future erected by Ugyen Wangchuck at the beginning of the century, and the **Temple of Chortens**, built on the place where the original temple stood. This temple contains the funerary *chorten* of Ngagi Wangchuk and some superb paintings of the Sixteen Arhats and of the Buddha Akshobya (Mitrugpa).

The *dzong* also houses a **printing house** where the printing of religious texts was done by the traditional xylographic method (see page 293). The Drukpa monastic community is about 200 members strong. Some of them spend the summer at Kurje monastery in the Choekhor Valley of Bumthang .

If you can visit the *dzong*, try to go through the door on the right, on the level below that of the small police post. In the old days, this door marked the end of the hard climb up from the river to the entrance of the *dzong*. To experience what it must have been like, go down the slippery steps along the precipice and then look up at the *dzong*. Its size and power are completely overwhelming and it is easy to understand the psychological effect it had upon travellers arriving at Trongsa.

Today the *dzong* is the administrative seat for Trongsa district, but in the 19th century it could have been considered the capital of Bhutan due to the importance and power of its governors, the Trongsa *Penlops*. They controlled all of eastern and central Bhutan, including the fertile strip in the south. In the middle of the 19th century, one governor became more powerful than any of the others. He was Jigme Namgyal, the father of Ugyen Wangchuck who was to be the 1st King of Bhutan. Jigme Namgyal came from the region of Kurtoe (now Lhuentse district) but he made his whole career at Trongsa *dzong* and played a dominant national role as well. His son, Ugyen Wangchuck, became *Penlop* of Trongsa in his turn and from that time on, the Crown Princes of Bhutan have received the title of Trongsa Penlop, recently changed to Chhoetse *Penlop* after the religious name of the *dzong*. Jigme Dorje Wangchuck, the 3rd King of Bhutan, was born in Trongsa in 1928 and the house of his birth can be seen on the left of the road, in the U-turn which leads to the main street.

The watchtower, the Ta *dzong*, stands on the side of the mountain east of the *dzong*. Unlike that of Paro, which is round, the Trongsa watchtower has a fairly narrow tower section and two wings which project in a V shape from the main part of the building. Its most important temple, established in 1977, is dedicated to King Gesar, the hero of a great epic and warrior god.

TRONGSA VILLAGE

Up until 1982, the three or four old houses that made up the village of Trongsa lay in the shadow of the *dzong* on a narrow piece of land near the stream, to the left of the entrance to the *dzong*. Today, the impressive size of the town houses, built in Bhutanese style, makes them appear like a rampart overlooking the *dzong*. Due to the configuration of the landscape, the town was built in the mid-eighties and Trongsa is hardly more than one street lined by well-stocked little shops and small friendly restaurants. Trongsa had a total 'facelift' in October 2004 at the time of the ceremonies of the dzong reconsecration followed by the investiture of the Chhoetse (Trongsa) *Penlop*.

A lot of Trongsa's shopkeepers are Bhutanese of Tibetan origin, and the restaurants are likely to serve Tibetan specialities such as fried dumplings stuffed with ground meat (*shabale*) and steamed bread with a soup (*trimono*). One place that can be heartily recommended is Yangkhyil, on the right at the end of the street. Aum Dralha, the owner, is a fine cook and the rooms are simple but clean and cheap. In winter, a wood stove heats the common room, which is much needed as Trongsa is always somewhat damp, hemmed in as it is by the mountains. Her children built a posh resort, **Yangkhyil Resort**, on a slope two kilometres before Trongsa, while coming from Thimphu. All the rooms are very comfortable and have a fabulous view of Trongsa.

A hotel that opened in a new building in town, the **Norling** (tel. 975-3-521171), offers decent rooms and cuisine. Above the *dzong*, there is the **Sherubling/ BTCL guest-house** (tel. 975-3-521107) and outside Trongsa, on the Bumthang road, the **Puenzhi** has a family atmosphere, a superb view in a lovely setting.

ZHEMGANG REGION (KHYENG)

Trongsa lies at the junction of the east–west road with the southern road. The road to the south runs for 237 tortuous kilometres (147 miles) to the southern agricultural zone and the commercial border town of Gelephu. This road crosses

THE DZONGKHA LANGUAGE

Dzongkha, Bhutan's national language, means 'the language spoken in fortresses'. Historically it is the language of western Bhutan, and was not spoken beyond the Pelela Pass in the Black Mountains. Today, however, it is Bhutan's language of administration and it is taught in all schools. Teachers are trained at the institue near Simtokha *dzong* in the Thimphu valley.

Dzongkha was formerly only an oral language: the written language was Choekey, the 'religious language' known to the western world as Classical Tibetan. The remarkable feature is that Choekey has remained practically unchanged since the eighth century and was the common written language of a vast geographical area including Bhutan, northern Nepal, Sikkim, Ladakh, Tibet and Mongolia. An enormous literature has been written in this language over the centuries by monks who were the only people with access to education.

Dzongkha has been a written language for the last 40 years or so, and the govemment has made great efforts since the 1960s to standardize it, and encourage its use. Linguistically related to Tibetan (both languages belong to the Tibeto-Burman subgroup of the Sino-Tibetan language family), Dzongkha uses the same writing system. This system, invented around the seventh century, is adapted from an Indian alphabet of that period, with 30 consonants and four vowels, reading from left to right.

One of the big problems of learning Dzongkha, which also holds true for Choekey, arises from the complexity of its orthography, which requires a great deal of memorization. Dzongkha is, in fact, a monosyllabic, two-tone language with an alphabet superimposed onto it.

To tell the difference in writing between words that have the same pronunciation but differing tones, certain 'subterfuges' had to be invented. These are additional prefixes and suffixes that are written but not spoken, or letters added above or below a word which can sometimes totally change the sound of the consonant to which they are attached! To deal with this, it clearly becomes necessary to learn each word by heart. Thus, a word pronounced '*la*' may in fact be written *lha, bla, la,* or *lags* depending on whether it means 'a god', 'life energy', 'a mountain pass' or 'yes'. The number 'eight', pronounced '*gye*', is written *brgyad* and 'Choekey' is *chos skad*!

The name of a person, written phonetically in the Latin alphabet as Rinzin Wangchuk and pronounced as it reads, is written *Rigs 'dzin dband phyug* in Dzongkha. The inventiveness of the orthography of proper names, written solely as a way to indicate pronunciation, is enough to throw the unprepared mind into total confusion. It turns out that the *dzong* pronounced Jakar can also be written as Byakar, but the proper spelling is *Bya dkar.* In the Roman alphabet, *Rdo rje* becomes Dorji or Dorje: *Rig dzin* becomes Rigzin, Rinzin or Rizzy; *Dpal 'byor* becomes Penjor or Peljor or Paljor; *Chos gron* becomes Choden; Choeden or Chogron; *Stob rgyal* becomes Tobgyey, Tobgye or Tobgyel; *Rnam rgyal* becomes Namgye, Namgyal, and so on.

An effort to standardize the orthography has been undertaken by a government office called the Dzongkha Development Commission which publishes books and dictionaries. Films and songs are very popular and do a lot for the spread of Dzongkha.

part of a large region formerly known as Khyeng, which nowadays is divided into the district of Zhemgang to the west and part of the district of Mongar to the east.

For the first 15 kilometres (9 miles) or so, the southern route runs parallel to the Thimphu road, which is on the other side of the gorge, then turns towards the southeast. It follows the side of the mountain and offers some fine, clear views over the Mangde River valley.

Some 20 kilometres (12 miles) south of Trongsa, **Kunga Rabten**, the nice winter palace of the 2nd King, Jigme Wangchuck, can be seen below the level of the road. It is worth stopping and going into the inner courtyard to look at the woodwork and decorations. An important Education campus is being built at Taktse not far from there.

The road passes through quite a few small villages and two other small palaces (Samdrupchoeling and Encholeing) which, in the first half of the 20th century, were used by the Royal family coming from Bumthang during the winter. The slope on this side of the mountain is relatively gentle, allowing rice cultivation. Then the valley narrows and the road descends into the river gorge, to an elevation of 1,400 metres (4,595 feet). This part is rather wild and little populated.

Zhemgang finally comes into view at the top of a ridge. It is only 107 kilometres (66 miles) from Trongsa but the poor condition of the road means that four hours of driving are required to reach it. Zhemgang is built on an open ridge, which gives it the advantage of an unbroken view over the whole area. The disadvantage is that it gets battered by the wind and in spite of its relatively low altitude of 1,900 metres (6,235 feet), it can be cold there.

A Tibetan Drukpa lama, Drogon Shangkyeme, built the first temple on the site of the Zhemgang *dzong* as early as 1163. The temple took his name as Shang Gang, 'Shang's mountain', which local pronunciation turned into Zhemgang. His youngest brother was the chaplain of the king of Khaling in eastern Bhutan. This king behaved very badly towards his subjects, so the lama wrote to his brother advising him to leave the king's service and come to join him at Zhemgang. He also wrote to the king saying that he was unwell and wanted his brother to come and visit him.

Unfortunately the two letters got mixed up as they were being delivered. The king was furious to read what the lama of Zhemgang had written to one of his subjects and sent assassins to kill the lama. But even after his death, Drogon Shangkyeme's temple continued to prosper. In 1963, when Zhemgang district was created, the 3rd King, Jigme Dorje Wangchuck, ordered that Zhemgang *dzong* be restored.

THE ANCIENT REGION OF KHYENG

In 1963, the ancient region of Khyeng was divided into the districts of Mongar and Zhemgang. It is a land of steep, forest-covered mountains except for plateaus such as Buli where rice is cultivated. The rivers cut deep gorges and valleys are rare. The people speak Khyengkha, a language which is a dialect of Bumthangkha, and they are highly regarded for their knowledge of forest plants.

Descending in steps from 1,900 metres (6,235 feet) to 200 metres (655 feet), most of the district is covered by a semi-tropical forest that conceals rare orchids and carnivorous plants. This is where most of Bhutan's production of bamboo, cane and rattan ware takes place. Many plants which still grow wild form an important part of the people's diet: bananas, mangoes, yams, bamboo shoots, young ferns, certain orchids and a very rare plant which tastes like potatoes when it is boiled, and even, in hard times, certain poisonous roots of fern or poisonous beans which, once they have been boiled or left to soak, become edible. Though Zhemgang may be lacking in spectacular historical sites, it makes up for that by being a paradise for botanists and ethnobotanists (see *Flowers of Bhutan* by K Nishioka and S Nakao, Tokyo, 1984).

The beautiful villages of Korphu and then lower down, Nabji, are two days' walk from Ri'utala on the Zhemgang road. In the temple of Nabji there is a stone pillar which is said to commemorate a peace treaty initiated by Guru Rinpoche between King Sendhaka (*Sindhu Raja*) and King Na'oche in the eighth century. This would make it one of the most ancient historical monuments of Bhutan. In this region, an ethnic community, the Monpas of the Black mountains, speak a distinctive language and are most probably amongst the first inhabitants of Bhutan. This area is excellent for short winter hikes and botanical treks.

The ancient region of Khyeng, which stretched east to Mongar and south practically to Gelephu, was divided into a multitude of petty kingdoms until the 17th century. The most important of these were Buli and Nyakhar. Buli, a village in a beautiful surrounding, was visited in 1478 and 1497 by the Nyingmapa saint, Pema Lingpa, who founded a temple there. After the Drukpa conquest in the middle of the 17th century, the kings lost whatever importance they may have had but their descendants still call themselves "king", as a purely honorific title. A feeder road now links Buli to the main road.

Here the ties with the Bumthang valleys went beyond simple language affiliation. The nobility of Chume and Choekhor in Bumthang owned land in the

Mules still transport goods in rural Bhutan.

Khyeng region and their herds of animals migrated there from Bumthang for the winter. It is also from Khyeng that Bumthang's weavers get their supplies of raw material for making vegetable dyes.

THE ROAD FROM TRONGSA TO BUMTHANG

It takes less than two hours to cover the 42 kilometres (26 miles) from Trongsa to the village of Gyetsa in the upper Chume valley of Bumthang. The road passes through Trongsa village just beneath the Ta *dzong* and then rises rapidly through a series of hairpin bends. The view over Trongsa and the *dzong* is superb on this side of the valley as well. After running across cultivated slopes for a few kilometres and passing the temple of Dorje Gonpa, the road enters a very ancient forest where the large trees are often bare but where magnificent rhododendron grow.

At a distance of 29 kilometres (18 miles) from Trongsa, the road reaches the Yutongla Pass (also spelt Yutola) at 3,400 metres (11,155 feet). After the pass, the landscape changes completely. The rhododendrons are still there, but a dense forest of conifers now stretches as far as the eye can see. After 13 kilometres (eight miles), the road comes out into a wide, open, cultivated valley. This is the Chume Valley, the first of Bumthang's four valleys.

THE BUMTHANG VALLEYS

A *bumpa* is an oblong-shaped lustral water vase and Bumthang means 'the plain shaped like a *bumpa*'. The religious connotation of the name aptly applies to the sacred character of the region. It would be difficult to find so many important temples and monasteries in such a small area anywhere else in Bhutan.

Bumthang is the general name given to a complex of four valleys—Chume, Choekhor, Tang and Ura—with altitudes varying from 2,600 metres (8,530 feet) to 4,000 metres (13,125 feet). Today it is a district with its administrative headquarters at Jakar (also spelled Byakar but always pronounced Jakar). Choekhor and Chume are mostly agricultural valleys; Tang and Ura are given over more to yak—and sheep—breeding but potatoes are now the important cash crop while the subsistance crops are still buckwheat (sweet and bitter), barley and wheat. Rice was introduced in Choekhor for the first time in 2004 as a trial.

Because the valleys are wide and open, and the mountains have relatively gentle slopes, there is a feeling of spaciousness that might be unequalled in any other part of Bhutan except the Phobjika valley in the Black Mountains. Bumthang is great for

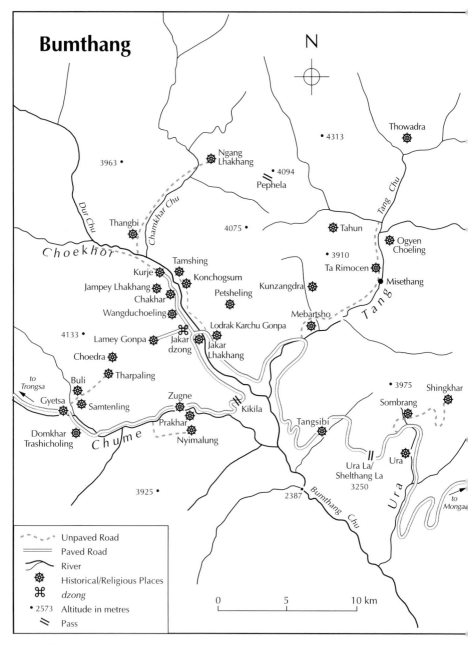

Bumthang

N

Thowadra

• 4313

Ngang
Lhakhang

3963 •

• 4094
Pephela

Dur Chu

Chamkhar Chu

Tang Chu

Thangbi

Choekhor

4075 •

Tahun

Ogyen
Choeling

Tamshing

Kurje

Konchogsum

• 3910
Ta Rimocen

Misethang

Jampey Lhakhang

Chakhar

Petsheling

Kunzangdra

Tang

Wangduchoeling

Lodrak Karchu Gonpa

Mebartsho

4133 •

Lamey Gonpa

Jakar
dzong

Jakar
Lhakhang

Choedra

to
Trongsa

Buli

Tharpaling

• 3975

Shingkhar

Gyetsa

Samtenling

Zugne

Kikila

Sombrang

Domkhar
Trashicholing

Chume

Prakhar

Nyimalung

Tangsibi

Ura

3925 •

2387

Bumthang Chu

Ura La/
Shelthang La
3250

Ura

to
Monga

```
- - - - -   Unpaved Road
=========   Paved Road
~~~~~~~     River
  ✹         Historical/Religious Places
  ⌘         dzong
• 2573      Altitude in metres
  ≈         Pass
```

0   5   10 km

© Airphoto International Ltd.

moderate hiking as the valleys are fairly flat, the slopes are usually gentle, and there are many hamlets where one can get some idea of what life in a rural area is like.

According to tradition, Bumthang was converted to Buddhism by Guru Rinpoche in the eighth century and was the temporary home of famous Tibetan saints of the Nyingmapa school such as Longchen Rabjam (1308–63) and Dorje Lingpa (1346–405). The most famous of all the religious men who taught in this area is Pema Lingpa (1450–1521), who was born in the Tang valley of Bumthang. His descendants scattered through central and eastern Bhutan and contributed to the spread of the Nyingmapa school. Dorje Lingpa and Pema Lingpa were also *tertons*, or 'discoverers of religious treasures' (*see* page 67).

After remaining more or less independent for centuries with a local religious nobility at the helm, Bumthang was conquered by the Drukpas in the middle of the 17th century. Bumthang keeps a strong sense of identity and its non-written language is very specific, belonging to the eastern Proto-Bodish subgroup of the large Tibeto-Burman family with many loan words from classical Tibetan.

In former times the Bumthang valleys were fairly poor and isolated, but since the construction of the east-west road the area has undergone significant economic development. Added to the road, tourism, projects financed by Switzerland such as potato cultivation and the small Indian hydro-electric station helped Bumthang to attain a good level of prosperity. This is now apparent in the number of superb new houses built in the last fifteen years and the abundance of products to be found now in the district centre, Jakar.

THE CHUME VALLEY

The Chume valley begins at Gyetsa and has an average altitude of 2,700 metres (8,860 feet). It is a wide valley dotted with villages and temples. People here grow wheat, barley, potatoes and particularly buckwheat, which used to provide the staple diet of Bumthang in the form of pancakes and noodles.

Just close to the village of Gyetsa on a small knoll to the left of the road, there is the ancient little **Buli Lhakhang** (still under restoration in 2005), founded at the beginning of the 15th century by a descendant of Dorje Lingpa. A small carpentry and painting training school has been established by the NGO, American Himalayan Foundation, in 2002. Tharpaling Monastery can be seen high up in the mountain and above Choedrak Monastery. A road now goes up to Tharpaling but it is not tarred and not always passable in rainy weather. On foot, it takes two to three hours to reach Tharpaling monastery from the valley.

Visit to the monastery.

THARPALING AND CHOEDRAK MONASTERIES

The site of Tharpaling (3,600 metres / 11,810 feet) was, it seems, first inhabited by Lorepa (1187–1250), a Drukpa Kagyupa lama from Tibet. The temple that he is said to have founded is a small building, lower than the main complex, and the paintings of Lorepa and of Tsangpa Gyare, the founder of the Drukpa school, dates, perhaps, from the 19th century.

In the 14th century, another temple was founded by Longchen Rabjam, the great philosopher of the Dzogchen, a religious movement of the *Nyingmapa* school. Longchen Rabjam (1308–1363) had to flee Tibet and lived in exile in Bumthang for almost ten years. He built several temples there, including Tharpaling built in 1352. Tharpaling was restored several times but most notably by the 1st King at the beginning of the twentieth century. The Eight Chortens commemorating events of the life of the Buddha (*Chorten Degye*) were consecrated in 2001. The temple on the ground floor, the **Tshogkhang**, is adorned with statues of Longchen Rabjam, Guru Rinpoche, Trisong Detsen, the eighth century Tibetan king who requested Guru to subjugate the deities of Tibet, Shantarikshita (Shiwatso), the Indian monk first invited to build Samye, as well as Jigme Lingpa. The small temple on the upper floor was restored in the time of the 1st King, Ugyen Wangchuck. It contains very beautiful paintings of the paradise of Amitabha; also of Longchen Rabjam, Shabdrung Ngawang Namgyal, and a rarely-seen form of Guru Rinpoche as Guru Dewa. The principal statues are those of Samantabhadra, Guru Rinpoche and Longchen Rabjam.

The monastery prospered and was always an active centre for Nyingmapa teachings and in 1985, a **monastic school** (*shedra*) was founded above the main complex. There are about 15 cells for monks; a hall with beautiful paintings of the Sixteeen Arhats and the lineage of Longchen Rabjam is well worth seeing.

Above Tharpaling monastery is **Choedrak** (3,800 metres). Guru Rinpoche had meditated at this spot and that is the reason why Lorepa (1187–1250), a Drukpa Kagyupa lama from Tibet, decided to live and build a temple there in 1234. Unfortunately, it is said that after his departure for Tibet, the place was besieged by a demon and nobody dared to go to Choedrak. It was not until the 18th century that Ngawang Trinley, the famous monk from Si'ula monastery in the Punakha region, succeeded in subduing the demon and repairing the monastery which had fallen into ruins.

From Choedrak, it is a good three hour walk crossing the ridge and down through a dense bamboo forest, to Lame Gonpa in the Choekhor valley.

On foot, on the way down from Tharpaling and Choedrak to the Chume valley, **Samtenling Monastery** is on a forested knoll not far from the path. It, too, was founded by Longchen Rabjam in the 14th century. Severely damaged by a fire in the mid-1980s, it is now restored.

The tarmac road follows the middle of the valley and a few kilometres after Gyetsa it comes to the village of Domkhar where, on the right side of the road, slightly above the village, stands the palace of **Domkhar**. Like Kunga Rabten in the Trongsa region, this was a royal palace built in 1937 as the summer residence of the 2nd King. Nowadays, Domkhar belongs to the government and has been restored in 2004 as the residence of the Chhoetse *Penlop*, the Crown Prince. Behind Domkhar palace, **Trashicholing**, a monastic complex, now disused, was built in the sixties for the 16th Karmapa. It still contains excellent paintings.

Four kilometres (two and a half miles) beyond Domkhar, the road runs alongside the buildings of the valley's large secondary school, then reaches below **Chorten Nyingpo Lhakhang**, founded in 1587 by Tenpe Nyima, the grandson of Pema Lingpa. Here a small hydroelectric power-station which barely provides for Bumthang's needs was finished in 1989 with aid from India.

ZUGNE VILLAGE

Just after the power-station comes the village of Zugne. This village is worth a stop for there are many weavers here. With scarves tied on their heads in the Bumthang style, they weave woollen *yatras* on pedal looms as well as belts on backstrap looms. *Yatras* are rolls of patterned twill-weave woollen cloth which are Bumthang's speciality and which can be used as bed covers, cushions or even garments. The Chume valley is famous for the quality of its *yatras*, two workshops line the road with brightly coloured woollen textiles: Thogmela and Khampa Gonpo.

Besides its *yatra* cloth, Zugne has another claim to fame. The tiny temple on the right side of the road is said to have been founded by the Tibetan king, Songtsen Gampo, in the seventh century, as part of a scheme to pin down a gigantic demoness. The principal statue in the sanctuary is that of Buddha Vairocana (Nampar Nanze) which is generally a sign of antiquity for a temple. Vairocana can be recognized by the wheel which he holds in his hands. The splendid new paintings were created in 1978 by Lam Pemala, a venerable monk, who is a native of Zugne.

PRAKHAR (PRA)

Two kilometres (just over one mile) beyond Zugne, the road skirts **Prakhar**, or **Pra**, a picturesque village perched on a small plateau in a bend of the river. Prakhar was built at the end of the 16th century by Tenpe Nyima who was not the father of the Shabdrung but the grandson of Pema Lingpa, the Nyingmapa saint. Tenpe Nyima had a vision and knew that he must construct a temple on this spot. As he built it, the temple seemed somehow to be growing in size at night as well, and the villagers observed that white monkeys were working on the temple after dark. The place takes its name from this event: Prakhar means 'white monkey'. Tenpe Nyima's father, Lama (*Thugse*) Dawa Gyeltsen (1499– ?), is embalmed in a *chorten* housed in a chapel next to the main temple. This room contains superb paintings and was restored by the Royal Grandmother, Ashi Phuntsho Chogron (1911–2003) who was the daughter of the Lord of Chume, a descendant of Pema Lingpa. The descendants of this lineage have given Bhutan many great reincarnations and eminent personages on both regional and national levels.

The private festival of Prakhar is called a *durchoe* and commemorates in the 9th lunar month the death anniversary of *Thugse* Dawa Gyeltshen.

Hidden in the woods half an hour's walk from Pra (or 15 minutes by car) is the Nyingmapa monastery of **Nyimalung**, closely associated with Prakhar. It was founded in 1938 by Doring *Trulku* (1902–1952), a lama with a volatile temper who came from Dartsedo, Kham in Eastern Tibet. In Chume, one of his foremost patrons was Dasho Gonpo, the Lord of Chume. The 2nd King whose wife from Prakhar helped to complete the monastery in the 1960s.

The monastery underwent complete restoration in 2002 and since 1994, has a new large *thangka/thondroel* that is shown to devotees at the time of the festival in the 5th lunar month. It was donated by Japanese devotees.

This monastery has acquired a high reputation for the quality of its teachings, for the virtuosity of its musicians (who uphold the great musical tradition of Mindroling monastery in central Tibet) and for the discipline which prevails there. Nyimalung has about one hundred monks. About forty of them come to dance during the (private) Prakhar festival in the autumn and then move to Gelephu in the south for the winter.

The last village in the Chume valley is **Nangar**. From there, a new road is being built and it will go straight to Ura bypassing the Choekhor valley and therefore Jakar.

From Nangar the present road starts to climb towards the **Kikila Pass** at 2,900 metres (9,515 feet), which separates the Chume valley from the Choekhor valley where Jakar *dzong* serves as the district seat. In the Chume valley, the road covers 18 kilometres (11 miles) from Gyetsa to Kikila. Below the pass, in clear weather the view on the vast sweep of Choekhor valley is magnificent: Jakar *dzong* rises on a spur on the far the left, the great Kurje monastic complex bars the head of the valley to the North, and in the distance snowy peaks stand out against the sky.

THE CHOEKHOR VALLEY

There are barely nine kilometres (five and a half miles) from Kikila to Jakar *dzong*, or rather the village of Chamkhar, which has grown up on the flat ground at the base of the Jakar *dzong* hillock. A roundabout situated on the east-west road in the centre of the village is the meeting point where people can wait for a vehicle or bus going in any direction. Although the village is named Chamkhar, it is more normally referred to as Jakar by foreigners.

On the right, towards the river, a broad, somewhat boggy area regards itself as the market area. The Bank of Bhutan sits half-way up the street. Numerous wooden sheds house small stores that sell everything—bars, a bakery and a pizzeria, telephone counters, crafts shops and two internet places. A lot of the shopkeepers are Bhutanese of Tibetan origin.

Chamkhar (Jakar) is in the process of urbanization and the new town will be on the right bank of the river, north, beyond the hospital.

After crossing a wind-battered bridge built in 2002, the road on the right leads to the Tang and Ura valleys and onwards to eastern Bhutan.

Just above the bridge, a large new religious complex is worth visiting: **Lhodrakarchu** monastery, which belongs to Namkhe Nyingpo Rinpoche, a reincarnation of one of Guru Rinpoche's disciples.

The road on the left of the bridge over the Chamkhar chu follows the left bank of the river towards the north. It runs through the farm of a former Swiss project and a mechanical workshop which is the only place for 400 kilometres (250 miles) where you can get a punctured tyre mended! A small shop sells delicious cheese made by the Swiss method (Gouda & Emmenthal), butter, apple or peach brandy, cider and apple juice, honey and beer (weissbier). The road continues up to Tamshing monastery, five kilometres (three miles) from the 'Swiss farm'.

From the mechanical workshop, a narrow rough road climbs up for a good kilometre (nearly a mile) above the farm to the Karsumphe plateau, where the **Swiss Guest House** is located. A little farther is the splendid complex of the Renewable Natural Resources (RNR) where archeological findings can be seen.

HOTELS AND INNS

The mid-1990s saw the establishment of several guesthouses. Until then there was only the **Wangduchoeling Guesthouse**, which was demolished to make way for the luxurious **Amankora–Bumthang** resort (tel. 975-2-331333; www.amanresorts.com). Unfortunately, this resort overshadows the historical Wangduchoeling palace.

The other guesthouses in traditional style are charming, but plumbing and electricity should not be expected. All the inns, run by families, are very friendly and offer very good meals. The **Karsumphe Swiss Guesthouse** (tel. 975-3-631145) is above the Swiss project's farm; **Tamshing Lodge** near Tamshing monastery; and the **Gongkar Lodge** is below the Lhodrakarchu monastery—all three being on the left bank of the river.

Aum Leki's Lodge, **Tshering Guesthouse** and **Karma Tobden Mountain Lodge** (tel. 975-3-631255) are close to each other, near the hospital. The **Siddartha** is a little farther towards Jampa Lhakhang. The **Village Lodge** is perched on a spur near the *dzong*, the **Riverview** and the **Wangduechoeling (BTCL)** (tel. 975-3-631107) are on slopes at the entrance of the town. **Kaila Choenzom Guesthouse** (tel. 975-3-631219) more commonly known as Kaila Guesthouse, is between the *dzong* and the village. It is especially popular with people living in Bhutan and serves the best French fries in the Himalayas! All these are on the right bank of the river.

The proprietors and staff of all these inns do their best to please visitors, under sometimes trying, material conditions.

(Left) *Two yaks grazing amidst rhododendrons.*

(Bottom) *Panoramic view of the Great Himalaya Range from the ridge between Paro and Thimphu.* (*Western Bhutan*)

A WALK IN THE VALLEY

The road which continues beyond the 'Swiss farm' offers the chance of a fine walk in the valley. Five kilometres (three miles) to the north it comes back to the river where there is a bridge over to the right bank. In this way one can make a loop on foot of about ten kilometres (six miles) over flat terrain. This walk should preferably be taken in the morning because it often rains in the afternoon or the wind may blow in gusts. (It is possible, however, to go as far as Tamshing Monastery by car.) Just after the farm there is a good view of the buildings on the other side of the river: Wangduchoeling Palace which dates from 1857 and the small houses containing prayer wheels, as well as above the palace, the Jakar *dzong*, then the hospital, a large building with remarkable architecture.

A little beyond the farm at Batpalathang is the superb RNR (Renewable Natural Resources) building. During the construction of this building in 1999, old structures were found, one of which, made of stone, dates from the 8th century. A short series of archaeological excavations, the first in Bhutan, was conducted in 2000 by a Swiss team.

The road goes through fields, and about three kilometres (two miles) further, at a place where the opposite bank of the river forms a cliff, you will see the 'iron castle' **Chakhar**. According to Bhutanese tradition, this was the residence in the 8th century of King Sendhaka, the king who invited Guru Rinpoche to Bhutan.

One kilometre (just over half a mile) further, the road skirts a tiny temple surrounded by a wall, on the right. It is **Konchogsum Lhakhang** (also called Tsilung) this was founded, according to the saint Pema Lingpa, as far back as the eighth century. This temple is famous for its bell, which bears an inscription from the eighth century inside and which must have been cast for the Tibetan royal family so that they could hear 'the sound of Buddhism'. The bell was stolen and transported to Bhutan where its chimes could be heard all the way to Tibet. The Tibetan army was sent to fetch it back but the bell was so heavy that the soldiers could not lift it and they let it fall, which explains why it is broken. The bell remained in Bhutan.

In 1039 Bonpo Dragtshel, the first active *terton* ('discoverer of religious treasures') in Bhutan, discovered texts which had been hidden by Guru Rinpoche at this spot. It is said that the king of the water deities rose out of the lake beneath the temple and offered Bonpo Dragtshel a stone pillar and a stone scroll.

Another story in the oral tradition claims that the saint Pema Lingpa in the 15th century also discovered religious treasures here, which he found in the subterranean lake. He then sealed up the entrance with a block of stone and set his lotus seal on it. The stone can be seen in the middle of the courtyard. As for the pillar which stands in front of the surrounding wall, it is perhaps an ancient megalith reconverted, such as one often finds in Bhutan and especially in this region.

The main statue in the sanctuary is Buddha Vairocana, which seems to point to the antiquity of the temple. The other statues are of Guru Rinpoche, Avalokiteshvara, and the great Nyingmapa masters who have been mentioned earlier on: Pema Lingpa and Longchen Rabjam. On the walls there are paintings of Guru Rinpoche as well as Pema Lingpa, Longchen Rabjam and Jigme Lingpa. The caretaker of this temple is from Tamshing monastery.

TAMSHING LHAKHANG

Tamshing Lhakhang, founded in 1501 (completed in 1505) by Pema Lingpa, is important on more than one count. It contains paintings of fundamental interest for the history of painting in this region and it is also, along with Gangtey Gonpa in the Black Mountains, one of the only places where Pema Lingpa's tradition of religious teachings still continues today. A small monastic community which came from the mother-monastery of Lhalung in Lhodrak (southern Tibet) in 1959 has settled at Tamshing, and young monks are being educated in the tradition of Pema Lingpa.

This small private monastery has a peaceful and studious atmosphere. New buildings and toilet facilities have been built with the help of a European donor, thus allowing the children and the monks to live in healthier conditions.

The temple was restored at the end of the 19th century, probably at the time of the 8th reincarnation of Pema Lingpa, by Kunzang Tenpe Nyima (1843–1891), since he is the last historical personage to figure in the paintings. He was the first king's uncle. The temple itself is made up of a vestibule and two sanctuaries, one above the other, with a path for circumambulation running around it. A restoration project proposal has been put up to UNESCO.

Ground Floor: The 36 paintings in the vestibule on the ground floor date from the same period as the construction of the temple and are still in relatively good condition. Since they are probably the oldest extant paintings in Bhutan, they are of enormous interest for the history of both art and religion, and by some miracle they have escaped the repaintings which are so frequently sponsored by the faithful as acts of piety. Each painting consists of a central figure surrounded by smaller personages who form his entourage and are placed on either side in small horizontal compartments. The colours are evenly applied and the lines are drawn

(Left) *Young monks resting at* dzong *above Thimphu.*
(Right) *Monks at* dzong *above Thimphu.*
(Bottom) *Monks walking to religious ceremony at Thimphu* dzong .
(Bottom right) *Young cheeky monk at* dzong *above Thimphu.*

firmly and clearly. All the figures conform to the iconographic canons laid down by Pema Lingpa.

On the left of the vestibule, starting from the door, there are: the Wheel of Life; the goddess Mahakali; the indigenous deity Shangpa Marnak; Sogdu, a divinity from Lhamo's entourage; the indigenous deity Shangpa Ngamo; Pema Lingpa, always recognizable by his hat which is like Guru Rinpoche's, and the Vase of Long Life which he holds in his hands; the seventh Karmapa Choedra Gyamtsho (1454–1506); Guru Rinpoche's consort Yeshe Tsogyel; Guru Rinpoche; Jampel Shenyen, the direct disciple of Garab Dorje and holder of the Dzogchen teachings; Garab Dorje, the first to receive the Dzogchen teachings directly from Buddha Vajrasattva; the blue Buddha Vajradhara; the white Buddha Vajrasattva; the green Buddha Amogasiddhi; the red Buddha Amitabha; the yellow Buddha Ratnasambhava; the blue Buddha Akshobya; the white Buddha Vairocana holding a wheel; and a painting which is nowadays effaced.

At the exit of the circumambulation path, the series resumes with Amitayus, in sexual embrace, Guru Dragpo, a terrifying form of Guru Rinpoche in red, holding a scorpion in his left hand; a form of Avalokiteshvara in sexual embrace, Hayagriva in sexual embrace; Samantabhadra in sexual embrace; followed by his terrifying form, also in sexual embrace; Manjushri; the deity Yama in sexual embrace; Avalokiteshvara; Vajrapani; Prajnaparamita; Vajrakila (Phurpa) the dagger-deity in sexual embrace; Vaisravana; Mahakala; Ekajati, the deity with one eye and one tooth; and Rahu (Za), the eclipse-deity whose body is covered with eyes; the two latter deities are both protective deities of the Nyingmapa school.

In the **circumambulation path**, the paintings cannot be dated. On the interior wall they represent Pema Lingpa's lineage and on the exterior wall the Sixteen Arhats separated by the Buddha of Medicine.

The **sanctuary on the lower floor** is dedicated to Guru Rinpoche and his Eight Manifestations. The right-hand wall displays paintings of the Norbu Gyamtsho, a lineage of Guru Rinpoche particular to Pema Lingpa. The left-hand wall has the lineage of Pema Lingpa himself, ending with this eighth incarnation, Kunzang Tenpe Nyima (1843–1891). These paintings were restored on the initiative of the Royal Grandmother, Ashi Phuntsho Chogron (1911–2003).

In the **vestibule in front of the sanctuary** there is a coat of mail attributed to Pema Lingpa, who had knowledge of metallurgy. Tradition says that if a person walks three times around the sanctuary wearing this coat of mail, a part of his sins will be wiped away.

Upper Floor: The ceiling of the upper floor is extremely low. It is said that Pema Lingpa was a short man and that his measurements were used as the gauge for the temple. The upper floor would thus have been scaled to his size.

The first paintings in the **left-hand gallery** are of the Thousand Buddhas followed by the Twenty-One Taras, feminine emanations of Avalokiteshvara. The outside wall of the circumambulation path is covered with pictures of the Three Bodies of Buddha (Amitabha, Avalokiteshvara and Padmasambhava). They are simple figures elegantly drawn in yellow on a red background. On the inner wall are paintings of the religious cycle called Sampa Lhundrup, very popular with the Nyingmapas, in which 13 protecting forms of Guru Rinpoche are represented. Next, the Eighty-Four Mahasiddhas are painted in a landscape of green hills. The right side of the gallery is taken up by a continuation of the Thousand Buddha images. The west part of the gallery over the entrance is occupied by the Gonkhang, the temple of fearsome deities.

The main temple of the upper floor is dedicated to Buddha Amitayus whose statue graces the inner sanctuary. The wall on the right is decorated with a painting of the primordial Buddha Samantabhadra, coloured dark blue. He is surrounded by the Four Bodhisattvas and several eminent Nyingmapa lamas, among them Jamyang Khyentse Wangpo (1820–92) and Kongtrul Lodroe Thaye (1813–99). The left-hand wall has a painting of Buddha Vajrasattva coloured white, holding a diamond-thunderbolt and a bell; he is surrounded by the other Four Bodhisattvas. Like the paintings in the sanctuary below, these date from the end of the 19th century.

From Tamshing Monastery there is an excellent view of the Kurje complex on the other side of the river. A little bit north of Tamshing, a footbridge crosses the river and from there it is only a ten-minute walk to Kurje.

Shortly after leaving Tamshing on the way to the footbridge, you will notice, about 100 metres (328 feet) above the road, the small **Padmasambhava Lhakhang** which was erected on one of Guru Rinpoche's meditation sites. It was founded by Pema Lingpa in 1490 and its name at that time was Dekyiling. It was restored by the Royal Grandmother, Ashi Pema Dechen in the 1950s and is under going renovation.

For more details of Tamshing, see Y Imaeda and F Pommaret *Le monastère de Tamzhing au Bhoutan central* in *Arts Asiatiques* t.XLII (Paris, 1987) pages 19–20; and M Aris *The Temple-Palace of Gtam Zhing as Described by its Founder* t.XLIII (Paris, 1988) pages 33–9.

THE KURJE MONASTIC COMPLEX

In addition to the walking route, a tarmac road accesses this complex, leaving from the village of Jakar and following the right river bank. Kurje is one of the most sacred sites in Bhutan as Guru Rinpoche meditated here and left the imprint (*jey*) of his body (*ku*) on a rock.

In the eighth century, Bumthang was under the rule of a king named Sendhaka (*Sintu Raja*) whose home was the 'iron castle', Chakhar. This king was at war with his southern neighbour, King Na'oche. The latter killed the son of King Sendhaka, who became so distraught that he forgot to worship his personal deity, Shelging Karpo. The angry god withdrew the king's vital principle and as a result he fell gravely ill. As a last resort, his ministers decided to call Guru Rinpoche, whose supernatural powers were well-known throughout the Himalayas.

When Guru Rinpoche arrived in Bumthang, he went to a place a short distance north of Chakhar where there was a large rock resembling a diamond-thunderbolt on the summit. Here lived the deity Shelging Karpo. Guru Rinpoche meditated there for a while, leaving the imprint of his body on the rock. Then he asked the king's daughter, whom he had taken to be his wife, to go and fetch some water in a golden ewer. While she was going so, he changed into his Eight Manifestations and began to dance in the meadow. So amazing was this spectacle that all the local divinities, except Shelging Karpo, came to watch.

When the king's daughter came back, Guru Rinpoche transformed her into five princesses, each holding a golden ewer in her hand. The ewers reflected the sun's rays directly at Shelging Karpo's rock. Curious about this unusual flashing, Shelging Karpo decided to take the form of a white lion and come out to see what was going on. This was the moment Guru Rinpoche had been waiting for.

Turning himself into a holy griffon, *garuda* (*jachung*), he swooped down, seized Shelging Karpo and forced him to give back the king's vital principle. At the same time he made him promise not to cause any trouble for Buddhism and to become a protective deity. Guru Rinpoche planted his pilgrim staff in the ground where it grew into a cypress tree which has a descendant said to stand to this day in front of Kurje Lhakhang.

As for Shelging Karpo, he is still the deity of Kurje. King Sendhaka recovered his health and converted to Buddhism. Guru Rinpoche compelled the two kings to meet each other and make peace at a place in the Black Mountains called Nabji, where a stone pillar commemorates this meeting (*see* page 217). This episode constitutes the first conversion to Buddhism in Bumthang.

(Following pages) *A village isolated by heavy snow.*

THE CUPBEARER

Three small benches, similar to that before the Raja, were brought and placed before us; and presently a servant came, bearing a large tea-pot of white metal, embossed, and highly ornamented with some other metal, of a yellow colour. He approached the Raja, and then giving a circular turn to the tea-pot, so as to agitate and mix its contents, he poured a quantity into the palm of his hand, which he had contracted to form as deep a concave as possible, and hastily sipped it up. To account for a custom which has so little either of grace or delicacy, in its observance, however recommended by extensive fashion, we are obliged to have recourse to the suspicions suggested in remoter times, by the frequent and treacherous use of poison. Hence originated a caution, in which the national character of this people readily disposed them to acquiesce; and the same jealousy and distrust, which have birth to its adoption, has contributed inviolably to preserve it to the present day; so that however humble, or exalted the rank of the person, who introduces to his guests the refreshment of tea, the cupbearer, which is an office of the first credit, never presumes to offer it, without previously drinking some of the liquor that he brings.

The Raja held out, upon the points of the fingers on his right hand, a shallow lacquered cup, of small circumference, which was filled with tea. Three cups had been sent, and were set down before us: the Raja directed his servant to fill them also; still holding the cup in his right hand, he repeated, in a low and hollow tone of voice, a long invocation; and afterwards dipping the point of his finger three times into the cup, he threw as many drops upon the floor, by way of oblation, and then began to sip his tea. Taking this as a signal, we followed the example, and partook of the dishes of parched rice, that were served up with it. We found this liquor extremely unlike what we had been used to drink, under the same name; it was a compound of water, flour, butter, salt and bohea tea, with some other astringent ingredients, all boiled, beat up, and intimately blended together. I confess the mixture was by no means to my taste, and we had hitherto shunned, as much as possible, these unpalatable libations, yet we now deemed it necessary to submit to some constraint; and having at last, with a tolerable grace, swallowed the tea, we yet found ourselves very deficient in the conclusion of the ceremony. The Raja with surprising dexterity turned the cup, as he held it fast betwixt his fingers, and in an instant passed his tongue over every part of it; so that it was sufficiently cleansed to be wrapped in a piece of scarlet silk, which bore evident marks of having not been very recently devoted to this service. The officers, who entered with us, were not permitted to partake of this repast, and, but for the honour of it, we would willingly have declined so flattering a distinction. They spoke several times during our visit, delivering themselves deliberately in a ready flow of language, by no means inharmonious, with confidence, but at the same time with profound respect.

The Raja descanted on the very limited produce of his mountains, and magnified greatly the scarcity of provisions, yet begged me to command every thing that the country could supply. Trays of fruit were placed before us, consisting of oranges, dried apples, walnuts, vegetables, and some preserved fruits of China and Cashmeer. He delivered to the Zempi, or master of ceremonies, a silk scarf for each of us, which being thrown across our shoulders, he dismissed us, with many admonitions to be careful of our health, and wishes that it might suffer no injury from the change of climate.

Samuel Turner
(18th century)

The actual Kurje complex is made up of three temples facing south. The **first temple** on the right is the oldest and was built on the rock where Guru Rinpoche meditated by Minjur Tenpa in 1652 while he was Trongsa Penlop and before he became the 3rd *Desi* of Bhutan. Below the roof there is a carving of Guru Rinpoche as Garuda subduing the white lion (*see* page 233). The temple has two sanctuaries. The upper one is dedicated to the Past, Present and Future Buddhas, whose images stand in the sanctuary. On the wall to the right are painted the Twenty-One Taras and on the left are various deities associated with riches.

The lower sanctuary is the holiest because this is the site of a cave containing a rock with the imprint of Guru Rinpoche's body. The cave cannot be seen as it is concealed by a large statue of Guru Rinpoche. His Eight Manifestations are displayed on the altar.

Just to the left of the entrance is the figure of Shelging Karpo and an altar dedicated to him. On the right of the door, a thousand statues of Guru Rinpoche are lined up against the wall accompanied by three large statues: of the white Tara, the Goddess of Compassion; Guru Rinpoche; and either Pema Lingpa or Dorje Lingpa—the identity of this image is uncertain.

The wall opposite the door, on the right of the altar, is covered with clay, high reliefs commissioned by the Royal Grandmother, Ashi Phuntsho Chodgron, in the 1930s. They represent Guru Rinpoche and his Twenty-Five Disciples, his Eight Manifestations and various other forms accounted for in the tradition of Pema Lingpa. The ceiling is decorated with a magnificent mandala dedicated to the teaching of the Gondu.

Leaving the sanctuary, you will notice two holes in the rock to the left of the entrance. They offer a way to purify sins. The sinner is supposed to enter on one side, worm his way as best he can through the rock and come out the other side. If he gets stuck it is because he has committed too many sins and will only be able to free himself by saying prayers. (Just in front of the steps leading to the temples there is a fairly small rock with a hole which you could also try to go through!)

The **second temple** was built in 1900 by Ugyen Wangchuck, the 1st King, while he was still the *Penlop* of Trongsa. The temple was built to house a monumental statue of Guru Rinpoche. It was modelled under the advice of the great Nyingmapa lama, the Bakha *Trulku*, Rigzin Khamsum Yondrol. He said that the blessings brought about by the presence of this image would contribute to the prosperity and stability of the whole country. The image of Guru Rinpoche is about ten metres (over 32 feet) high and is surrounded by his Manifestations as they appear in the Sampa Lhundrup text. An image of the historical Buddha sits on the left side of the altar and Zangdopelri, the paradise of Guru Rinpoche, is on the right. Facing the entrance, a second, smaller statue of Guru Rinpoche was commissioned by Tamshing Jagar, in the early 1960s.

To the left of the window there is a large painting of the 4th reincarnation of Pema Lingpa, Ngawang Kunzang Dorje (1680–1723), and on the right is a painting of Shabdrung Ngawang Namgyal with on his right by *Umze* Tenzin Drugye (1st *Desi* of Bhutan from 1651 to 1656), and on his left by Pekar Juney (1st *Je Khenpo*).

The porch at the entrance to this temple contains particularly fine paintings of the Guardians of the Four Directions and various indigenous deities who were subdued by Guru Rinpoche and transformed into protectors of Buddhism. Here we find Dorje Legpa red in colour, holding a diamond-thunderbolt and riding on a goat; Ekajati, dark red, with one tooth and one eye; Yakdu Nagpo, the guardian deity of the valley, coloured black and mounted on a black yak; Kyebu Lungten, the guardian deity of the Four Valleys of Bumthang, red, wearing armour and mounted on a red horse; and of course Shelging Karpo, Kurje's deity, coloured white and riding a white horse.

A **third temple** was consecrated in June 1990. It was sponsored by HM the Queen Mother of Bhutan, Ashi Kesang, who also commissioned 108 small stone *chortens*. These enclose the Kurje complex, transforming it into a three-dimensional *mandala* along a pattern set by the Samye Monastery in Tibet. This temple is never open for visits.

In front of the temples there are **three** *chortens*, one of them made up of a heap of stones which are dedicated to the three Kings of Bhutan. Some of the monks from Trongsa spend the summer at Kurje and perform numerous rituals here including a *tshechu* festival (*see* page 108–120).

A little away the main complex and on the footpath to Jampe Lhakhang, HM the Queen Mother of Bhutan, Ashi Kesang, is commissioning the building of a beautiful new temple. It is designed according to Zangdopelri, Guru Rinpoche's paradise, and the master painter is *Lopen* Tashi Wangdi who also did the wall paintings at Lhodrakarchu monastery.

THANGBI LHAKHANG

North of Kurje temple is Thangbi temple. A very pleasant half-hour walk takes one there and a vehicular road will soon reach the temple. Sheltered in a grove and surrounded by houses, the temple has a pastoral air about it. The 4th Shamar

Rinpoche of the Karmapa religious school came to Bumthang from Tibet in the 15th century in order to establish a monastery. In 1470 he founded Thangbi, located in the middle of a wide, fertile plateau overlooking the river. Following a quarrel with Pema Lingpa, Shamar Rinpoche had to leave Thangbi. The iron chain curtain hanging in the entrance is said to have been forged by Pema Lingpa who took over the monastery.

The temple has two sanctuaries and a rather large temple of terrifying deities, the *Gonkhang*. The sanctuary on the ground floor contains recent statues of the Past, Present and Future Buddhas and three clay statues which probably date from the end of the 15th century. Of exceptional craftsmanship, these are portraits of lamas, one of whom is the fourth Shamar Rinpoche (1453–1524).

On the upper floor, the vestibule of the sanctuary contains remarkable paintings: Zangdopelri, Guru Rinpoche's heaven, the paradise of Amitabha (the Buddha of Infinite Light) and Guru Rinpoche removing obstacles. The main statue in the sanctuary is that of Maitreya (Jampa), the Buddha of the Future.

NGANG LHAKHANG

A road leading north of Choekhor valley is now been constructed and the end of the road marks the beginning of the historical trail leading Bumthang across the mountains to Lhodrak in southern Tibet. The road passes in front of Thangbi and continues till Ngang lhakhang on the right bank of the river to the north. However, if possible, it is really nice to walk to Ngang lhakhang from Thangbi. It is an easy flattish walk and although one can follow the new road, the nicest way is on the left bank of the Chamkhar river where the trail goes through forests and meadows.

It takes about 2 hours to walk to Ngang, so Ngang can be a one day walk (round trip) from Jakar. Before Ngang, in the mountain, one can see the ruins of Draphe *dzong*; it was the residence of the Choekhor *Penlop* who was ruling the valley before the Drukpa conquest in the 17th century.

Ngang lhakhang, the "Swan temple" is in a lovely location on a knoll on the right side of the valley which is, at that point called Choekhortoe or 'upper Choekhor'. This private temple was built in the 16th century by a Tibetan lama Namkha Samdrup who also built Namkhoe lhakhang in the Tang valley. The trail to the Tang Valley via the Phephela pass starts from nearby Ngang. In 2004, the friendly owners were enlarging their family home to add four guest-rooms.

JAMPA LHAKHANG

From the Kurje complex, a tarmac road heads south along the right bank of the river to the temple of Jampa (Maitreya) and beyond that to the village of Jakar. It is equally possible to return to the village on foot, five kilometres (three miles) away.

Like Kyichu Lhakhang in the Paro valley (*see* page 131), this temple is said to be the first that King Songtsen Gampo of Tibet constructed in Bhutan in the seventh century. It is one of the 108 temples built by him throughout Tibet and the Himalayas to overcome a giant demoness. While Kyichu Lhakhang was erected on the demoness's left foot, and was one of the temples built 'to subjugate regions beyond the frontiers', Jampa Lhakhang was placed on the left knee and was one of the temples built 'to subjugate the frontiers'.

When Guru Rinpoche came to Bhutan, it is said that he preached the teachings of the *Kagye* cycle to King Sendhaka and his court from the roof of the temple. In addition to the main sanctuary containing the statue of Jampa, four more sanctuaries were added after the middle of the 19th century, creating a closed courtyard in front of the main sanctuary. A caretaker from the Trongsa monastic community looks after the temple.

The exact dates of the founding and restoration of the different sanctuaries are not clear, except that the whole complex was partially restored by Ugyen Wangchuk's brother-in-law, the Jakar *Dzongpon*, Chime Dorje, in 1905 (J C White, *Sikkim and Bhutan*, reprint).

Outside the temple, a long building was erected in 1999 to serve as an assembly place during the great annual prayer (Monlam Chenmo) instituted that year, and it is in front of this building that, in the autumn, the Jampe lhakhang festival (*Grub*) now takes place. More buildings were being built in 2005.

INSIDE THE COMPLEX

It is not known exactly when **the main sanctuary** was restored, but it was probably at the beginning of the 20th century judging by the style of the paintings. Like all very ancient temples, the sanctuary consists of a central shrine with a circumambulation path. The central shrine contains a large statue of Maitreya, framed on either side by Four Bodhisattvas. On one side of the doorway leading into the main shrine there is a painting of the historical Buddha and, on the other, a painting of the Eight Manifestations of Guru Rinpoche. The circumambulation walls are is covered with paintings of the Thousand Buddhas, 1,004 to be precise.

Doma, made from betel and areca, is offered as a sign of friendship.

The **sanctuary of Duki khorlo**, or **Dukhor** (*Kalacakra*), is on the right of the main sanctuary, forming the right side of the courtyard. It was built by Jigme Namgyal or his son Ugyen Wangchuk, it is not clear who, at the end of the 19th century.

Kalacakra, the Wheel of Time, is considered to be the most complex of the cycles of Tantric teachings, and is the one most recently propagated. According to Himalayan tradition, it was preached by Buddha and then kept secret for several centuries in the fabled kingdom of Shambala. After reappearing in India around AD 966, it was introduced into Tibet in 1026.

The deity who symbolizes *Kalacakra* is coloured dark blue, with 32 arms, one yellow leg and one red leg. He is in sexual embrace with his consort, who is orange. The temple's main image represents this deity and the smaller statues represent his entourage. The splendid paintings devoted to the Karling Shitro cycle are of 'the peaceful and terrifying deities according to Karma Lingpa' who appear in the intermediary state between death and rebirth.

The *Gonkhang* is situated near the Dukhor sanctuary is never open for visits. The **Chorten Lhakhang** is in an extension of the Dukikhorlo Lhakhang. It was built by Ashi Wangmo, the present King's great-aunt, who became a Karmapa nun. This temple is dedicated to the 1st Benchey Lama, a reincarnation of the Karmapa school who died around 1940 and was one of the Wangchuck family's chaplains. His *chorten* is in the middle of the temple. On the right-hand wall there is a painting of the lineage of the Karmapas, and the left wall depicts the Thirty-Five Buddhas of Confession.

The **Guru Lhakhang** forms the left side of the courtyard. It was founded by the Jakar *Dzongpon*, Tsondru Gyeltsen, in the middle of the 19th century. The main statue is of Guru Rinpoche flanked by images of Avalokiteshvara and Amitayus. On the wall to the right are the Twenty-One Taras. On the left-hand wall are Avalokiteshvara with a thousand eyes and a thousand hands, and Sukhavati—the Western Heaven of Amitabha. On the right of the window there is a painting of Pema Lingpa and, on the left, the protective deity Gonpo Maning (one aspect of Mahakala).

The **Sangye Lhakhang** is above the complex main entrance. This 'temple of Buddhas' was founded by the 2nd King, Jigme Wangchuck. The main statues represent the Buddhas of the Seven Ages. The wall on the right depicts the cycle of Gondu. On the left are Guru Rinpoche and his Eight Manifestations, Avalokiteshvara and the Medicine Buddhas whose principal figure is dark blue, holding a myrobolan fruit (*Terminalia Chebula*) in his hand.

CHAKHAR

Not far from Jampa Lhakhang, set back on the edge of the plateau overlooking the river, is the residence of Chakhar, where King Sendhaka's 'iron palace' stood in the eighth century. A temple seems also to have been founded on this spot by the saint Dorje Lingpa in the 14th century. The head of the family who lives at Chakhar is said to be descended from Dorje Lingpa and he bears the name of Chakhar Lama. He takes care of the annual festival of Jampa Lhakhang, with which bonds continue to survive after many centuries. The house dates from the beginning of the 20th century but was entirely restored in 1999.

Approaching Jakar/Chamkhar village, to the left of the road, one can admire the architecture of the regional hospital built in 1989 with Swiss aid. This hospital has an allopathic unit and a traditional medicine unit.

Right against the hospital is the Sekargutho temple. This is a small temple from the 1960s, built at the time for the community from Sekargutho monastery in Chodrak (Southern Tibet), which is famous for having been a residence of Marpa and the place where Milarepa built his tower on the orders of his master, Marpa.

WANGDUCHOELING PALACE

As the road approaches the village of Jakar, and just after the hospital, (beyond the archery range) the structure of the Wangduchoeling Palace—built on a site called Chamkhar, already inhabited in the eighth century—is now largely hidden by the Amankora–Bumthang resort (tel. 975-2-331333; www.amanresorts.com). This palace was constructed in 1857 by the Trongsa *Penlop*, Jigme Namgyal, whose son, Ugyen Wangchuck, the future 1st King, was born here.

JAKAR DZONG

The road leading to Jakar *dzong* splits off from the main road, above the primary school. Jakar *dzong* (also written Byakar) sits on a little spur overlooking the valley. The '*dzong* of the white bird' is very elegant and more modest in size than the *dzong*s mentioned so far. It is the administrative seat of the district and, since 1998, has a Drukpa monastic community.

The place was founded by the Shabdrung's great-grandfather, the Drukpa lama, Ngagi Wangchuk. After he had founded Trongsa, Ngagi Wangchuk came to Bumthang where with the help of donors, he started to build a monastery. One day he saw a white bird flying over the construction site towards the ridge where the *dzong* now stands, and he bird landed there. Ngagi Wangchuk took this to be a good omen and he decided to change the location of the monastery. In 1549 the monastery was finished and he named it 'the monastery of the white bird'.

After Shabdrung Ngawang Namgyal had firmly established his power, he ordered the Trongsa *Penlop*, Minjur Tenpa, to repair the monastery and build it into a *dzong*, which he did in 1646. During the struggle for effective control of central Bhutan which took place in the 1650s after the Shabdrung's death, the *dzong* was damaged. It was repaired much later in 1683 by the 4th *Desi* of Bhutan, Tenzin Rabgye, who added a tower as a water reservoir. The *dzong* was badly damaged again in the earthquake of 1897 and was rebuilt on a smaller scale by the future 1st King, Ugyen Wangchuck, in 1905 (see JC White, *Sikkim and Bhutan*, reprint).

Coming into the *dzong* through the courtyard for administration, you will pass below the central tower which contains a temple to Maitreya. A second temple, dedicated to the lineage of the Drukpa lamas, has as its principal statue a representation of Tenpe Nyima, Shabdrung Ngawang Namgyal's father. A passage then leads to the courtyard formerly reserved for monks. The part on the right was the *Kunre*, the monks' assembly hall, containing a statue of the deity Phurpa.

Four kilometres (two and a half miles) above the *dzong* stood the palace—monastery of Lame Gonpa, 'the unsurpassed monastery', which was home to a Forest Institute. It was one of the finest examples of palatial architecture in Bhutan. Lame Gonpa was built at the beginning of the 19th century by the Trongsa *Penlop*, Sonam Drugel, who was King Ugyen Wangchuck's maternal great-grandfather. The King restored Lame Gonpa, and the place became the residence of his two daughters, both very pious. The palace's main tower had to be destroyed for structural reasons.

JAKAR LHAKHANG

Many houses have recently been built along the road that runs from the base of the hill where the *dzong* stands to the roundabout in the village. However, on the left side of the road, near **Kaila's guesthouse** (tel. 9753-631219) and only minimally distinguished by the gold ornament on its roof, is Jakar Lhakhang, one of the oldest temples in Bhutan.

Founded in 1445 by a descendant of Dorje Lingpa, it contains some very fine paintings of the deity of Victory and Long Life, Ushnishavijaya (T*sugtor Namgyalma*) represented in a *chorten*. The temple appears to have been restored at the end of the 19th century since there is a painting of Shabdrung Jigme Choegyel (1862–1904). The principal statue is of Guru Rinpoche.

LHODRAKARCHU MONASTERY

This monastery immediately comes to one's notice partly because of the extent of its buildings, and partly because of its dominant position above the village on the other side of the river. It faces the *dzong* and its terrace provides a superb view point over the *dzong* and village.

Its construction began in the mid–1990s, with the help of foreign and Bhutanese donors, and is not yet finished. Its style is closer to that of a Tibetan monastery than a Bhutanese monastery. It bears the name of a great monastery in Lhodrak (Southern Tibet), practically on the border with Bhutan and whose reincarnated lama took refuge in Bhutan and died there. This lineage is that of Namkhe Nyingpo Rinpoche, whose origin goes back to a disciple of Guru

A DAY IN THE LIFE

*T*his day the Rajah paid us a visit; a tent was pitched for his reception on the open ground before our house, consisting of a small silken pall, with two high silken parti-coloured kunnauts. He arrived about eleven, preceded and succeeded by followers amounting to less than a hundred. On reaching the ground, he was carried or shuffled off his horse and deposited in the tent amid most terrific screechings. He took an immense time to arrange for our admission. We found him seated on a shabby throne, with a head priest, a coarse looking man, on his right, on a less elevated seat. Brass cups, etc. were arranged before him. Our chairs occupied the left; a present of fruits, onions, etc., the floor. The meeting was friendly, and he promised us coolies in two days. He is a youngish man with a square face, and was well dressed.

After we had taken leave, he feasted his attendants and the spectators with salt fish and rice. He departed about 2 pm. The procession was as follows, both going and returning—

A large, black, shaggy dog led by a chain.

A drum and drummer; a gong with a melodious sound; a clarionet played by an old and accomplished musician, rivalling in its strains that beautiful instrument the bagpipe; a man bearing a wooden painted slab on a pole, on this was an inscription; a banner looking like a composition of rags; a white flaglet; fifteen matchlockmen; fifteen bowmen; the Dompa of Roongdong; five horses and one mule led.

The household; Natchees; guitar; sundries. Personal attendants, looking like yeomen of the guard in red cloth dresses, variegated with yellow; the Rajah wearing a chinese copper hat.

Lastly, the priests, of whom there were about six.

These were the best clothed and best mounted, and evinced satisfactory tokens of being corporeally well off. Their dress consisted of a sombre jacket with no sleeves, with either a yellow or red silk back, over this is a sombre scarf. They are great beggars, and the headman was well pleased with a present of four rupees. In return, he gave P. two, B. and myself each one paper of salt, similar to those given to the lookers–on.

The ponies were all poor, excepting two or three of the Rajah's awn, which were handsomely equipped; these had their tails raised on end, exactly like hobby–horses. In addition to this, each was supplied with supernumerary yâk tails, one on either side.

The whole people collected did not amount to more than 300. The arms, at least were wretched, consisted of culverins, which went off with an enormous report, and matchlocks with short rests, like the end of a pitchfork. The bows were long and good. The helmets were worn on the head when going and coming, but were allowed to sling on the back while resting here; they are rude iron things, like bowls, but covered for some way up the sides with cloth in a most unbecoming way. Dirt and noise were predominant; the dancing women, evidently not what they should be, had clean faces, but horridly dirty feet, and were very plain. The dancing was poor, consisting chiefly of ungraceful motions of the hands and forearms; the singing pleasing, harmonious but monotonous.

William Griffith, Esq, FLS, Bhutan 1837–1838

Rinpoche. The present reincarnation, who comes from Eastern Bhutan, is very respected. Many children have joined this monastery, whose monks now number about 250.

The recent paintings in the assembly hall are magnificent and are the work of Tibetan monk in residence, *Lopen* Trashi Wangdi. They describe episodes in the life of Guru Rinpoche. Another assembly hall was built in 2000 and contains statues of Guru Rinpoche, the Buddha, and the great Tibetan treasure discoverer, Rigzin Goedem (1337–1409), to whose lineage this monastery's teachings are linked. The paintings, finished in 2004, are very beautiful and are also the work of Lopen Trashi Wangdi and his helpers. On the western wall, there is a painting of the 5th Dalai Lama (1617–1682), who was very close to the Nyingmapa teachings and in particular to the tradition of Rigzin Goedem. Since 2001, the monastery has had a large religious banner (*Thondroel*), which is displayed on certain occasions.

THE TANG VALLEY

From Jakar, the road crosses the bridge over the Chamkhar Chu and branches to the right, following the left bank of the river southwards. Five kilometres (three miles) further, the road turns to the east and enters the southern end of the Tang valley, whose average altitude is 2,800 metres (9,185 feet). The road passes Dechenpelrithang, a sheep-breeding farm, and after crossing a bridge over the Tang Chu, goes up, in a series of sharp bends, towards the Ura valley.

The unpaved road into the Tang valley branches off to the left, one kilometre (half a mile) beyond the sheep farm, and climbs steeply to cross over the first line of hills. From here the valley stretches out northwards.

It is also possible to reach Tang on foot from the Choekhor valley. The shortest route is the one which starts above the Swiss farm and climbs up to **Petsheling Monastery** then follows the ridge to a small pass after which it comes down not far from **Kungzandra Monastery**. This hike takes about four hours. Another route is through the Pephela pass (3700m), north of Choekhor.

The Tang valley is still relatively poor compared to the other Bumthang valleys. Its agricultural yields are meagre and people there used to raise sheep but the potato cultivation has improved their income and sheep rearing is on decline. The unpaved road now reaches part of the valley, but since the north is a dead end, it lies some distance off the east–west axis of road connections. One can still see old women wearing a black sheep skin on their back, the garment serving as a coat, a raincoat and a cushion for sitting on the ground.

MEBARTSHO

The Tang River cuts through the first line of hills, forming a narrow gorge which contains one of the great pilgrimage sites of Bhutan—Mebartsho, 'the flaming lake'.

This is where Pema Lingpa, born close by, found treasures hidden by Guru Rinpoche and thus became a *terton*, a 'discoverer of religious treasures'. The story is well known in Bhutan, and goes as follows. One day, in the year 1475, when Pema Lingpa had gone to look for mushrooms in the forest, he met a stranger who said he had come to see him, gave him a scroll and disappeared. The scroll declared that Pema Lingpa should go and fetch the religious treasures hidden in a rock called Naring on the opposite side of the river. So Pema Lingpa headed for the gorge, accompanied by five friends. Just before arriving there, Pema Linga began to behave strangely, as though he were in a trance. He plunged into the river, went over to the rock, fetched the books and came back to the other side again. His friends were absolutely amazed.

In the autumn of that same year, Pema Lingpa returned to the gorge and, in the presence of a large number of people, stood at the edge of the river with a lighted lamp in his hand, saying: 'If I be a demon, let me die! If I be the spiritual son of Guru Rinpoche, let this lamp not go out and let me find the religious treasures!' Having said that he plunged into the river and came out with a statue of Buddha and a skull sealed full of miraculous substances. And the lamp was still burning. So that seems to be how the place got the name of Mebartsho, 'the flaming lake'. This name also refers to a prophecy contained in the *Pema Thangyig*, a text discovered a century earlier by Ogyen Lingpa (1329–67), the Tibetan lama.

Mebartsho, in fact, is not a lake but a gorge through which the river rushes. It is a great pilgrimage site; visitors launch small lighted lamps on the water. Images of Pema Lingpa and his two sons have been carved on the rock. There is no sanctuary, only a small altar. A little farther up the Tang road, a nunnery has been established by the Gangtey *Trulku*.

KUNZANDRA MONASTERY

This monastery, at 3,350 metres (10,990 feet), is located in the hollow of a cliff which rises above the valley floor. One needs about one and a half hours to reach it on foot. It is one of the places where Guru Rinpoche meditated, as did his disciple Namkhe Nyingpo, and a little temple is said to have been established there at the end of the eighth century. However, the present site was founded in 1488 by the saint Pema Lingpa who was born close by at Chel, and he made it one of his residences. Apart from Pema Lingpa's living quarters, the monastery consists of three temples: the Wangkhang, in which the principal statue is Avalokiteshvara with a thousand eyes and a thousand hands; Oezerphug, the meditation cave of Pema Lingpa's son, Dawa Gyeltsen; and the Khandroma Lhakhang, which contains a gilded copper statue of Pema Lingpa.

TA RIMOCEN

Few kilometres from the foot of the Kunzandra cliff, beyond the school and the recent village of **Misethang**, the road passes by Ta Rimocen (temple). This temple is dominated by an enormous rock which was one of Guru Rinpoche's meditation places. He left numerous marks on it, and the name of the temple means 'the one with drawings (or marks)'. The religious master Longchen Rabjam predicted in the middle of the 14th century that a temple would be built on this spot. At the end of the 14th century, the saint Dorje Lingpa erected a little temple which was restored at the end of the 19th century by one of his distant descendants, the Trongsa *Penlop*, Tshokye Dorje who was from Tang Ogyenchoeling. It contains some remarkable paintings, including one of Milarepa.

A beautiful *chorten*-gate marks the road, which continues northward, and soon you see, on the left bank of the river, on top of a small hill, Ogyenchoeling. Three kilometres (two miles) beyond the *chorten*-gate, the road passes in front of two small shops and there is, on the right, a small wall, a beautiful *chorten* and a bridge.

If you cross the bridge on foot and then pass through the village of Kyizum, a good half-hour walk brings you to Ogyenchoeling, where you overlook the whole Tang Valley. A village is clustered closely around the manor.

A feeder road to Ogyenchoeling was built in 2004 and a bridge over the Tang river is expected to be completed in 2006, making it possible to access the place by car.

OGYENCHOELING MANOR

The site was occupied in the middle of the 14th century by the Nyingmapa master, Longchen Rabjam, who built a little retreat there. At the end of the 14th century, the saint Dorje Lingpa decided to settle at the place where the great master had meditated and there he discovered numerous religious treasures. Of all the places in Bhutan where Dorje Lingpa lived, Ogyenchoeling seems to have been his favourite. His descendants took over and contributed to the spread of his teachings, keeping close ties with his other residence in Chodrak (Southern Tibet).

The original monastery seems to have been preserved up until the middle of the 19th century when Tshokye Dorje, the Trongsa *Penlop* and the 15th blood-descendant of Dorje Lingpa to be born at Ogyenchoeling, built the palace which is seen today. The structure was very badly damaged in the earthquake of 1897 and Tshokye Dorje's grandson, the Jakar *Dzongpon*, Ugyen Dorje, had to rebuild a large part of it at the beginning of this century. The people of the valley respectfully refer to the manor as the *dzong*, and the lords of Ogyenchoeling experienced a golden century from the time of Trongsa *Penlop* Tshokye Dorje up to the middle of the 20th century. Ogyenchoeling is still a private property owned by the same family.

The large building on the right is the *Jokhang*, which contains two temples with spectacular statues and exceptional paintings dating from the beginning of the 20th century and done by Tibetan artists. The temple on the ground floor is dedicated to Tara, the Goddess of Compassion, and the one on the first floor to Jowo, the Buddha as a young prince. In the antechamber of the ground floor, the paintings of auspicious symbols done were in a very original style, in 2000, by the sacristan, Ngawang Jampel. On the first floor landing, at the top of the staircase, remarkable painting dating from the beginning of the 20th century represents the realm of Shambhala.

In May 2001, a very interesting museum of the history and life of Ogyenchoeling was opened through the initiative, finances and work of the family itself. Allow one to two hours to visit this museum, which occupies several floors of the central tower, the *utse*. This is a unique opportunity to get to know life in a lord's mansion before 1950: granaries, kitchen, reception rooms, trade room, religious dances costumes room, library and printing-room, every room gives the intimate feeling of stepping into a bygone way of life. In the weaving and dying rooms set up outside the central tower, there is a tiny shop, which offers basket wares typical of this valley.

A small guesthouse, with six simple rooms, has been established in an old building in the garden adjoining the main residence, and the lady of the family is an excellent cook. There is a wonderful view on the Tang valley from the large stone *chorten* near the guesthouse. It is a serene, magical place.

Other temples and villages are scattered along the Tang Valley beyond Ogyenchoeling towards the north: *Anu Lhakhang* at Gamling, from which one can also get to Ogyenchoeling, Kharab, Namkhoe and Langmalung. To the west a rough road goes until the livestock farm of Wobthang and Tahun, a lovely village high up in the mountain from where the trail via Phephela pass leads to Ngang Lhakhang in the Choekhor valley.

THOWADRA MONASTERY

Beyond Ogyenchoeling, at least four hours' walk to the north, another monastery nestles into a cliff that appears to block the Tang valley. Thowadra, meaning 'the highest rock', is at an altitude of 3,400 metres (11,155 feet). It was blessed by the presence of Guru Rinpoche who came there to meditate. This is where Guru Rinpoche is said to have left behind a wooden bird which he used to expel a wicked king from the Khenpalung (also called Khenpajong) valley north of Bumthang. Thowadra is also one of the 'gates' leading into this secret valley, which was sealed up by Guru Rinpoche after he drove out the king.

Thowadra was founded in 1238 by Lorepa (1187–1250), the Drukpa Kagyupa lama who had established Choedrak Monastery at another of Guru Rinpoche's meditation places. A Nyingmapa monastic community was established here at the end of the 18th century by Changchub Gyeltsen (also called Jigme Kundrel), a disciple of the great Tibetan Dzogchen master, Jigme Lingpa (1730–98).

THE URA VALLEY

From Tang it is 50 kilometres (32 miles) across a pass to the Ura valley, the last and highest of the Bumthang valleys. To get there the road climbs through amazingly open countryside, only occasionally running into a forest.

Large sheep pastures line the road 20 kilometres (12 miles) beyond the southern tip of the Tang valley, and the big village of Tangsebi can be seen below the road level. Five kilometres (three miles) further is the Urala Pass at 3,600 metres (11,810 feet), marked by a *chorten*. About one kilometre (half a mile) before reaching the top of the pass, and to the North there is a magnificent view in clear weather of Bhutan's highest peak, **Gankar Puensum**, at 7,541 metres (24,596 feet), its massive white summit etched against the sky.

The road descends into Ura by long loops across fields and pastures. Villages in the region of Ura characteristically have very closely clustered houses, which is rather unusual in Bhutan. Ura people's main occupation was raising sheep and yaks, but the introduction of potato farming **fifteen** years ago has brought a degree of prosperity to the peasants living in the harsh climate of this valley. Since the advent of the monarchy, the families of Ura have also given Bhutan many high-ranking civil servants who contribute to its prosperity.

SOMBRANG AND SHINGKHAR

Just before the road reaches the floor of the valley, above the road on the left can be seen the village and monastery of Sombrang, where Pema Lingpa's ancestors settled in 1228. In front of the temple are some megaliths. The forestry road continues beyond the little hill that overlooks Sombrang and then descends to the superb village of Shingkhar (3,400 metres/11,155 feet). Its temple was founded by the Nyingmapa master Longchen Rabjam about 1350. To visit the temple, one must pass through the village, and admire its beautiful stone houses.

The temple was entirely restored in 2000 under the patronage of Dasho Shingkhar Lam, the local lama who had a long career in the royal administration. He is a font of knowledge concerning Bhutan, but is also a true artist and has done the paintings in the temple himself.

The temple has two sanctuaries. The one on the ground floor has three *gonkhang*, which are never open to visits. The main statues are those of the Buddhas of the Three Times and the paintings represent the *tertons*, the "great discoverers of religious treasures", surrounding Guru Rinpoche, as well as the three great fundamental cycles of the Nyingmapa school: the *Lama Gondu*, the *Kagye* and *Phurpa* (*see* in contrast, the Memorial Chorten page 171). During the rebuilding of this temple, a stone seat was found and it is considered to be the throne of Longchen Rabjam. A clay statue of the 14th century master was built over the throne, hiding it from view.

The main statue in the sanctuary on the upper floor represents Guru Rinpoche, and the main painting, Guru Rinpoche and his manifestations in the *Sampa Lhundrup* cycle. Also of note are the mandalas that decorate the ceiling.

A small inn with five simple rooms has been put up near the old residence of Longchen Rabjam, at the top of the hillock overlooking the village. For the time being, the small climb up to the inn is made on foot. Nearby, you can visit the residence of Longchen Rabjam, which was restored in 1967. This is a temple containing statues of this Nyingmapa master, Guru Rinpoche and Jigme Lingpa (1730–98), the other great philosopher of the Dzogchen religious movement, as well as paintings of the twenty-five disciples of Guru Rinpoche and of *tertons*, the "great discoverers of religious treasures".

URA VILLAGE

The village of Ura **is** on the right side of the main road as one travels east. Situated at an elevation of 3,100 metres (10,170 feet), the village is made up of large houses squeezed up against each other and covered with shingles.

Overlooking the village, a new temple dedicated to Guru Rinpoche was inaugurated in 1986. The main statue is a very large figure of this master and the remarkable paintings in the two sanctuaries illustrate the great religious cycles of the Nyingmapa school (cf. the Memorial Chorten, and Shingkhar).

A pastoralist.

EASTERN BHUTAN
THE ROAD FROM URA TO MONGAR

The mountains of eastern Bhutan can be seen in clear weather. From the pass, the road plunges down in a long series of bends through a dark coniferous forest. The whole descent is dizzying, taking a good three hours, and at the bottom the lowest point has a surprisingly low altitude of only 650 metres (2,130 feet). The distance from Ura to Mongar is 141 kilometres (88 miles). At the far end of the Ura valley, the road starts to climb towards the highest pass in Bhutan, the Thumsingla, at 3,800 metres (12,465 feet), and passes through a conifer forest with an underbrush of rhododendron. The pass, which lies about 30 kilometres (19 miles) further, is often hidden in mist, or covered with snow in winter. A sign put up by a road construction crew used to invite all comers simply to 'BASH ON REGARDLESS!' This kind of sign, and others warning about unexpected curves even though the road is nothing but curves, are a delight to newcomers.

From the pass, the forest lasts for about 20 kilometres (12 miles), then the road comes out at 3,000 metres (nearly 10,000 feet) on to a large open meadow where Sengor is situated. This is the last village where Bumthangkha is spoken as it was a grazing ground for the herds belonging to the people of Ura.

After this brief opening out of the landscape, the road enters a forest once more, this time composed of both deciduous trees and conifers, the latter disappearing progressively before the road comes into the semi-tropical zone at about 1,800 metres (5,900 feet). Bamboo and creepers then take over the scene. The 20 kilometres (12.5 miles) between Sengor and Namning is perhaps, for the uninitiated, the most hair-raising stretch of road in Bhutan. The route is literally dug out of the rock and bordered by a vertiginous drop. The heavy atmosphere is made worse by the constant humidity, the frequent fog and the absence of any human activity. A small memorial has been put up for the 247 Indian and Nepalese workers who lost their lives while constructing this road.

Namning is scarcely more than a name and marks the spot where the road enters the semi-tropical zone. More houses are to be seen from here on, some roofed with bamboo matting, the typical roofing material of eastern Bhutan.

The first fields of maize, eastern Bhutan's staple food, now appear by clumps of bamboo and banana trees while cows lazily graze foliage. The temperature rises noticeably and it is really warm by the time the road reaches the maintenance camp at Lingmithang, 37 kilometres (23 miles) beyond Namning.

Shortly before Lingmithang, near an area called Saling, **the ruins of Shongar** *dzong* can just be seen peeping through the thick jungle on the right. This fortress, built in 1100 by a lord from Ura, was abandoned around 1800 when Mongar *dzong* was established. Up until that time it had been one of the most important *dzongs* of eastern Bhutan, as it controlled the route between the centre and the east of the country.

Four kilometres (two and a half miles) further, the road reaches its lowest point of 650 metres (2,130 feet) at the bridge over the Kuru River. The big *chorten* here, built in Nepalese style, was founded about 1800 by the last Shongar Dzongpon, Kunzang Wangdu, who enshrined the precious religious objects of Shongar *dzong* inside it when the *dzong* was abandoned in favour of Mongar.

After crossing the river, a road branches off, leading to Gyalposhing, where a big hydro-electric station was built on the Kuruchu. The way to Mongar is to take the road that climbs and zigzags up the side of the mountain to where this town is located.

Thirteen kilometres (eight miles) from the bridge, a road branches off to Lhuntse *dzong*, sixty-five kilometres (forty miles) to the north. The Mongar road continues to climb, through a fairly open forest of broad-leaved trees and chir pines, to arrive twelve kilometres (seven miles) further up at Mongar (1,700 metres / 5,575 feet).

MONGAR

Mongar is the district headquarters and was for a long time, hardly more than a resting place surrounded by fields of maize. While coming from the west, it is also the first town encountered which is built on a mountainside instead of in a valley. This is characteristic of eastern Bhutan where the valleys are usually little more than riverbeds and the mountain slopes, which rise abruptly from the rivers, flatten out as they approach their summits. Looking up at those steep slopes from a river, one would never imagine that the upper parts of the mountain were so densely populated.

The western and southwestern parts of Mongar district used to belong to the ancient district of Khyeng (*see* pages 217). The true land of the 'Eastern People', the Sharchopas, begins beyond Mongar. The language of these people is very different from Khyengkha and, although it is commonly called Sharchopkha, its correct name is Tsanglalo.

Mongar *dzong* was at built the beginning of the 19th century when the site of Shongar was abandoned. The present *dzong* dates from 1953, when it was founded on orders from the 3rd King, Jigme Dorje Wangchuck. Besides its function as an administrative centre, it houses the region's Drukpa monastic community. The *dzong's* central tower contains two temples.

Zhongar Lodge (tel. 9754-641107), near the *dzong,* is a large inn, simple but with a very pleasant garden and a view of the whole region. The main street is below the *dzong,* and the shops offer the usual products and the small bars are popular. At the end of the main street, near the *chorten,* is the **Druk Kuenphen**, a small, simple inn. The **Druk Zhongar** is a suitable place to stay too. Mongar has the good fortune of having a good hospital, but its restaurants are far from renowned! The town is now growing rapidly and new buildings are popping up.

THE ROAD FROM MONGAR TO LHUENTSE

Mongar is only 77 kilometres (48 miles) from Lhuentse but the road is so bad that it often takes more than four hours to cover this distance. Even worse, the Mongar road is sometimes cut off for weeks on end and then Lhuentse becomes one of the most isolated districts in Bhutan. The road to Lhuentse branches off from the Bumthang–Lingmithang road 12 kilometres (seven and a half miles) below Mongar. After running for a few kilometres through open countryside on the side of the mountain, the road turns north and goes down into the gorge of the Kurichu, following its left bank at an altitude of 950 metres (3,610 feet). The landscape is spectacular, with cliffs and a coniferous forest from which turpentine is extracted. Lemon grass also grows in abundance.

The first village is Aotsho, followed by Gurgaon, both of them recent settlements which came into being after the road was built. The old villages are higher up on the mountainside, invisible from the road. Lhuentse, like Mongar and Trashigang, is a densely populated district but you have to climb for hours in the mountains to realize this.

After about 30 kilometres (19 miles), the road reaches Tangmachu at 1,150 metres. Here a bridge crosses over the Kuri Chu to the right bank, giving access to Lhuentse *dzong* which lies 13 kilometres (eight miles) beyond it. The *dzong* perches on a spur and appears to block the end of the narrow valley completely. The road which leads to it is very steep, climbing from 1,350 to 1,700 metres (from 4,430 to 5,570 feet) in only four kilometres (two and a half miles).

Lhuentse has only deserved to be called a village since the mid-1990s, and there is a small, simple inn there. Before this date, it amounted to a *dzong* and a school. It is the headquarters of Lhuentse district which, from Tangmachu up north, was formerly called Kurtoe. The language spoken in the Kurtoe region is closely related to Bumthangkha and Khyengkha. Indeed several families from Bumthang migrated to Kurtoe in the 16th and 17th centuries. In particular, Kurtoe is the cradle of the Wangchuck Royal Family. Their exact point of origin is the village of Dungkhar, two days' walk north of the *dzong*, where one of Pema Lingpa's sons emigrated in the 16th century. A feeder road is being built.

The region is famous for its weavers who, in the dim light of their homes, make superb dresses called *kushutara*, woven with a brocading technique (see page 97). The village of **Gonpa Karpo**, a four-hour walk east of the *dzong*, and **Dungkhar** village are especially renowned for the fine quality of the fabrics they produce.

LHUENTSE DZONG

The original foundation of Lhuentse *dzong* seems to go back to Pema Lingpa's son, Kunga Wangpo, in 1543. Then in 1552, the Drukpa lama, Ngagi Wangchuk, who had already established temples at Trongsa and Jakar, arrived in Kurtoe and set up a little *dzong* at a place called Linglingthang. After a successful military campaign against the lords of Kurtoe in 1654, the Trongsa *Penlop*, Minjur Tenpa, had a *dzong* constructed at Lhuentse (Lhundrup Rinchentse) in 1654. The *dzong* was restored in 1962 and again between 1972 and 1974. It is the administrative centre of the district and it houses a monastic community of about a hundred monks.

The *dzong* contains five temples and a *Gonkhang*. The three temples in the central tower are a temple dedicated to Guru Rinpoche, the *Gonkhang* dedicated to Mahakala and the temple dedicated to Amitayus, the Buddha of infinite life. The assembly hall of the monks, the *Kunre*, is on the upper floor in the wing on the right. Its principal statues represent the Past, Present and Future Buddhas. On the ground floor of this wing there is a temple dedicated to Avalokiteshvara. The upper floor of the left-hand wing contains a temple of Akshobya. The woodwork on the railings of the galleries is extremely fine.

To see and appreciate Lhuentse district properly, with its many small villages and ancient temples, one should really explore it on foot, but from May to early October, leeches are rife!

THE ROAD FROM MONGAR TO TRASHIGANG

This trip of 96 kilometres (60 miles) takes three hours and generally presents no serious difficulties since the Korila Pass is only 2,450 metres (8,000 feet) high. The first part of the journey is through a leafy forest filled with ferns. The Korila lies 18 kilometres (11 miles) beyond Mongar; it is marked by a pretty *chorten* and a stone (*mani*) wall. Seven kilometres (four miles) after the pass comes the village of **Nagtshang** where one of the petty kingdoms of eastern Bhutan was located before the Drukpa conquest in the 17th century and where, today, there is a small monastic school.

The road descends rapidly through corn fields and banana groves and arrives, about ten kilometres (six miles) below, at the famous zigzags of Yadi. **Yadi**, a settlement which grew up in the 1980s beside the road at 1,500 metres (4,920 feet), is composed of shops and a school. After 20 kilometres (12 miles) of interminable bends through a sparse forest of conifers, the road reaches the bridge over the Sherichu, its lowest point on this section of the journey, at 700 metres (2,300 feet). The small sheds along the road are where lemon grass oil is extracted.

The Sherichu is a small tributary of the Drangmechu which flows below Trashigang and after flowing into the Manas river, goes on into the Assam plains. Halfway up the mountain facing the Sherichu bridge, there is a large *chorten* in Nepalese style.

The road now follows the Drangmechu northwards. An unsurfaced road branches off 13 kilometres (eight miles) beyond the bridge over the Sherichu to the large monastery of Drametse. This hairpin-bend road climbs for 20 kilometres (12.5 miles) before reaching Drametse, at an altitude of 2,400 metres (7,875 feet). From here, Sherubtse College, the higher education institution, situated at Kanglung, can be seen on a plateau on the opposite mountain.

Once more it becomes evident that in most cases in eastern Bhutan, due to its peculiar geography without open valleys, the distance in kilometres or miles on the motor road has very little to do with the actual topography. It is a 60-kilometre (40-mile) drive, passing by way of Trashigang, to get from Sherichu to Kanglung and Sherubtse College!

DRAMETSE MONASTERY

Drametse, on a plateau at the top of a hill, is the biggest and most important monastery of eastern Bhutan, where Pema Lingpa's teachings were faithfully transmitted. Drametse Ogyenchoeling, to use its full name, is a Nyingmapa monastery which became state property in 1982.

The history of the founding of Drametse is very complicated and there are several versions. It is said to have been founded in 1511 by the nun (Ani) Choeden Zangmo who was a great-granddaughter of Pema Lingpa. She escaped from Tamzhing, in Bumthang, after she was pressured by the Chhokhor ruler, Kuenthub, to become his wife. It is here that Choeden Zangmo's brother, Kunga Nyingpo had his vision of the famous dance, the 'Drummers of Drametse', which has become the dance symbolizing Bhutan. The family line started by Choeden Zangpo was called the 'Drametse Choeje' and many eminent Bhutanese lamas, including three Shabdrungs (Jigme Drakpa (1791–1830), Jigme Norbu (1831–1861) and Jigme Choegyel (1862–1904) and a Gangtey *Trulku*, were born into this family.

The monastery was restored at the end of the 17th century because it has the architecture of a *dzong*, and again at the beginning of the 20th century because there are paintings of the

Old Bhutanese farmer.

Shabdrung Jigme Choegyel (1862–1904) and the 1st King, Ugyen Wangchuck. Some of the paintings were completely redone in the 1950s. Further restorations were carried out in 1985 and major renovation work done in the early 2000s with five new temples added. A large banner (*thondroel*), consecrated in 2001, depicts the famous saint Pema Lingpa (1450–1521), the 'treasure revealer' surrounded by 14 small images. The monastery was reconsecrated in April 2004.

The temples are located in the central tower. On the top floor is the *Gonkhang* and below it a temple dedicated to the 'Five Sisters of Long Life', indigenous goddesses who became protectors of Buddhism. The ground floor is occupied by a large Guru *Lhakhang* that contains the funerary *chorten* of the temple's foundress, Choeden Zangmo.

Apart from a few ordained monks, the main religious community consists of 78 *gomchens* who live around the monastery with their families, as is the case at Bhutan's other great Nyingmapa monastery, Gangtey Gonpa in the Black Mountains. The monastery is owned by the state and the head of the monastery is the Peling Sungtrul (born in 1968), the reincarnation of Pema Lingpa. A large *thangka* (*thondroel*) which liberates on sight, was consecrated in the Autumn of 2001.

TRASHIGANG

The road from Thimphu to Trashigang, earlier known in Bhutan as the 'Lateral Road', covers a distance of 580 kilometres (360 miles). It was begun in 1965 but the difficulties encountered during its construction were so great that it was not finished until 1975. The paving of the surface took another ten years.

The town of Trashigang lies 20 kilometres (12.5 miles) beyond the point where the Drametse road branches off. The road follows north the right bank of the Drangme River and then enters Trashigang district, the most densely populated district in Bhutan with over 150,000 inhabitants.

As soon as the road crosses the new bridge, which replaced the "iron bridge", Trashigang *dzong* comes into view at the top of a spur overlooking the river. The upper slopes of the mountains throughout Trashigang district are covered with small villages, and the deforestation there has been extreme. After a steep eight-kilometre (five-mile) climb, the road reaches Trashigang where the altitude is 1,150 metres (3,775 feet).

Trashigang is the centre of a region where several international development projects have been implemented and is the largest mountain town in Bhutan after Thimphu. It has a true atmosphere of its own which helps to make it one of the most pleasant towns in Bhutan. The mild climate and flowering bougainvillea contribute to this atmosphere: people chat on their doorsteps or in front of their stalls, women stop to gossip in the middle of the road, bistros are full until quite late at night, people from the Merak and Sakteng valleys stroll about with their little yak-hair hats pulled down on their heads; everybody watches the arrival of cars or the evening bus in the small square in the middle of town. It is somehow reminiscent of a village in the south of France, except for the costumes!

The topography of Trashigang town, built on a spur and backing on to the side of a mountain, defies any precise description. The commercial district is immediately at the back of the spur where the *dzong* stands, while the school, the hospital and the tourist guesthouse have been built somewhat higher and more to the north, in a kind of small circuit.

In the small square, where the prayer wheel is located, in addition to a number of shops, is a clean, simple restaurant called Phuensum, a bakery and a small hotel-restaurant. Accomodation is still not a strong point of Trashigang. The town has a guest house that is very simple but with a magnificent view of the *dzong*.

TRASHIGANG DZONG

The *dzong* stands at the extreme end of the spur, overhanging the river by more than 400 metres (1,300 feet). Unlike most other *dzongs*, it has only one courtyard. It serves as the administrative seat for the district and the Drukpa monastic community also occupies part of it.

The *dzong* was built in 1659 by Pekar Choepel on orders from the Trongsa *Penlop*, Minjur Tenpa, after eastern Bhutan had finally been conquered by the Drukpas. The *dzong* was named Trashigang, the 'fortress of the auspicious mountain'. The site had probably been occupied since the 12th century when Serdung, one of the kings of eastern Bhutan, settled there and built a fort which he named Bengkhar.

The *dzong* commands a remarkable view over the surrounding countryside. Furthermore, it is practically impregnable, being protected on three sides by the river and ravines, and from behind by the mountain. It was enlarged by the 4th *Desi* of Bhutan, Tenzin Rabgye (1680–94), and restored in around 1950 by *Dasho* Dopola.

The building includes a *Gonkhang* and several temples: the Lam *Lhakhang* dedicated to the Eight Great Indian Masters of Buddhism; the Guru *Lhakhang*; the Tshogshing *Lhakhang* where the lineages of the Drukpa, Karmapa, Nyingmapa, and Dzogchen Nyingmapa lamas are represented; and the assembly hall of the monks—the *Kunre*. In the central tower are the *Gonkhang* dedicated to Mahakala; the *Tshechu Lhakhang*, where images of Guru Rinpoche and his Eight Manifestations are displayed for worship; and a meditation room.

A large *Thongdroel* depicting the Buddha Shakyamuni, surrounded by his 16 followers (*Neten chudrug*) was ordered to commemorate the silver jubilee of His Majesty the King's coronation in 1999 and consecrated in 2003.

If you have a car and a whole day at your disposal, it is worth making a trip to Chorten Kora by way of Gom Kora and Trashi Yangtse. The distance is 50 kilometres (31 miles), which takes about two hours when the road is good.

GOM KORA

From Trashigang, one drives back down to Chagzam, the 'iron bridge' which was initially constructed by the Tibetan lama *Thangton Gyelpo* in the 15th century (see page 138), and replaced with a new bridge in 2000. Then one takes the road on the right which follows north the right bank of the Kulong river. The bottom of the gorge, formed by the denuded mountains, has an altitude of only 750 metres (2,460 feet) and it can get very hot.

24 kilometres (15 miles) from Trashigang, the temple of **Gom Kora** is set on a small alluvial plateau overlooking the Kulong river on the right of the road. Behind the small temple is an enormous black rock surrounded by rice fields and clumps of banana trees. It is like an oasis in an arid landscape.

Gom Kora is one of the famous places where Guru Rinpoche meditated in order to subdue a demon who dwelt in the big rock. It was vanquished after Guru Rinpoche turned himself into a *garuda* (*Jachung*). The big rock contains the special feature of a 'sinner's path' through which a person must wriggle in order to expiate personal sins. The little temple, which was established in the second half of the 17th century on orders from Minjur Tenpa, contains statues of Guru Rinpoche and Avalokiteshvara. The temple is renowned for its festival held in the 2nd lunar month which draws people from the region as well as from Tawang in India. A new *thondroel*, depicting the eight manifestations of Guru Rinpoche was installed at the temple in 2001 and is shown at each festival.

Two kilometres (just over one mile) after Gom Kora, the road arrives at Doksum, a small place at a spot where two valleys come together. In certain seasons many of the women sit weaving outside their houses. Doksum is the only place in Bhutan where one can still see a bridge made of iron chain that would have been built by the Tibetan religious figure *Thangton Gyelpo* in the 15th century.

The left-hand road rises rapidly into a gorge. Six kilometres (four miles) from Doksum, a road branches off to the right and leads after eight kilometres to the ridge of Ranthong Woom, at 2,100 metres (6,890 feet), where **Tsenkharla**, a ruined castle, stands. It is possible that this site was the one occupied in the ninth century by Prince Tsangma when he fled from Tibet to take refuge in eastern Bhutan.

TRASHI YANGTSE DZONG

The road now goes through the Kulongchu gorge, filled with lush vegetation where one can sometimes see monkeys playing. Road blocks are frequent. Some 20 kilometres (12.5 miles) further, the small and ancient Trashi Yangtse *dzong* comes into view on the left, on the far side of the river. Trashi Yangtse *dzong*, at an altitude of 1,850 metres (6,000 feet), was established just after the Drukpa conquest in around 1656 but was renovated in the 1970s but the district headquarters have been moved up north to a wider area. A beautiful old bridge still stands above the narrow river.

(Following pages) *The impressive* Chorten Kora *in the lush valley of Trashi Yangtse in eastern Bhutan.*

In former times Trashi Yangtse was important because it lay on one of the caravan routes leading from western and central Bhutan. Instead of going from the Ura valley (Bumthang) to Trashigang by way of Mongar, muleteers would go from the Tang valley to Lhuentse via the Rodonla and from there to Trashi Yangtse before coming down to Trashigang.

CHORTEN KORA AND TRASHI YANGTSE VILLAGE

Still heading northwards in the gorge, the road passes near a pretty little *chorten*, and four kilometres (two and a half miles) further it opens out into a circuit with terraced rice fields all along the gentle slopes. Near the river, the large *Chorten Kora* finally appears. Trashi Yangtse village is in the middle of rice fields. Today Trashi Yangtse is the administrative centre of the district of the same name and a new *dzong* was built and inaugurated in 1997.

Constructed in Nepalese style, this *chorten* is entirely whitewashed. It is said that after Guru Rinpoche had overcome the demons in the Bumdeling valley, of which Chorten Kora forms the southern tip, he predicted that a great *chorten* and a temple would be built at this spot. Local tradition has it that a Bhutanese brought a model of this *chorten* from Nepal carved in a radish. The *chorten* is believed to have been founded by the 13th *Je Khenpo*, Yonten Thaye, in 1782. The *chorten* was restored at the time of the 2nd King, Jigme Wangchuck.

Under the porch leading to the little temple near the *chorten*, there is a very unusual rendering of the Wheel of Life. The main statue in the temple is of Guru Rinpoche.

A great religious festival takes place annually at Chorten Kora mid-March and it is followed by the one at Gom Kora. People from all parts of eastern Bhutan come for these celebrations and, in particular, the pastoralists of the high Merak and Sakteng valleys and the Tawang people, both having distinctive costumes.

Just north of the *chorten* is the new town, with its small shops, where you will find bowls and other containers made of turned wood, the speciality of the region.

A little to the east, below Trashi Yangtse village, is the *dzong* inaugurated in 1997, and the interesting Rigne School, also called 'The School of Traditional Arts', whose students receive training in some of Bhutan's traditional arts. Founded in 1997 and having about forty students who have completed an initial elementary schooling, this government institute is now affiliated with the School of Traditional Arts in Thimphu. Currently, six forms of art are taught: painting, pottery, sculpture in wood, wood-turning, lacquer-work and embroidery. A small stall sells the items made by the students.

A two hour walk northward from Trashi Yangtse village takes you to the beautiful valley of **Bumdeling**, where black-necked cranes come in winter. An eight kilometres access road is being built. Higher up at 2800 metres and three hours walk away from Bomdeling, the temple of Rigsum Gonpa is one of the holiest in Bhutan, being one of the meditation spots of Guru Rinpoche. Built in the 18th century, it was restored and reconsecrated in 2004. A meditation school (*gomde*) was established in 2001.

THE RADHI-PHONGME (GAMRI RIVER) VALLEY

From Trashigang town, an upaved road leads east along the Gamri river into the beautiful valley of Radhi and Phongme. The view on Trashigang *dzong* just before descending into the valley at 800 metres is superb. This part of the valley and the road are often damaged by flood during the monsoon.

A 16 kilometres long, rough, hairpin road climbs up above the right bank of the river to a plateau where the large Bartsham village (2,200 metres) is located. From there the view on Eatern Bhutan is superb in clear weather. Bartsham is well known for its religious laymen (*gomchen*), well versed in scriptures, and has a holy temple, the Chador *Lhakhang*.

If one follows the main road along the left bank of the Gamri chu, the village of Ranjung is next at 1,100 metres, 16 kilometres from Trashigang. It boasts the private Oeselchoeling monastery, established in 1990 by Garab Rinpoche as well an hydro plant set up by the Austrians.

The road continues east through beautiful rice and maize fields and after eight kilometres reaches the village of Radhi (1,600 metres). Women weave raw silk cloth in small bamboo sheds. Nine kilometres later the road stops at Phongme (1800 metres), the last village before starting the trail which takes two days to reach the high valleys of Sakteng and Merak. In Phongme, like in Radhi, houses dot a landscape of rice and maize fields and there is a small temple. One comes across the Sakteng people, called by the generic term of 'Brokpas' (herdsman), coming down to winter in this warm region. Men have a specific costume of sheep or deer skins and leather trousers, while women wear knee-length poncho dresses. Both wear a black hat made of yak hair felt with spikes prodding out to be rainspouts.

This one-day excursion from Trashigang is well worth the trip if one is in Eastern Bhutan and wants to see the rural life of this region, but the monsoon period should be avoided because of landslides.

THE SOUTHEAST: TRASHIGANG TO SAMDRUP JONGKHAR

The construction of 180 kilometres (119 miles) of road from Trashigang to Samdrup Jongkhar started in 1963 and finished (unpaved) in 1965. Today it is paved, and the trip south takes six hours, but the southern region (Pemagatshel and Samdrup Jongkhar) was not open to foreigners in 2005. Access may open in 2006.

Unlike western Bhutan where the road goes over passes between one valley and another, here it follows ridges almost the whole way and is marked throughout with stone chortens. Some houses are still on stilts and covered in bamboo matting, although they are being more and more replaced by the standard Bhutanese style, which was developed in the 1980s.

The town of **Kanglung** is located on a ridge 25 kilometres (16 miles) south of Trashigang. This is the site of the first institute of higher education, Sherubtse College, founded in 1978 and where, from its earliest beginnings as a school in 1968 until 1988, the principals were Canadian Jesuits (Father Mackey, Father Leclaire). The vast campus takes up most of the ridge and it houses more than 800 students in Arts, Sciences, Information Technology and Commerce. The Zangdopelri Temple was built in 1978 by the late Minister of Home Affairs, Tamshing Jagar and the ground floor contains superb images of Guru Rinpoche and his manifestations in the *Sampa Lhundrup* cycle.

A post office, a few shops and several small restaurants are located near the temple and the campus gate which looks like an ancient Indian gate as the campus was built with Indian assistance.

The old village of Kanglung is after the campus. It has few shops, the primary school and a hospital.

The road passes near Khangma agricultural project and continues to climb, up to the pass of Yonphula (2,300 metres / 7,545 feet), often shrouded in mist. Nearby is a major Bhutanese army camp and a temple, **Yonphula** *Lhakhang*. The spot was offered to the great saint Pema Lingpa when he visited Eastern Bhutan and it contains superb paintings from the life of Guru Rinpoche.

Nearby on the ridge there is an airstrip, which is never used because it is too dangerous. But the tarmac is a great place to learn how to drive a car !

A little further down is the pretty place of Barshong and below down the slope, Udzarong. Iron ore used to be mined for local use in both places.

For most of the trip the road goes from ridge to ridge, giving lovely glimpses of the surrounding countryside. Some 32 kilometres (20 miles) from Kanglung, the village of **Khaling** nestles in a mountain hollow at 2,100 metres ((6,890 feet); besides the usual shops, it has a weaving centre, a government school for the blind and a large secondary school. The pastoralists (*Brokpas*) of the Merak valley come to this region in winter with their herds of sheep. About ten kilometres (six miles) further, the road reaches its highest point, hardly 2,450 metres (about 8,000 feet)– a low altitude for Bhutan.

Some 20 kilometres (12.5 miles) from this high point, the road goes through the village of **Wamrong**, at 2,100 metres (6,890 feet), then a forestry and immigration check-point, and then passes the Riserboo Hospital established by Norwegian missionaries in the early 1970s largely to fight leprosy which was endemic in this region. After another 20 kilometres (12.5 miles) the road reaches Tshelingor where a road branches off to Pemagatshel, a district created thirty years ago.

PEMAGATSHEL

Pemagatshel is the smallest district in Bhutan. It is a low altitude semi-tropical area (1500–1800 metres) which is wonderful to visit from October to March and easy village treks could be developed there.

It covers part of the ancient region called Dungsam and was on the trade route between Trashigang and Assam. The name Pemagatshel, 'the blissful lotus grove', was given by the great lama Dudjom Rinpoche (1904–1987) in 1970 when he conducted a general blessing of the people in the area.

Pemagatshel is essentially a rural district dotted with gypsum mines. The Tshebar village is the reknowned home to craftsmen of musical instruments. Several temples are located in the region; Chungkhar, Bar, Kheri and Khar having historical interest. The Shalikhar dzong, now in ruins, is north of the present Pemagatshel dzong and controlled the main road from Trashigang to the Indian plains. It seems to have been destroyed at the time of the Duar war in 1864–1865 by Indian soldiers under British command.

The monastery of Yongla (or Yongle) is located at the top of a hill, standing almost by itself. By clear weather, the view from there is amazing: on 360° one can see the central Bhutan ranges on the west, the great Himalaya to the north, the eastern Indian hills on the east and the Assam plains in the south.

The place may have been visited by Yap Tenpey Nima, the father of the Shabdrung Ngawang Namgyal, in the late 16th century. However the monastery was established in the 18th century by Jigme Kundrel, a Bhutanese disciple of the great Tibetan Nyingma master Jigme Lingpa (1730–98). When Jigme Namgyal visited Yongla at the time of the Duar war, he found it damaged . He had it repaired but further problems arose and the temple fell into disrepair. In 1967, Tamshing Jagar, the late Home Minister had it repaired. Several great lamas offered prayers at the place including Dudjom Rinpoche who started the *drubchen* annual ceremony in 1970 and lama Sonam Zangpo (died. 1982) also resided there. In 1990 on the present king's order, repair work started on the monastery, three new statues of Guru Rinpoche in wrathful protecting forms (Guru Dorje Droloe, Phurpa et Guru Horsog Jigpa) were installed. The consecration took place in 2000 in presence of the King and the Queens and was conducted by lama Kunzang Wangdi from Bartsham.

Note: In mid–2005, Pemagatshel and Samdrup Jongkhar districts were still closed to tourists following the problems between the Bodos/ULFA and India. But there are indications that the south/eastern exit through Samdrup Jongkhar, and onto Assam, would reopen in the near future.

DEOTHANG

Eighty kilometres (fifty miles) beyond Wamrong and fifty-five kilometres after Tshelingor, the road reached the last ridge before the plains and the town of Deothang (870 metres/2,855 feet). Deothang offers little of interest but it is home to an important Royal Bhutan Army camp. Until 1865 an important fort marked the ridge and kept watch on the road. This fort, which was then called Dewangiri, was dismantled by the British forces during the Anglo-Bhutanese war of 1865. They had suffered a bitter defeat there and when they retook Dewangiri, they erased all traces of their humiliation.

The descent to the plain is rather steep and passes through thick tropical forest, where teak, ferns and bamboo grow in abundance. A check-post exists on the road in the forest, just before Samdrup Jongkhar.

SAMDRUP JONGKHAR

This small frontier town is situated 18 kilometres (11 miles) south of Deothang at the precise point where the mountains meet the Assamese plain. It is the headquarters of a district boasting a new *dzong*, although it is basically a town of small shopkeepers who serve all of eastern Bhutan as far as Mongar and Lhuentse. The tropical heat gives it a languid air which is accentuated by a lack of busy traffic.

There are three simple but decent hotels. The **Shambala** and the **Peljorling** are side by side on the main street and have an Indian atmosphere. The old government **tourist guesthouse**, now privatized, is situated in a garden. From Darranga , the Indian district on the other side of the border in Assam, it is a four-hour drive to Gauhati, which is connected by air to New Delhi and Calcutta.

Trekking and Mountaineering

General Advice

Depending on the programme chosen, trekking in Bhutan is pretty much reserved for the adventurous! Indeed, in Bhutan, it presents elements very different from those encountered in other regions of the Himalayas. It is a little late sometimes when one realizes that there is a huge gap between accepting, in the comfort of a Western travel agent's office the idea of difficulties posed by the terrain, and actually being confronted physically and psychologically by these difficulties.

The climate is much windier, damper and colder than Nepal. The changes in weather are spectacular, and when bad weather moves in it may last for several days. The valleys are narrow, and once the clouds have set in, they seem unwilling to be dislodged. The monsoon arrives around the middle of June and does not really finish until the end of September, leaving only a short time for high-altitude treks above 4,000 metres (13,000 feet) before snow starts falling.

The starting points of treks in Bhutan are generally higher by about 1,000 metres (more than 3,000 feet) than in Nepal, a factor which should not be taken lightly, and the quick changes in elevation make the treks strenuous.

Furthermore, it is unthinkable to go trekking alone or without the help of somebody who knows the way. Bhutan is sparsely inhabited, there are no detailed trekking maps and none of the routes are properly marked. It is easy to get lost by taking paths that peter out in pastures or forests, and there is noone to ask for directions. The scarcity of houses means also that there is nowhere to spend a night and you must carry food for several days, as well as utensils. Even if you should happen upon a village, it is most unlikely that the inhabitants would agree to give up their own provisions, even for money. In some places rice is an excellent barter item, but rice is heavy to carry! Of course, there is always the option of using extreme restraint like the famous Robert Rieffel who went off on a seven-day trek in the mid 1980s with three kilos (six pounds) of raisins as his only source of food! So, you do need to go with a guide, have a tent, and take provisions.

The Bhutanese who go along on the trek also need their rations of rice and hot peppers or else they won't walk or, at the very least, will be bad tempered. They loathe having to eat a snack lunch of sandwiches in the middle of the day; either they settle down, light a fire and prepare a hot meal and curse these crazy

(Following pages) *The gorge of Barshong, north of Thimphu.*

Westerners who are always hurrying to get to some destination which they are going to reach sooner or later anyway; the 'middle path' is to prepare a hot lunch in the morning and carry the food in 'hot cases'.

The last point of difference with Nepal is the question of carrying the gear. In Bhutan there are no porters. Farmers and herdsmen have enough to do at home and do not need to hire themselves out as porters in order to earn a living. They don't want to leave their fields during spring and autumn, the busiest agricultural season, which happen to coincide with the trekking seasons.

Some people rent their horses, mules or yaks as beasts of burden. However, they may be late, very late indeed, or have forgotten where they were supposed to meet the trekkers, or have any number of good excuses for not showing up. It all becomes more complicated when you realize that it is obligatory to change animals whenever you enter a new district, and the boundary lines may be in the middle of nowhere. A certain degree of patience and a philosophical outlook are necessary, especially if you are above 4,500 metres (14,500 feet) in some desolate area, far from any village or means of communication, and the yaks which should have been waiting for you are not present.

Finally, the possibilities for evacuation are limited and can take a lot of time because the authorities have to ask permission from the Indian army to use one of their helicopters and the latter, naturally, only fly in calm weather. Besides, the helicopter will not usually take more than two people at a time. The price is around US$1,000 an hour and you have to count on at least four or five hours and good weather for an evacuation.

Logistics and organization in Bhutan, in contrast to Nepal, are fairly complicated and should not be underestimated. However, if you want to walk on trails where you do not meet a Westerner every hundred metres, and pass through truly wild countryside, you should come to Bhutan.

The price for trekking identical to that of cultural tours is officially US$200 per day per person (in 2005), which includes a guide, horses, cook, helpers, food, mats and tents. Trekking personnel are dedicated and prepare, in general, sumptuous meals in conditions that are precarious, to say the least. The helpers put up and take down the tents, prepare tea, carry water in the morning, etc.

It is not possible to describe here, in detail, each trek offered in Bhutan; you will find, however, some information (*see* page 276) on the most classic treks.

Be careful not to leave any refuse of any kind. Tour operators' personnel are trained in eco-tourism and this desire and effort to keep the mountains clean must be encouraged. Because of concern for the preservation of the environment, bonfires are not always possible, and cooking has to be done with portable gas or kerosene stoves.

WHAT TO BRING?

The travel agencies are responsible for the material organization of the trek and provide tents and foam mattresses, but you must have your own sleeping bag and all your own personal equipment.

You need a strong bag (as much waterproof as possible) to be carried by the mules and a rucksack/backpack for personal belongings during the day. Do not forget to carry with you a fleece jacket, a windbreaker or down jacket depending on the season and the altitude, a hat and gloves. Never set out for the day without a jacket to protect you from sudden changes in weather, an umbrella, a torch (flashlight) and a water bottle.

An umbrella is, in my opinion, more practical than a poncho, under which you sweat, but this is matter of personal preference. Clothing and hiking boots made of Goretex are perfect for Bhutan, but sneakers and canvas shoes are totally unsuitable because there is always water running on the trails. In Thimphu you can buy excellent umbrellas which triple as sunshades and walking sticks, as well as plastic sheets to cover your backpack. Wrap everything in plastic rubbish bags inside your bag and backpack, and bring extras with you as this kind of bag is not always available in Thimphu.

Also bring toilet paper (available in all the towns), a torch (the head-lamp type with a halogen bulb is the most practical for trekking with extra batteries), all your own photographic equipment, a water flask, a multi-purpose pocket knife, a hat, glasses, a towel, wet wipes (towelettes), sunscreen lotion, band-aids, antibiotic ointment and an antihistamine cream for leeches or insect bites, as well as earplugs to counter the barking and howling of dogs at night. A small plastic water jug (available in Thimphu) is useful for washing in the stream. Binoculars are useful for bird watchers.

As in Nepal, leeches can be a nuisance in the rainy season. You make them drop off by dabbing them with salt, and then disinfect the wound thoroughly. The bites are not painful but they bleed for a long time and can easily become infected.

THE CLASSIC TREKS

Detailed routes are available from travel agencies.

DRUK PATH

This is a short, four-day trek which leads from Thimphu to Paro or vice versa, crossing the chain of mountains that separates the two valleys. Although there are very few houses to see, there are wonderful lakes teeming with fish at 4,000 metres (13,000 feet) and spectacular rhododendrons that bloom in May. In winter and in clear weather, there is a magnificent view over the high Himalayas. This trek can be done in all seasons, but the best time is from October to the end of May.

BUMTHANG-LHUENTSE VIA RODONGLA

This trek can be longer or shorter than four days, depending on whether or not it is combined with the previous trek. The trek leaves Ogyenchoeling in Tang and gets to Lhuentse *dzong* by way of a long and arduous descent after crossing Rodong La (4,160 metres/13,650feet). There are many flowers in season and dwellings and to see along the way.

BUMTHANG TREK

This two-day trek is ideal for average walkers as the altitude does not go over 3,400 metres (11,155 feet) at Phephela pass between Choekhor and Tang valleys There are no views over the high peaks, but the trek visits several villages and winds through the Bumthang countryside, giving an exceptional opportunity to be in contact with rural life. This trek can be done in October and November or from February to May. Add another day to visit Ogyenchoeling and its museum.

GANGTEY GONPA TREK

This is another good trek for average walkers. It takes three days and gives you a chance to visit the isolated valleys of Gangtey Gonpa/Phobjika, Gogona and Kothoka. Although this trek can be done any time from October to May, it is best done in April and early May when the rhododendrons are flowering.

Mount Masagang seen from the trail to Laya.

PUNAKHA TREK AND SAMTENGANG TREK

These two treks are perfect for beginners. They take only three or four days, altitudes are low, at 1,500–2,000 metres (5,000–6,500 feet), and they go through several villages.

JOMOLHARI TREK

This is a superb seven-day trek for experienced walkers. It goes into northern Bhutan to the land of yak-herders, to the base of Mount Jomolhari, at 7,316 metres (24,000 feet) and on to remote Lingshi *dzong*. There are fabulous views of the mountains and exceptional flora. You will encounter many yak-herders but few villages. The maximum altitude is 4,900 metres (16,000 feet). This trek can be done from the end of April to November, with the possibility of snow during these two months.

There are three possibilities for the return: take the same trail back to Paro; return to Thimphu, although the trail from Shodu to Thimphu is bad and sometimes makes the trek not very pleasant; return to Paro via Yaksa, which is the most beautiful of the routes. The best time to go is October, but August and September are the best months for seeing the high altitude flora if one does not mind the rain or the occasional snow fall.

LAYA TREK

This trek takes about eight days and goes from the sub-tropical Punakha valley, at 1,300 metres (4,265 feet), up to the high Laya region, at 4,000 metres (over 13,000 feet), where yak-herders live at the foot of Mount Masangang, at 7,200 metres (23,620 feet). The route passes by hot springs and Gasa *dzong*, and through different levels of vegetation before reaching the village of Laya, where the women wear black yak-hair costumes and strange, conical bamboo hats. This trek combines a variety of landscapes, villages, and beautiful views of the peaks. It can be made in May, June, September, October and November, the best season being October.It is not advisable to go during the monsoon because leeches swarm in the jungles between Tashinthang and Gasa.

LUNANA TREK

This is the most difficult and the longest trek (18 days) and it requires not only excellent health but also a high spirit of adventure and self control. It starts off taking the same route as the Laya Trek. After reaching Laya, it turns eastwards and crosses the Ganglakarchung Pass, at 5,100 metres (16,730 feet), into the Lunana region where habitation is concentrated in the villages of Thargza and Chezo. It is the most difficult region of Bhutan to reach, lying at 4,000 metres (13,000 feet) at the foot of peaks that soar up to 7,000 metres (23,000 feet). The inhabitants are farmer-herders who are famous for their difficult character. The trek then heads south, and after crossing the Rinchenzoe Pass, at 5,220 metres (17,125 feet), another possibility is to continue on to Bumthang, via the base camp of Gangkar Puensum (7,541 metres) and the Dur hot springs. The trek can be done from mid-June to mid-October, but there is always the possibility of snow.

SNOWMAN TREK

The Lunana trek can be combined with the Jomolhari and Laya treks and becomes the **Snowman Trek**, a long trek taking more than three weeks and considered to be one of the most difficult in the world, with a distance of 356 kilometres (221 miles), eight passes, three of which are more than 5,000 m (16,405 feet) and an average altitude of 4,000 metres (13,125 feet).

Several routes are possible but one should be warned of the strenuous efforts that this trek entails; a thorough medical check-up is highly advisable.

Note: More regions are being opened to trekkers, especially the Ha valley. Ask your Tour Operator about new options.

MOUNTAINEERING

Bhutan was open for mountaineering around 1983–85 but then closed down after local people complained citing religious reasons.

Peaks below 6,000 metres (19,700 feet) can be climbed without prior permission in the course of treks.

Bhutan's mountains are not as high as those in Nepal but they are reputed to be difficult, due undoubtedly to the harsher climatic conditions and to the fact that proper reconnaissance still remains to be done.

NATIONAL PARKS AND NATURE RESERVES

Bhutan is very conscious of the need to protect its environment and has been included in the list of the world's "hot spots" for conservation of biological diversity. Starting its development later than most countries means that Bhutan has been able to learn from the mistakes of others. Its emphasis is on the conservation of forests and rare flora and fauna. Many animals are protected: musk deer, takin, red panda, black-necked crane, blue sheep, snow leopard, golden langur, *masheer* fish, monal pheasants, etc. An NGO, the Royal Society for the Protection of Nature (RSPN) has been established. It works with the Nature Conservation Department of the Agriculture Ministry and the World Wide Fund for Nature (WWF). The latter gives funds and technical assistance for developing parks and nature reserves, and helps to promote an awareness of ecology among children. For information: www.rspn-bhutan.org and www.wwf.org.

PARKS AND NATURE RESERVES

32 per cent of the country has been declared protected land and 9% is made of bio-corridors.

1. **Jigme Dorje Wangchuck National Park**, 4,349 km^2 (1,679 mi.^{2}), created in 1974. This park occupies a large part of Bhutan's northern band.
2. **Trumshing La National Park**, 786 km^2 (303 mi.^{2}).
3. **Kulung Chu Nature Sanctuary**, 1,300 km^2 (502 mi.^{2}), created for the protection of the sambar deer and black-necked cranes.
4. **Sakteng Nature Sanctuary**, 650 km^2 (251 mi.^{2}), on the border with the Indian state of Arunachal Pradesh.
5. **Black Mountains National Park**, covers 1,723 km^2 (665 mi.^{2}) and two ecological zones.
6. **Manas National Park**, 1,023 km^2 (395 mi.^{2}), created in 1966. It extends from the southern limits of the Black Mountains National Park towards the south, as far as Assam.
7. **Phibsoo Nature Sanctuary**, 278 km^2 (107 mi.^{2}), created in 1974. On the border with India, it is a conservation area for the Sal (*Shorea robusta*) forests.
8. **Khaling/Neoli Nature Sanctuary**, 273 km^2 (105 mi.^{2}), created in 1984, for the protection of animal species in the semi-tropical zone.
9. **Torsa Reserve**, 644 km^2 (249 mi.^{2}), in the western part of the country, on the border with the Chumbi Valley of Tibet.

SOME BHUTANESE CUSTOMS AND ETIQUETTE

A whole book could be written about Bhutanese customs, but here there is only space to highlight those that may be problematic to you.

Showing Respect

As in most other Asian countries, a sense of hierarchy and respect for superiors or older people plays an important part and conditions people's attitudes. This respect is mixed with awe when it comes to religious personages. It shows itself in various ways in daily life: the body inclined slightly forward if one is standing up; legs held straight against the chair, knees covered with the ceremonial scarf when sitting down; right hand placed in front of the mouth to avoid defiling the air with one's breath when speaking; no smoking. Using the word 'la' at the end of a sentence (even in English!) is another sign of respect.

Important religious figures are greeted in the same way as deities, with three prostrations. It is good to leave small offerings of money in temples and monasteries, just as it is advisable not to speak too loudly and to take off one's shoes as a sign of respect for the holiness of these places. Umbrellas and hats are not allowed in monasteries or *dzongs*.

The head is considered the most sacred part of the body and the feet are the most impure, which means in practice that you must never touch another person's head, nor extend your feet out in front of you. Thus, when sitting on the ground, you should sit cross-legged, or with legs folded to one side if the first position is too uncomfortable, and avoid crossing your legs when sitting on a chair.

Face

The rules of politeness and honour are complex and some of their manifestations may cause you bewilderment. For instance, it is impolite to say 'no', so a Bhutanese will answer any question in the affirmative, or he may evade it altogether if he sees that he is going to have to say 'no' and thus lose face in front of his questioner, or make the questioner lose face.

It is also bad manners to appear too sure of oneself or too firm in one's opinions since that leaves no honourable way out in case of disagreement or failure. The word 'perhaps' and conditional clauses are therefore widely used. A suggestion is more congenial to the Bhutanese way of thinking than a statement.

Exchanging Presents

Exchanging presents is much more important here than in the West. There are three ways of designating a gift according to social status: from an inferior to a superior, from a superior to an inferior, or between people of the same rank. A present should always be reciprocated after a certain length of time unless it came from a superior. When food is given in a receptacle, the latter must be returned with some sweets (candy) in it because an empty container infers an absence of prosperity. Gifts should never be opened in front of the donors, so do not expect your gift to be opened and appreciated in your presence. It is not the custom to send a thank-you note.

When the great events of life take place (marriage, promotion, death) it is the traditional custom to present three or five, seven or nine—depending on the status of the donor—pieces of cloth called *zon* accompanied by a white scarf, a *kata*. Today, the white scarf is still obligatory but some people prefer to give money in an envelope instead of the pieces of fabric, which entail a very good knowledge of the proper ceremonial practices.

It is also the custom to give presents when somebody is leaving on a trip. This can be anything from a bottle of local alcohol to a fine piece of cloth or a little pocket money for the children.

Host and Guest

To receive a guest without offering a cup of tea or a glass of alcoholic drink is the height of rudeness. In a private home, a guest should take at least two cups or glasses (sips can suffice) of whatever beverage is offered. You should not accept what is offered too quickly. If you are playing host, don't take a guest's initial refusal at face value, but go on insisting.

When you are invited to a meal with a family at home, different drinks with appetizers will be served before the meal (*see* Food and Drink, page 37) and this 'cocktail hour' may last for more than an hour. Very often, if you are visiting a humble family that you do not know very well, the hosts will not stay with their guests but will disappear until it is time to serve the meal. Much to their surprise, guests are left alone in the 'parlour', which is most likely to be the private chapel. The master of the house may then be present at the meal but not eat with the guests. There is no necessity to make conversation during the meal as there is in the West. Eating is a serious business which does not allow for distractions, so conversation is supposed to take place before it starts.

When the meal is over, guests do not sit around and chat as they do in the West, but get up and go almost as soon as they have swallowed their last mouthful. This rule holds for official banquets as well, and the guest of honour should always be the one to give a signal when it is time to leave or nobody else will dare to move. Since many foreigners do not know about this custom of leaving as soon as the meal is finished, the situation can become a little awkward as an air of impatience subtly overtakes the Bhutanese guests. 'Disappearing without notice' is customary and tends to infuriate Westerners.

Attending a Ceremony

One of the most important official customs, obligatory for both Bhutanese men and women, is the wearing of ceremonial scarves to visit *dzongs* or monasteries or to attend official ceremonies.

The most common official ceremonies are of two kinds. The first is a ceremony of blessing and prosperity, called *Shugdrel*, performed by monks. The second, conducted by a layman or a monk, is a ceremony of propitiation to the protective deity Mahakala, the *Marchang*. A container filled with local beer (*chang*), and decorated with four horns made of butter on its rim, is placed on a tripod. A local official or monk then takes a little of the alcoholic liquid in a ladle and after raising it towards the sky and saying a prayer he pours a small amount of it on the ground. Then a prayer flag is blessed.

(Following pages) Gomchens *blowing the long telescopic horns.*

PERSONAL NAMES

B hutanese personal names are few but singularly complicated for Westerners, not only by the way they are written or their pronunciation but by a number of other factors as well.

In Bhutan there are only about 50 personal names in existence. The same names appear over and over again, but this does not mean that the people bearing them are in any way related to each other. There were traditionally no family names. There are a great many Dorjes and Wangchuks but they are unrelated to any of the branches of the Royal Family.

Among the commonest names are: Chime, Chencho, Choeden/ Chogron, Choekyi, Dago, Dawa, Dechen, Dekyi, Dorje, Drolma, Gyamtsho, Gyeltsen, Jamyang, Jigme, Jinba, Karma, Kezang, Khandro, Kunley, Kunzang, Lhendrup, Nima, Norbu, Pema, Penjor, Phub or Phurpa, Phuntsho, Rinzin, Sangye, Singye, Sonam, Tashi, Tenzin, Thinley, Tobgye, Tshering, Tshokyi, Ugyen, Wangchuk, Wangdue, Wangmo, Yangkyi, Yeshe, Yoedoen, Yonten and Zangmo.

To make things more difficult, the great majority of names are given without distinction to boys and girls. However, there are a few names that are typically feminine: Choeden, Choekyi, Dekyi, Drolma (*Dem* in spoken Dzongkha), Tshokyi, Wangmo (*Om* in spoken Dzongkha), Yangkyi, Yoedoen and Zangmo (*Zam* in spoken Dzongkha).

People are always called by two names, each of which can be in the first of second position in the combination (for example: Karma Dorje or Dorje Wangdue). A foreigner abroad may says: 'I know a Bhutanese whose name is Dorje (or Wangdue or Yeshe)' but that is like saying 'I know somebody named Smith' in England. Some Bhutanese differentiate themselves from others with the same name by adding the name of their village or office as a prefix to their name.

To complicate things even further, a woman does not take her husband's name but keeps her own, and the children have names that are totally different from their parents and different from each other. This means that a man called Tenzin Dorje and his wife Phuntsho Choeden may have a son named Nyima Wangdue and a daughter Kezang Wangmo.

Nicknames are common and it is not unusual to meet someone whose nickname has, by continued use, come to replace his original name, even if it is something like 'idiot' or 'animal'.

Once again, when it comes to personal names it is all a question of everyday use, memorization and practice!

So where do the names come from? Names are not chosen by the family but are given by a monk a few weeks after birth. The name almost always has some meaning or a religious connotation: Dechen means 'Supreme Happiness' and refers to the name for a Heaven; Tashi means 'Good Auspices or Good Luck'; Sonam means 'Religious Merit'; Chime is 'Immortality'; and Tenzin is 'Holder of the Faith'.

Names in southern Bhutan work according to a completely different system, because the society is strongly influenced by Hinduism. Here family names, or rather names of castes or tribes, do exist and are transmitted to the male children, while women take their husband's name.

First names, or two first names in the case of men, are likely be the names of Hindu deities: Devi, Lakshmi, Shiva, Vishnu. Last names designate the caste (or sub-caste) or the tribe to which a person belongs. For instance: Basnet, Chetri, Katwal are names for the Kshatriya caste; Adhikari, Bandhari, Sharma, Upadhya are Brahman names; Gurung, Tamang, Limbu, Rai or Sherpa are tribal names. Here again the number of names is limited, so it is important to remember the initials that precede the last name in order to know which Sharma or Gurung one is referring to or addressing.

ARCHERY AND OTHER SPORTS

Archery

A rchery is Bhutan's national sport and is played practically all year. Spectators marvel at the dexterity of the Bhutanese and gasp at other members of a team who stand close to the target and sidestep the flying arrows with amazing speed. Archery is an integral part of all festivities and is usually accompanied by a banquet.

Bows and arrows are made of a special kind of bamboo and the tension can be as high as 60 pounds. Two painted wooden targets 30 by 120 centimetres (12 by 47 inches) are placed at each end of the range which measures 120 metres (394 feet) in length! The two targets are used alternately. Two teams of 11 archers compete, each man shooting two arrows, and the first team to get 33 points wins the match. There are three sets and the method of scoring is complicated because arrows that land within an arrow's length of the target also count.

Each team is encouraged by its supporters and 'cheer leaders'. These are women who dance and sing, extolling their team while teasing and mocking the adversaries with bawdy comments to make them lose their concentration.

Women are not allowed to touch a bow. The day before an important match, the archers will not only make offerings to their local deities but will refrain from sleeping at home. The best archers wear multicoloured scarves tied to the back of their belts, and each time an arrow hits the bull's-eye a short victory dance is performed by the team. Western-style archery was introduced in the 1980s and is played by both men and women who compete in international tournaments.

Charming sketches of an archery contest—the shooting and victory dance.

Dego

Dego is a traditional sport played by monks, since archery is forbidden to them. It is a game something like bowls or the French game of 'petanque', which involves throwing a stone of a certain weight underhand to get it as close as possible to a small stick driven into the ground. A competitor can also dislodge his opponent's stone.

Pundo

Pundo is a game played by laymen which consists of throwing a stone weighing about one kilo (over two pounds) as far as possible. This time the throwing movement is from the shoulder, with the stone held flat in the hand.

Kuru

Kuru is a game like darts played outdoors with the target some 20 metres (65 feet) away.

Soksom

Soksom consists of throwing a javelin a distance of 20 metres (65 feet).

Games of Strength

Keyshey and Sherey parey are games of strength that pit two men against each other. The first one resembles wrestling, while the second is more like 'iron hand'; one fighter's fist is clasped in the two hands of his opponent and if he can get it free he is declared the winner.

Others

Nowadays, two Western sports have found favour with the public: football (soccer) and basketball. A Korean sport, Taekwondo, has also made a remarkable breakthrough. Badminton, golf, tennis, cricket, table tennis and squash are also played.

AN UNPLEASANT ENCOUNTER

On the 14th of January the Jungpen paid Mr Eden a visit, came accompanied by a disorderly band of about two hundred followers, consisting of musicians, match lockmen, and standard bearers—the latter carrying boards with inscriptions on them. The interview and its results Mr Eden describes as follows: "The Jungpen on arriving at my tent, was seized by the legs by some of his followers, and after being twirled round in the air twice was carried to the tent, as it was thought below his dignity to walk. He was a fat, uncouth, boorish, ignorant man. He assumed airs of great dignity for a time, but was unable to resist asking for some brandy. On receiving this he became very talkative; his chief topic, however, was the quantity of spirits he could drink; he repeatedly called for more brandy, and finding that it was taking effect upon him, I gave him leave to go; nothing, however, would induce him to leave; he stayed for four or five hours, and at length was taken away forcibly by his servants, who saw that I was annoyed. Later in the day he left the camp; but whilst going through it he saw some coolies, who after receiving large advances of pay had deserted us and had been brought back, being flogged. He insisted on their being released. Captain Lance and Dr Simpson, who were present, said they could not do so without my orders; he then drew his knife and rushed into the ring with his followers, threatening to cut down the Commissariat-sergeant who was in attendance, and behaving with great violence. The men of the escort ran to their arms and fell in, and the bullying and violence of the Jungpen and his followers was immediately changed to abject fear. Seeing me approaching, he ran to meet me, trembling with fear, and begged for forgiveness. I ordered him out of camp, and the whole party ran off to the fort in a most undignified manner. I declined to receive any further visits from him until he sent me a written apology for his conduct, and this he did the next day."

Surgeon Rennie MD
Bhotan And The Story of The Dooar War, 1866

THE ART OF BOOKS

Most historical writing in Bhutan has been religious. A religious book is sacred because it represents the speech of Buddha, and must be treated with respect—blessings are coming from it. It is considered extremely beneficial to own religious books at home. The great importance given to books is reflected in the care that goes into writing and making them.

Paper is made from the inner bark of two shrubs, *Daphne* and *Edgeworthia*, that grow in abundance in Bhutan. The bark is reduced to pulp and mixed with ashes while it goes through a long cooking process. The pulp is then beaten and two methods are used for obtaining the finished sheets.

One method, widely used throughout the Himalayas, produces paper called *resho*, 'cotton paper'. The process begins with the pouring of the pulp onto a cotton screen; it is then spread over the cotton surface while it is floating in water. This manoeuvre requires dexterity and practice. The screen and the pulp are then left to dry, which takes half a day, before the sheet of paper can be taken off.

The second method is only used in Bhutan and produces a kind of paper called *tsasho*, 'bamboo paper'. A screen made from slim bamboo sticks is lowered into a vat of pulp; the paper-maker then lifts it out and deftly spreads the pulp over the surface of the screen while it is out of the water. The screen is subsequently turned over, and the sheet that has formed on it drops off and is put on a growing pile of freshly-made paper. At the end of the day, a stone is placed on the pile to help the water drain out of it during the night. The next day, the paper-maker peels the sheets

Centuries-old bookshelves.

off one by one and sticks them directly on to the earthen walls of a hut built for this purpose. By the end of the day, the sheets are dry and fall off the wall.

Bhutanese paper is of excellent quality and impervious to insects. Unfortunately, insects love the ink, which is made from soot, herbs, yak-blood and animal-based glue.

The sheets of paper are cut to the size of book pages and the text is then either written by a calligrapher or printed by xylography. Xylography, or woodblock printing, entails carving the text in reverse on a wooden board, coating the plank with ink and then pressing a sheet of paper on to it with a roller; the printed text appears on the page the right way around. Certain texts are written in calligraphy with ink made from gold dust and illuminated like medieval manuscripts in Europe.

When the printing or calligraphy of a whole text is completed, the pages are not bound but simply pressed between two wooden boards. The upper board, which makes the cover, may be a work of art in itself because it is often carved with religious subjects and perhaps covered with a sheet of wrought, gilded copper.

It is possible to see some of these books, printing boards and paper at the National Library in Thimphu. Established in 1969, the library was moved in 1984 to a new building constructed in traditional style. It contains about 6,100 Tibetan and Bhutanese books, both manuscripts and xylographs, and a collection of 9,000 printing blocks.

For a more in-depth look at books in Bhutan, read *Papermaking in Bhutan*, by Yoshiro Imaeda (Kasama, 1988).

GLOSSARIES

The definitions in this glossary are given in the Bhutanese context, and do not take into account connotations or meanings these terms might have in other Himalayan countries.

HISTORICAL FIGURES, SAINTS AND OTHERS

Ani	nun
Ashi	Title given to women of the royal family; can be translated as "princess".
Aum	(Pronounced 'Am' term of respect when addressing an elder woman
Banchung	Small double basket made of bamboo.
Bodhisattva	(In Dzongkha: *Changchub Sempa*) "Enlightened being", a person who has the spiritual possibilities to obtain the state of Buddhahood, but has voluntarily reincarnated to help beings leave the cycle of reincarnation.
Brogpa	(Or *bjop*) Yak and sheep pastoralist.
Bura	Bhutanese raw silk.
Cham	Religious dances.
Changkhang	Bar.
Choesham	Private chapel inside a house.
Chorten	Buddhist funeral or commemorative monument (Sanskrit: *stupa*).
Chu	Water, river.
Dasho	Non-inheritable title given by the king to certain officials; indicated by the wearing of a red scarf and a sword; title also given to the men of the royal family.
Desi	(In the past, called *Deb Raja* by the British) Temporal ruler of Bhutan in the time of the *Shabdrungs* (from 1651 to 1905).
Doma	Quid composed of areca nut, lime and a betel leaf.
Druk Yul	Dzongkha name for Bhutan; "Land of the Drukpas"; Druk also meaning "dragon and thunder", it is often translated as "Land of the Dragon".
Drukpa	Official religious school of Bhutan; belonging to the major school called *Kagyupa*, of Mahayana Buddhism; founded in Tibet in the 12th century by Tsangpa Gyare.
Drukpa	Name given to the Bhutanese who practise Tantric Buddhism; by extension, the name for Bhutanese citizens.
Duar	"Door"; the traditional eighteen points of access into Bhutan from the Indian plain.
dzong	Fortress, seat of civil and religious power.

Dzongda	Literally "master of the *dzong*"; district head, governor.
Dzongkha	National language of Bhutan; also called *Zhungkha*.
Dzongkhag	District/province.
Gang	Mountain, summit.
Gup	Village head.
Gelong	Ordained, celibate monk; wears the monk's robe.
Go	Man's dress.
Gomchen	Lay religious practitioner; can be married.
Gonpa	Monastery.
Goenkhang	Temple of terrifying protective deities.
Guru Rinpoche	Also known as Padmasambhava, Ugyen Rinpoche and Pemajune; saint originally from Swat (now in Pakistan) who converted Tibet and Bhutan to Buddhism in the 8th century.
Hemadatsi	Chilli and cheese; national dish of Bhutan; formidable for the uninitiated.
Je Khenpo	Spiritual head of Bhutan; head of the *Drukpa Kagyupa* religious school in Bhutan.
Kabne	Man's ceremonial scarf.
Kada / Kata	White scarf, given on official or religious occasions.
Kadrinche	Thank you. Note: There is no word for "please"; a different form of the verb produces the polite form of a request.
Kera	Belt.
Kira	Woman's wrap-around dress.
Koma	Clasps that hold the woman's dress together at the shoulder.
Kousouzangpo	Hello (literally 'you are well').
La	Pass.
La, lasso la	Polite terms used to end a sentence or added to a person's name as a mark of respect.
Lama	Religious master; can be celibate or married, and may or may not, therefore, wear the monk's robe. Equivalent to *guru* in Sanskrit.
Lha	Deity.
Lhakhang	Temple, sanctuary.
Lopon	(Pronounced 'Lopoen') Literally (master); title given to any person who has received a traditional education and, most particularly, to learned monks.
Lyonpo	(Pronounced 'Loenpo') Minister; wears an orange scarf and carries a sword.
Mandala	(In Dzongkha: *khyil khor*) Mystical or cosmic diagram.
Ngalong	Name traditionally given to Western Bhutanese.

Nyingmapa	Important religious school of Central and Eastern Bhutan; follows the teachings of Padmasambhava (Guru Rinpoche). Guru Rinpoche.
Onju	(Or *gyenja*) Woman's blouse.
Patang	Straight sword worn by dignitaries.
Pema Lingpa	(1450–1521) *Nyingmapa* religious figure and 'treasure discoverer' (*terton*) from Central Bhutan; he played a very important religious role through his founding of temples, his writings and his visions; many influential families descend from Pema Lingpa, in particular, the royal family.
Penlop	Governor; title given from 1651 to 1905 to governors of the three large provinces of Paro, Trongsa and Daga; today abolished except for the title of *Trongsa/Choetse Penlop*, which is given to the crown prince.
Rachu	Woman's ceremonial scarf, usually red.
Rinpoche	honorific title given to a reincarnated or a learned lama.
Sakya Thupa	Historical Buddha
Sangye	Buddha.
Shabdrung	'At whose feet one prostrates'; title given to Ngawang Namgyal and then to his reincarnations who succeeded one another as leader of Bhutan until 1904. Shabdrung Ngawang Namgyal (1594–1651) is the lama of the Drukpa Kagyupa religious school who unified Bhutan in the 17th century and gave it its institutions.
Sharchopas	'Easterners'. Name given to Eastern Bhutanese by Western Bhutanese. They call themselves Tshangla.
Sharchopkha	Name often given to the language of Eastern Bhutan; the real name of the language is Tshanglalo.
Shedra	monastic school
Gomde	meditation centre
Terton	'Discoverer of religious treasures', the *terma*, hidden by Guru Rinpoche and destined to be discovered by a predestined person for the benefit of beings.
Thangka	Religious banner; can be painted, embroidered or appliqué.
Thondroel	Large religious banner that brings 'liberation by sight'.
Toego	Woman's jacket or man's shirt.
Torma	Sacrificial cake offered to deities during ceremonies.
Trulku	Literally "Body of transformation". Reincarnated lama. Can be married.
Tshechu	"Tenth day"; religious celebration in honour of Guru Rinpoche.
Tsho	Lake.
Tshongkhang	Store.
Utse	Central tower of a *dzong*.

DEITIES OF THE BUDDHIST PANTHEON AND THEIR SANSKRIT NAMES

Dzongkha/Tibetan	Sanskrit
Chagton Chenton	Avalokiteshvara with a thousand hands and a thousand eyes
Chana Dorji/Chador	Vajrapani
Chenrezig	Avalokiteshvara with four arms
Demcho Khorlo Dompa	Cakrasamvara
Donyondrub	Amogasiddhi
Dorje Jigje	Vajrabhairava, Yamantaka
Dorje Legpa	a protector of Buddhism
Dorje Phagmo	Vajravarahi
Dorjechang	Vajradhara
Dorjesempa/Dorsem	Vajrasattva
Drolkar	White Tara
Droljang	Green tara
Drolma	Tara
Drubthob	Siddha
Dukyikhorlo/Dukhor	Kalacakra
Ekajati/Ngasungma	a protector of Buddhism
Ging	belongs to Guru Rinpoche's retinue
Gompo Jarodonchen	Mahakala with a raven's head
Gompo Maning	Aspect of Mahakala
Guru Rinpoche	Padmasambhava
Jampa	Maitreya
Jampelyang	Manjusri
Jomo	goddess
Kuntu Zangpo	Samantabhadra
Kyedorje	Hevajra
Menlha	Baishajyaguru (Buddha of Medicine)
Mitrugpa	Akshobya
Namparnanze	Vairocana
Namthoese/Namse	Kubera, Jambhala, Vaishravana
Oepame	Amitabha, Buddha of the Infinite life
Palden Lhamo	Mahakali, Sri Devi
Pehar	a protective deity
Phurba/Phurpu	Vajrakila
Rinchenjune	Ratnasambhava
Shakyatupa	Shakyamuni
Sangdu	Guyasamaja
Sangye	Buddha
Shinje Choekyi Gyelpo	(Lord of the dead) Yama Dharmaraja
Tamdrin	Hayagriva
Tchuchije	Avalokiteshvara with eleven heads
Tshepame	Amitayus

Tsheringma	goddess of eternal life
Tsugtor Namgyalma	Ushnishavijaya
Yeshe Gompo	Mahakala
Yum chenmo	Prajna Paramita
Za	Rahu

COMMON TREES AND PLANTS

Botanical Name	Local Name	English Name
Abies densa	Dunshing	Fir
Acer	Chalam	Maple
Aconitum orochryseum	Tsenduk/sorig	Aconite
Albezzia	Kabasisis	Silk Tree (in tea plantations)
Alnus	Gamashing	Alder
Areca	Domashing	Areca nut
Artemisia	Khempa	Wormwood
Betula utilis	Latap	Birch
Cannabis satatavia	Keha	Marijuana
Castanopsis	Sokey	Chestnut
Cinnamomum	Patashing	Camphor
Citrus	Humpa	Lemon
Cordyceps sinensis	Yartsagunbu	'Summer plant, winter worm' mushroom
Cornus capitata	Phatsishing	Dogwood
Cosmos	Jaga Meto	Cosmos
Cupressus corneyana (National tree)	Tsendenshing	Weeping Cypress
Daphne	Deshing Nap	Daphne
Datura	Dushing	Datura
Delonix regia	Gulmohan	Flame Tree
Diospyros	Andey	Japanese Persimmon
Duabanga	Lampatey	—
Edgeworthia	Deshing Kap	Edgeworthia
Erythrina	Chatseshing	Coral Tree
Euphorbia wallichii		Euphorbia
Eucalyptus	—	Eucalyptus
Ficus religiosa	Pipal	Pipal/ Bodhi tree
Gerardina hitrophylla	Zocha	Nettle
Gentiana Lureii	Pangen meto	Gentian
Juglans regia	Tashing	Walnut
Juniperus recurva (Cupressaceae)	Shup	Juniper (tree)
Juniperus squamata (Cupressaceae)	Shup	Juniper (shrub)
Juniperus pseudo-sabina (Cupressaceae)	Shup	Juniper (shrub/tree)

Larix griffithiana	Zashing	Himalayan Larch
Magnolia campbellii	Kashing	Magnolia
Meconopsis grandis	Euphel meto oem	Blue poppy
Oroxyllum indica	Tsampakha meto	No equivalent
Picea spinulosa	Sheshing	Eastern Himalayan Spruce
Pinus bhutanica	Tongphushing	Bhutan pine
Pinus roxburghii	Thaythongshing	Chir Pine
Pinus wallichiana	Tonphushing	Blue Pine
Populus ciliata	Kashing	Poplar
Primula denticula	Chukameto	Primrose
& Biocarpum himalayica		
Quercus griffithii	Sishing	Oak
Quercus semecarpifolia	Jishing	Oak
Rhododendron arboreum	Ethometo	red Rhodendron
Rhododendron ciliata	Ethometo	white rhododendrdon
Rhus	Chokashing	Asiatic Sumac (lacquer tree)
Salix	Changma/Lambashing	Willow
Santal	Tsenden kap	Santal
Shorea robusta	Sal	Sal
Tecoma grandis	Teak	Teak
Tsuga domosa	Bashing	Hemlock
Zanthoxyllum	Thinye	Sichuan Pepper

RECOMMENDED READING

ACHARYA, Sanjay, *Bhutan: Kingdom in the Himalayas* (Lustre Press/Roli books, New-Delhi, 1999).

ADAMS, Barbara S, *Traditional Bhutanese Textiles* (Orchid Books, Bangkok, 1984).

ALLENDE, Isabel, *Kingdom of the Golden Dragon* (Flamingo, London, 2004) (novel).

ALI, Salim & al, *Handbook of the Birds of India and Pakistan: Together With Those of Bangladesh, Nepal, Bhutan and Sri Lanka* (Vol 8, 1997).

ALI, Salim, B. Biswas, S. Dillon Ripley, *Birds of Bhutan* (Zoological 1996 Survey of india, Kolkatta, 2002).

AMUNDSEN, Ingun Bruskeland, *On sacred architecture and the dzongs of Bhutan. Tradition and transition in the architectural history of the Himalayas* (Oslo, Arkitekthoegskolen i Oslo (AHO), 2003).

ARIS, Michael, *The Raven Crown: The Origins of Buddhist Monarchy in Bhutan* (Serindia, London, 1994).

ARIS, Michael, *Views of Medieval Bhutan, The Diary and Drawings of Samuel Davis, 1783* (Serindia, London/Washington, 1982).

ARMINGTON, Stan, *Bhutan* (Lonely Planet Publications, Australia, 2002).

ASHI Dorji Wangmo Wangchuck, *Of Rainbows and Clouds: the Life of Yab Ugyen Dorji as Told to His Daughter* (Serindia, London, 1998).

AVIESON, Bunty *A baby in a backpack to Bhutan. An Australian family in the land of the Thunder dragon* (Pan Macmillan, Sydney, 2004).

BARKER, David K, *Designs of Bhutan* (White Lotus, Bangkok, 1985).

BARTHOLOMEW, Mark, *Thunder Dragon Textiles from Bhutan* (Tokyo, 1985).

BEAN, Susan & Myers, Diana, *From the Land of the Thunder Dragon: Textile Arts of Bhutan* (Serindia, London/Salem 1994).

BERRY, Steven K, *The Thunder Dragon Kingdom: A Mountaineering Expedition to Bhutan* (Marlborough/Seattle, 1988).

BLOFIELD, John, *The Way of Power: A Practical Guide to the Tantric Mysticism of Tibet* (London, 1970).

BOGLE, George, see Markham, Clements R.

BOSE, Kishen Kant, see Eden, Ashley.

CARPENTER, RUSS & BLYTH, *The Blessings of Bhutan* (Hawai University Press, Honolulu, 2002).

CHODEN, Kunzang, *Bhutanese Tales of the Yeti* (White Lotus, Bangkok, 1997).

CHODEN, Kunzang, *Folktales of Bhutan* (White Lotus, Bangkok, 1993).

CHODEN, Kunzang, *Dawa, The Story of a stray Dog in Bhutan* (Kunzang Choden, Ogyenchoeling, 2004).

CHODEN, Kunzang, *The Circle of Karma* (Penguin/Zubaan, New-Delhi, 2005)(novel).

CHODEN, Tashi & Penjore, Dorji, *Economic & political Relations between Bhutan and neighbouring countries* (CBS, Thimphu, 2004).

COLLISTER, Peter, *Bhutan and the British* (Serindia, London, 1987).

CROSSETTE, Barbara, *So Close to Heaven: The Vanishing Buddhist Kingdoms of the Himalayas* (Vintage Departures, 1996).

DARGYE, Yontan & Sorensen, Per K., *The biography of Pha 'brug sgom zhig po called the current of compassion* (National Library, Thimphu 2001).

DORJE, Gyurme, *Bhutan Handbook* (Footprint, Bath, 2004).

DORJI, Dasho Sithel *The origin and description of Bhutanese mask dances* (KMT Press, Thimphu, 2001).

DORJI, C T, *Gyalsay Tenzin Rubgye and his Reincarnations* (Prominent Publishers, New-Delhi, 1999).

DORJI, Chang, *The clear mirror of Archery in Bhutan* (Chang Dorji, Khasadrapchu, 2001).

DORJI, Kunzang, *Icons of awakened energy. An introduction to Bhutanese Iconography* (Department of Tourism, Thimphu, 2003).

DORJI, Jagar *Lhop, A tribal Community in South Western bhutan, and its survival through time* (NIE, Paro, 2003).

DOWMAN, Keith (tr), *The Divine Madman: The Sublime Life of Drupka Kunley* (London, 1987, Pilgrims publishing, Kathmandu, 2002).

EDEN, Ashley, *Political Missions to Bootan, comprising the reports of the Hon'ble Ashley Eden, 1864; Capt. R B Pemberton, 1837, 1838, with Dr. W. Griffith's Journal; and the account by Baboo Kishen Kant Bose. Calcutta, 1865* (Rééd.: Bibliotheca Himalayica, New Delhi, 1972, with the addition of Anonymous, *The Truth about Bootan by One who knows it,* originally published Calcutta, 1865).

FLETCHER, Harold, *The Quest of flowers: The Plant Exploration of F. Ludlow and George Sheriff* (Edinburgh University Press, 1975).

GREGSON, JONATHAN, *Kingdoms Beyond the Clouds : Journeys in search of the Himalayan Kings* (Macmillan, London, 2000).

GRIFFITH, William, *Journal of Travels in Assam, Burma, Bootan, Afganistan and the Neighbouring Countries* (Calcutta, 1847). Chapters XI, XII and XIII reprinted under the title: *Bhutan 1837–1838* (Kathmandu, 1975).

HARDING, Sara *The Life and revelations of Pema Lingpa* (Snow Lion, Ithaca-Boulder, 2003).

HELLUM, A.K. *A Painter's Year in the Forests of Bhutan* (The University of Alberta Press, University of Hawai'i Press, Edmonton-Honolulu, 2001).

HICKMAN, Katie, *Dreams of the Peaceful Dragon: A Journey into Bhutan* (London, 1987).

IMAEDA, Yoshiro, *Butan, kaze no inori (Faith and Festival at Nyimalung),* (Hirakawa shuppansha, Tokyo, 1996) (photos: Akira Tabuchi).

INSKIPP, Carol and Tim, GRIMMET, Richard, *Birds of Bhutan* (Helm Field Guides, Oxford University Press, New Delhi, 1999) *Paro Journal of Bhutan Studies*, Centre for Bhutan Studies, Thimphu (www.bhutanstudies).

KARAN, Pradyumna P, *Bhutan: A Physical and Cultural Geography* (University of Kentucky, Lexington, 1967).

KINGA, Sonam, *Gaylong Sumdar Tashi, Songs of Sorrow* (CAPSS, Education Division, Thimphu, 1998).

KINGA, Sonam, *Speaking statues, flying rocks. Writings on Bhutanese history, myths and culture* (DSB publication,Thimphu, 2005).

KOMATSU, Yoshiro et al, *Bhutan* (Children of the World) (Milwaukee, Wis, 1988).

LUMLEY, Joanna, *In the kingdom of the Thunder Dragon* (BBC books, London, 1997).

MARKHAM, Clements R, *Narratives of the Mission of George Bogle to Tibet and the Journey of Thomas Maning to Lhasa* (London, 1879. Reprint: New Delhi, 1971).

MYERS, Diana K, 'Costume and Ceremonial Textiles of Bhutan', *The Textile Museum Journal 1987* (Washington, 1988).

NAKAO, Sasuke, *Hikyo Butan* (Bhutan Unexplored) (Tokyo, 1959. Reprint: Tokyo, 1971).

NAMGYAL, Singye *The Language web of Bhutan* (KMT, Thimphu, 2003).

NIDUP, Tshewang and SORENSEN, Per K., *Sayings and Proverbs from Bhutan: Wisdom and Wit in Dzongkha Idiom ('Jig rten pa'i dpye gtam)* (Thimphu, 1999).

NISHIOKA, Keiji and SATOKO, *Shinpi no okoku* (Mysterious Kingdom) (Tokyo, 1978).

NISHIOKA, Keiji and NAKAO, Sasuke, *Flowers of Bhutan* (Asahi Shimbum, Tokyo, 1984).

OLSCHAK, Blanche C, *Ancient Bhutan: A Study on Early Buddhism in the Himalayas* (Swiss Foundation for Alpine Research, Zurich, 1979).

PALIN, Michael, *Himalaya* (Weidenfeld & Nicolson, The Orion Publishing Group, London, 2004).

PARMANAND, *The Politics of Bhutan: Retrospect and Prospect* (Pragati Publications, New Delhi, 1992).

PEARCE, N R and CRIBB, P J, *The Orchids of Bhutan* (Royal Botanic Garden and Royal Government of Bhutan, Edinburgh, 2000).

PEISSEL, Michel, *Bhoutan* (Reprint Olizane, Genève, 1992).

PEMBERTON, R Boileau, *Report on Bootan* (Calcutta, 1839. Reprint: New Delhi, 1976).

PENJORE, Dorji , *Bhutan's national bibliography* (CBS, Thimphu, 2002).

POLUNIN, Oleg & Stainton, Adam, *Flowers of the Himalaya* (OUP, Delhi, 1984).

POMMARET, Françoise, *Tibet : an enduring civilization* (Abrams, New York, 2003).

POMMARET, Françoise & Schicklgruber, Christian, *Bhutan: Mountain Fortress of the Gods* (London, Serinda Publications, 1997).

POMMARET, Françoise, *Bhutan Au plus secret de Himalaya* (Decouvertes Gallimard, Paris, 2005).

PRADHAN, Rebecca and WANGDI, Tandin, *Threatened birds in Bhutan* (Thimphu, 1999).

PRADHAN, Rebecca, *Wild Rhododendrons of Bhutan* (Thimphu, 1999).

PRADHAN, Rebecca, *Conifers of Bhutan* (RSPN-JICA, Thimphu, 2005).

RENNIE, David Field, *Bhutan and the Story of the Dooar War* (London, 1886. Reprint: Réed New Delhi, 1970).

RICARD, Matthieu, *The Spirit of Tibet* (London, 1996).

RICARD, Matthieu & Föllmi, Olivier & Daniele, *Buddhist Himalaya* (Thames and Hudson, London, 2002 & Abrams, NY, 2002).

RINZIN, Rinzin, *The talisman of good fortune and other stories from rural Bhutan* (Rinzin Rinzin, Thimphu 2002).

RONALSHAY, Earl of, *Lands of the Thunderbolt: Sikkim, Bhumhi and Bhutan* (London, 1923. Reprinted under the title *Himalayan Bhutan, Sikkim and Tibet,* Delhi, 1977).

ROSE, Leo E, *The Politics of Bhutan* (Cornell University Press, Ithaca, New York, 1977).

RUSTOMJI, Nari, *Imperilled Frontiers: India's North-Eastern Borderlands* (New Delhi, 1983. Reprint: Oxford University Press, 1996).

SINGH, Amar Kaur Jasbir, *Himalayan Triangle: A Historical Survey of British India's Relations with Tibet, Sikkim and Bhutan 1765–1950* (London, 1988).

SNELLING, John, *The Buddhist Handbook* (Century Paperbacks, London, 1987).

SOLVERSON, Howard, *The Jesuit and the Dragon: The Life of Father William Mackey S. J. in the Himalayan Kingdom of Bhutan,* (Ed. Robert Davies, Outremont, 1995).

STAPLETON, Chris, *Bamboos of Bhutan* (Royal Botanic Gardens, Kew, 1994).

STRICKLAND, Nancy and LOEDY, Jigme, *Going Home in the Rain,* Canadian Cooperation Office (Thimphu, 2000) (children's book).

THINLEY, Dorji, *The Boneless tongue* (Figurative proverbs, wise sayings and incidental remark), Dorji, Thinley (NIE, Samtse, 2005, bilingual publication).

TOGO FUMIHIKO, *Himaraya no Okoku Butan* (Bhutan: Himalayan Kingdom) (Tokyo, 1965).

TURNER, Samuel, *An Account of Embassy to the Court of the Teshoo Lama in Tibet: Containing a Narrative of a Journey Through Bootan, and Part of Tibet* (London, 1800. Reprint: Réed, Bibliotheca Himalayica, New Delhi, 1971).

UEDA, Akiko, *Culture and modernisation from the perspectives of young people in Bhutan* (CBS, Thimphu, 2003).

URA, Karma, *The Ballad of Pemi Tshewang Tashi* (Karma Ura, Thimphu, 1996).

URA, Karma, *The Hero With A Thousand Eyes* (Karma Ura, Thimpu 1995).

Ura, Karma, *Deities, archers and planners in the era of decentralisation* (Karma Ura, Thimphu, 2004).

URA, Karma & Galay, Karma(eds.) *Gross National Happiness and development* (CBS, Thimphu 2004).

VAN STRYDONCK, Guy; IMAEDA, Yoshiro; POMMARET, Françoise, *Bhutan: A Kingdom of the Eastern Himalayas* (Geneva, 1984. Reprint: London/New York, 1989). The 1984 book is now available as an interactive CD-rom (PC only) in English and French (National Library, Thimphu, 2005).

WANGCHUK, Ashi Dorji Wangmo, *Of Rainbows and Clouds: the Life of Yab Ugyen Dorji as Told to His Daughter* (Serindia, London, 1998).

WANGCHUK, Tashi, WANDI, Karma et al, *Field Guide to the Mammals of Bhutan*, (Ministry of Agriculture, Thimphu, 2004).

WHITE, John Claude, *"Castles in the Air"*, in *National Geographic*, vol. XXV, No.4, April 1914, pp 365–453.

WHITE, J Claude, *Sikkim and Bhutan: Twenty-One Years of the North-East Frontier, 1887–1908* (London, 1909. Reprint: Bibliotheca Himalayica, Delhi, 1971).

WILLIAMSON, Margaret D, *Memoirs of a Political Officer's Wife in Tibet, Sikkim, and Bhutan* (Wisdom, London 1987).

ZEPPA, Jamie, *Beyond the Sky and the Earth*, (Riverhead Books, New York, 2000).

ZÜRCHER Dieter and CHODEN Kunzang, *Bhutan. Land of spirituality and modernization. Role of Water in Daily Life* (New Dawn Press, Chicago-Slough-New-Delhi, 2003).

USEFUL WEBSITES

www.kuenselonline.com (Lots of links)	Kuensel, Newspaper
www.bbs.com.bt	Bhutan broadcasting Service
www.drukair.com.bt	National airline
www.druknet.bt (links, e-cards etc..)	National internet provider
www.rspn-bhutan.org	Royal Society for Protection of Nature
www.undp.org.bt	UN in Bhutan website
www.tourism.gov.bt	Tourism Department
www.bhutanstudies.org.bt	Centre for Bhutan Studies
www.bhutan.at	Exhibition website

RECOMMENDED MUSIC

DRUKPA, Jigme, *Endless songs from Bhutan*, Grappa music, Norway, 1998, HCD7143 (info@grappa.no)

DRUKPA, Jigme, *Folksongs of Bhutan*, 2003.

LEVY, John, *Tibetan Buddhist rites from the monasteries of Bhutan*, 4 vols.(1971), New York, Lyrichord 7258.

Large production of traditional and 'Bhutanese pop' music available only in Bhutan.

RESORT ACCOMMODATION

Recently, a number of luxury acommodation facilities have started to open and this looks like being a rapidly growing trend. The pathfinder projects are listed below.

COMO SHAMBHALA, UMA–PARO
PO Box 826, Phendeylam, Chubhachu, Thimphu
Tel. (975-2)326254, Fax. (975-2) 328718
E-mail. res.paro@uma.como.bz; www.uma.como.bz

AMANKORA–PARO
Balakha, Chento Geog, Near Drugyal Dzong, Paro
Tel. (975-8) 272333, Fax. (975-8) 272999
E-mail. info@amanresorts.com; www.amanresorts.com

AMANKORA–PUNAKHA
PO Box 333, Habisa, Punakha
Tel. (975-2) 584 222, Fax. (975-2) 584 555
E-mail. amankora@amanresorts.com

AMANKORA–THIMPHU
Near Kuenga Chhoeling Palace, Upper Motithang
Tel. Tel. (975-2) 331333, Fax. (975-2) 331999
E-mail. amankora@amanresorts.com

AMANKORA–BUMTHANG
Please refer to the website for this location.
Tel. (975-8) 272333, Fax. (975-8) 272999
E-mail. info@amanresorts.com

AMANKORA–GANGTEY
Please refer to the website for this location.
Tel. (975-2) 331333, Fax. (975-2) 331999
E-mail. amankora@amanresorts.com

(Left) *"Palace of Tassisudon [Tashichō dzong], Bootan". Engraving by J.B. Allen after William Daniell based on Samuel Davis, in Hobart Caunter, The Oriental Annual, 7 vols (London, 1834–40), v, plate 12.*

INDEX

Compiled by Don Brech, Records Management International Limited

A

Accommodation, 153, 156, 165, 168, 169, 181, 189, 193, 206, 213, 227, 244, 251, 307 (also *see* guesthouses)
administration, system of, 68–9, 74–5
agriculture (*see also* Royal Institute of Agriculture), 51, 52–3, 76, 219, 248
aid, foreign, 70, 80, 187, 195, 211, 223, 229, 243, 245
airport tax, 28
airports, 25, 156
alcoholic drinks, 33, 37, 42
altitude sickness, 33
American Himalayan Foundation, 221
Anglo–Bhutanese War, *see* Duar War
anims (nuns) (*see* also nunneries), 64
antiques, 29
archaeological sites, 226, 228
archery, 108, 135, 138, 152, 173, 288
architecture, 87, 90–1, 93–4, 160, 163, 164, 245
archives, 180
armour, 145
art (*see also* School of Traditional Arts)
    characteristics of Bhutanese, 81
art galleries, 153
Ashi Kesang, The Queen Mother, 131, 209, 259
Ashi Dorje Wangamo, Queen, 180, 191
Ashi Pema Dechen, Royal Grandmother, 232
Ashi Phuntsho Choegron, Royal Grandmother, 171, 178, 188, 224, 225, 231, 238

Ashi Sangay Choeden, Queen, 169
Ashi Tshering Yandon, Queen, 194
Ashi Wangmo, 243
atsaras (clowns), 109
Avalokiteshvara (deity), 142, 160, 184, 231
    statues of, 131, 133, 181, 184, 189, 193, 229, 243, 263
    temples dedicated to, 258

B

bamboo ware, 47, 98, 148
banks, 156, 169, 225
bargaining, absence of, 44, 95, 173
bars, 164, 165, 168
baskets, 47
beauty salons, 44, 168
Bhutan, 22–3 (map)
    climate, 33–4
    economy, 76–8, 80
    geography, 51–3, 58–9
    government, 68–9, 70, 71–2, 74–5
    history, 61, 65–72, 74–5, 173
    legal system, 68, 74
    membership of international organisations, 70–1
    name of, 61
    national integration policy, 52
    national symbols, 73
    population, 11, 14, 51
    statistics, 79
    unification of, 67–8

(Left) *William Daniell after an untraced original by Davis, engraved by J. Redaway, "The Palace at Wandechy—Bootan", 1834, engraving on steel. Source: Hobart Caunter,* The Oriental Annual, *7 vols (London, 1834–40), iv, plate 12.*

Bhutanese (language) (see also Dzongkha)
  meaning of terms, 295–7
  pronunciation, 17, 56
Bhutanese (people)(see also Drukpas), 15,
  71, 105
births, 125
Bitekha dzong, 50
Black Mountains, 53, 56, 203
Black Mountains National Park, 280
black–necked cranes, 59, 203, 267
books, 48, 180, 294
  religious, 87, 293
bookshops, 48, 153, 156, 168, 169
boots, 49, 176
bridges, 138, 173, 195, 261, 266
  concrete, 163
  covered, 149, 179, 209
  iron, 144, 160, 180, 261, 263
Buddha
  paintings of, 133, 188, 194, 241
  statues of, 133, 183, 188, 194, 212, 240,
    243, 258
Buddhism (see also Tantric Buddhism), 14,
  56, 65, 221
Buli Lhakhang, 221
Bumthang, 219, 220 (map), 221
Bumthang trek, 276
Bumthangkha (language), 58, 255, 258
Bunakha village, 187
Byabar, see Jakar

C
Cafes, 165
caravan routes, 266
carpets, 48
cell phones, see mobile phones
Central Bhutan, 50, 58, 211–54
Central Himalayas, 52–3, 56

ceremonies, 157, 236–7, 283
Chagzmapa, see Thangton Gyelpo
Chakhar residence ('iron castle'), 228, 233,
  243–4
cham, see religious dances
Chamkhar, see Jakar village
Changangkha Lhakhang, 181
Changchub Gyeltsen, 252
Changlimithang area, 172–3
Changlimithang temple, 50
Chapcha, 187
Chapcha dzong, 50
Chapcha Pass, 186
Chasilakha temple, 50
Chendebji Chorten, 209
Cheri monastery, 91, 179
Chhukha dzong, 187
Chhuzom, 129, 160, 199, 203
Chimakhoti village, 187
Chime Dorje, 241
Chime temple, 50, 192
Chirang region, 195
Choekey (written language), 214–5
Choeden Zangmo, 259, 260
Choedrak monastery, 221, 223, 252
Choekhor valley, 219, 225–6
Chorten Lhakhang, 243
Chorten Nyingpo Lhakhang, 223
Chorten Kora, 50, 262, 266
chorten–gate, 250
chortens, 14, 83, 90, 186, 209, 256
  as protection, 160, 194
  Eight Kinds of, 124, 149, 188, 222
  field of, 191
  funerary, 212, 260
  metal, 87
  stone, 239

Chume valley, 219, 221–5
Chuzomsa, see Chhuzom
cigarettes, 37
cinemas, 169
climate, 33–4, 271
clothes and clothing, 36, 45–6, 275, 276
communications, 31
conference facilities, 153
convention centre, 178
courier services, 181
crafts, see handicrafts
Crane Study Centre, 203
credit cards, 25, 30
cremation, 128
currency, 30
customs (government agency), 29
customs (traditions), 15, 281–3

D
Dametsi monastery, 91
dances (see also religious dances), 67, 121
Dasho Shingkhar Lam, 253
Dechenchoeling palace, 163, 178
Dechenchoeling temple, 178
dego (sport), 290
deities, 15, 100, 142, 231, 242, 298–9
Deothang, 270
development, economic, 77–8, 80
Dewangiri fort, 270
Dilgo Khyentse Rinpoche, 137
divorce, 127
Dobji dzong, 186
Dochu La Pass, 191
dogs, barking, 36, 37, 275
Domkhar palace, 223
Doring Trulku, 224–5
Dorje Lingpa, 67, 221, 245, 250
Drametse monastery, 67, 112, 259–60

drinks, 37, 41–2, 282–3
Druk Air Corporation Ltd, 25, 27–8, 30, 76
Druk Choeding temple, 153
Druk Path, 276
Druk Wangyal, 191
Druk Yul (Bhutan), 61, 67
Drukpa Kunley, 66, 177, 192
Drukpa school (of religion), 65, 66, 67,
    104, 113, 163, 181
Drukpas (Bhutanese), 56, 61
Drukyel dzong, 50, 137–8
dry cleaning, 36
Duar (Dooar) War, 69, 269, 270, 291
Dungkhar village, 258
Dungse Rinpoche, 171
Dungtse Lhakhang, 138, 142, 160
Dzongkha (national language), 122, 214–5
Dzongkha Development Commission, 215
dzongs, see fortresses

E
Earthquakes, 177, 193, 202, 211, 251
Eastern Bhutan, 50, 58–9, 255–70
economy, 76–8, 80
eco–tourism, 275
electricity (see also hydro–electric power), 37
e–mail, 31
embassies and missions, Bhutanese, 29
embroidery, 178, 180, 267
equipment and supplies, 36–7, 168, 274, 275
etiquette, 14, 36, 114, 281–3
evacuations, medical, 274
exports, prohibited, 29

F
Fabrics (see also Textile Museum, weaving),
    45–6, 49, 95, 97, 224
farmhouses, 94

fees, tourist services, 19
fax services, 30
festivals (*see also* religious festivals), 193,
    224, 241
fitness centres, 156, 165
Five Buddhas of Meditation, 142
flights, mountain, 25
flora and fauna, 58, 60, 148, 181, 191, 217,
    255, 278, 280, 299–300
    export prohibited, 29
Folk Heritage Museum, 180
food, 37, 40–1, 168, 221, 271, 274
foot–wear, 49, 76
    removal of, 36, 145
foreigners
    areas closed to, 268, 270
    visits to monuments by, 50, 129
forests, 56, 76, 192, 203, 219, 261
    checkpoint, 269
fortresses, 37, 53, 91, 93
    Central Bhutan, 211–3, 216, 244–5
    Eastern Bhutan, 256, 257, 258, 262, 263,
        266, 269, 270
    visits by foreign tourists to, 50, 129
    Western Bhutan, 138, 149, 176–7, 183,
        192–3, 195, 199, 209
funerals, 127–8

G
Gamri River, 267
Ganglakarchung Pass, 279
Gangtey Gonpa (monastery), 67, 91, 203,
    206, 229, 261
Gangtey Gonpa trek, 276
Gangtey palace, 153
Gangtey Trulku, 249, 260
Gedu, 187, 188
Geduen Rinchen, 198

geography, 51–3, 58–9
gifts, 282
go (men's garment), see kho
golf courses, 42, 160, 176
gomchens (religious category), 64
Gom Kora temple, 262
Gom Karpo village, 258
gonpas, see monasteries
Gongzim Sonam Tobgye, 70
government, system of, 68–9, 70, 71–2, 74–5
group travel, 19
Great Britain, 69, 70
Griffith, William, quoted, 246–7
Guardians of the Four Directions,
    paintings of, 131, 177, 183, 239
guesthouses
    Central Bhutan, 213, 227, 251
    Eastern Bhutan, 261, 262, 270
    Western Bhutan, 160, 165, 168, 181, 199
guests, 282–3
guides, 19, 271, 274
Guru Rinpoche, 61, 104, 136, 142, 172,
    217, 221
    Eight Manifestations of, 117, 120, 189, 241
    meditation sites, 136, 137, 232, 233,
        238, 249, 250, 252, 263, 267
    paintings of, 133, 142, 152, 229, 231,
        240, 241, 248, 268
    prophecy of, 192–3
    reincarnations of, 67
    statues of, 133, 177, 188, 189, 194, 222,
        229, 239, 243, 245, 248, 253, 263
    temples dedicated to, 133, 254, 258
Gyelchok, 148
Gyelwa Lhanangpa, 65, 176
Gyelzom, 148

H

Ha (district), 160–1
hair salons, 44
handicrafts, 44, 94–5, 153, 169, 173, 180
hats, 48, 267, 278
  removal of, 36
health, personal, 32–3
Himalayas, 88, 188, 191
  Central, 52–3, 56
  foothills, 51, 52
  High, 51, 59, 207, 276
history, 61, 65–72, 74–5
Hongtso Lhakhang, 191
Hongtso village, 191
Hospital of Indigenous Medicine, 141, 180
hospitals, 33, 171, 243, 257, 261, 268, 269
hot springs, 278, 279
houses, 36, 56, 58, 59, 90, 93–4, 195, 268
hydro–electric power, 53, 56, 187, 188,
  221, 224, 256

I

Iconography, 81, 86, 142, 194, 231
immigration checkpoint, 269
incense, 48
India, 80, 187, 189, 223
  Bodo and Assamese separatists, 71, 191,
  270
Indian nationals, 19
industries, 52, 76
inoculations, 32
Institute of Languages and Cultural
  Studies, 183
Internet, 31, 78, 156, 171, 225

J

Jakar *dzong*, 93, 244–5
Jakar Lhakhang, 245
Jakar village, 225

Jampa Lhakhang, 241–3
Jamyang Kunga Sengye, 178
Jamyang Khyentse Wangpo, 232
Je Khenpo, 75, 104
jewellery, 46, 97–8
Jigme Choegyel, Shabdrung, 179, 245, 260
Jigme Drakpa, 260
Jigme Kundrel, 269
Jigme Norbu, 260
Jigme Dorje Wangchuck, King, 70, 144,
  171, 177, 183, 212, 216, 257
Jigme Dorje Wangchuck National Park, 280
Jigme Lingpa, 223, 229, 252, 253, 269
Jigme Namgyel, 69, 211, 212, 242, 244
Jigme Singye Wangchuck, King, 70, 211,
  216, 243, 266
Jigmeling temple, 50
judicial system, 68, 74

K

Kagyupa school (of religion), 65, 142, 148,
  176, 179
Kamji temple, 50
Kanglung, 268
kata (ceremonial scarf), *see* scarves,
  ceremonial
Kazi Ugyen Dorje, 70
keyshey (game), 290
Khaling/Neoli Nature Sanctuary, 280
Khamsum Yuelley Namgyel Chorten, 194
Khangzang temple, 185
Khanling village, 268–9
Kharbandi temple, 50
Kharbandi monastery, 188
Khewang Lhakhang, 207
kho (men's garment), 45
Khyeng region (*see also* Zhemgang region),
  58, 216, 217, 219

Khyengkha (language), 58, 217, 256, 258
Kiki La Pass, 225
kira (women's dress), 45
Kongchogsaum Lhakhang, 228
Kongtrul Lodroe Thaye, 232
Kori La Pass, 258
Kulung Chu Nature Sanctuary, 280
Kunga Gyatso, 185
Kunga Nyingpo, 260
Kunga Rabten palace, 216
Kunga Wangpo, 67, 258
Kungzandra monastery, 67, 248, 249–50
Kunzang Tenpe Nyima, 229
Kunzang Wangdu, 256
Kurje monastery, 212
Kurje Lhakhang, 233, 238–9
Kurroekha (language), 58
kuru (darts), 290
Kuruthang, 192
Kyichu Lhakhang, 131, 133

L
Lam Pemala, 224
lamas, 64
Langchen Pelkyi Singye, 136, 137
Langdarma, King, 65
languages (see also Bumthangkha,
    Dzongkha, Khyengkha, Tsanglalo), 52,
    53, 58, 258
  study of, 52
'Lateral Road', 261
laundry, 36
Laya trek, 278
leeches, 187, 275, 278
legal system, 68, 74
leprosy hospital, 269
Lhakang Karpo, 160
Lhakang Nagpo, 160

Lhakhang, see temples
Lhakhang Sarp, 177
Lhapa school (of religion), 65, 66, 131, 176
Lhodrakarchu monastery, 226, 245, 248
Lhuentse district, 257–8
Lhuentse dzong, 257, 258, 276
Lingshi dzong, 278
livestock, 51, 53, 76
Longchen Rabjam (philosopher), 66, 67,
    221, 222, 223, 229, 250, 253
Lopen Tashi Wangdi, 239, 248
Lorepa, 252
Lunana region, 279
Lungten Zampa bridge, 163, 172

M
Malaria, 32
Manas National Park, 280
mandalas, 83, 152, 171, 177
manuscripts, 180
maps, 49, 271
markets, 47, 49, 173
marriages, 125, 127
Mebartsho gorge, 50, 249
medicines, 33, 275
  Bhutanese, 140–1
megaliths, 253
Memorial Chorten of the Third King, 171–2
military camps, 161, 185, 195, 268, 270
mines, 76, 203
Minjur Tenpa, 183, 193, 211, 244, 258, 263
missions, see embassies and missions
mobile phones, 31
monarchy, 70, 71
monasteries, 63, 137, 184–5, 206, 222–3,
    224–5, 226, 245, 248–53, 261, 269
  founding of, 66, 67, 206, 223, 224, 259
  restoration of, 179, 225, 260

types of, 91
visits by foreign tourists to, 50, 129
monastic communities, 63–4, 75, 194, 211,
   212, 229, 252, 257, 258
monastic schools (shedra), 206, 223
money, 30
Mongar, 256, 257
Mongar dzong, 50, 256–7
monkeys, 160, 203
monuments, religious
   photography, 37
   visits by foreign tourists to, 50, 129
Monpas (ethnic group), 217
Motithang area, 181
Mount Jomolhari, 137–8, 207, 278
Mount Masagang, 191, 278
mountaineering, 279
mountains (see also Himalayas), 191, 279
museums (see also Folk Heritage Museum,
   National Museum), 251, 276
music, 48, 121–2, 305
music shops, 168, 169
musical instruments, 48, 121

N

Nagtshang village, 259
names and naming, 15, 125, 286–7
Namkhoe Lhakhang, 240
Na'oche, King, 217
national airline, see Druk Air Corporation Ltd
National Assembly, 72, 178
National Commission for Cultural Affairs,
   29, 50, 129, 181
national day, 73, 108
national dress, 36, 45
National Environment Commission, 14
National Institute of Agriculture, 192
national language, see Dzongkha

National Library, 47, 48, 169, 180, 294
National Museum (Ta dzong), 50, 144–5,
   148
national parks, 280
national symbols, 73
nature reserves, 280
Nepal, 11, 71, 279
   imports from, 46, 169, 173
   trekking in Bhutan compared with, 274,
   275
Nepalese (people), 11, 52, 71
'New Years', 108
newspapers, 169
Ngagi Wangchuck, 66, 211, 212, 244, 258
Ngang Lhakang, 240
Ngawang Choegyel, 153, 178, 191, 192
Ngawang Kunzang Dorje, 239
Ngawang Namgyal, Shabdung, 66, 67, 68,
   104, 179, 244
   death, 68, 136, 193
   engraving of, 171
   fortresses of, 138, 148–9, 176, 183,
      192–3, 198
   paintings of, 133, 152, 194, 223, 239
   relations of, 144, 153, 179, 211, 244,
      245, 269
   residence, 178
   statues of, 188, 189, 194
Ngawang Trinley, 223
night life, 164
Northern Bhutan, 59
Norzim Lam (street), 165, 169, 176
nunneries, 185, 249
nuns, 64
Nyangtel Nyima Oezer, 172
Nyingmapa monastery, 224
Nyingmapa school (of religion), 64, 65, 66,
   172, 221, 222, 223, 253, 254

O

Oesel Choeling monastery, 267
Oesepang, 185, 189
Ogyen Dorje, 70, 251
Ogyenchoeling Manor, 250–1
Ogyenchoeling monastery, 50, 66, 250–1
Old Man of Long Life, 149
opening hours
  museums, 144
  shops, 48
  optician, 168

P

Padmasambhava Lhakhang, 65, 232
paintings, 149, 178, 184, 188, 189, 194,
  212, 223, 232, 239, 240, 241, 254, 268
  collections of, 142
  loss of, 137
  oldest, 229
  recent, 224, 248, 251, 253
  restoration of, 183, 260, 231
  school of, 221
  techniques and styles, 81–2, 86
  walls, on, 131, 133, 152, 181, 183, 229,
    231
Pangri Zampa temple, 178
paper, 47, 48, 98, 293–4
Paro, 153
Paro dzong, 93, 109, 144, 145, 148–9, 152,
  213
Paro valley, 129, 131, 132 (map)
Paro town, 152–3, 156
passes, mountain, 191, 207, 255
Pekar Choepel, 262
Pele La Pass, 207
Pema Karpo, 67
Pema Lingpa, 67, 206, 217, 221, 229, 231,
  249

relations of, 67, 223, 224, 231, 250, 259
statue of, 250
temples founded by, 217, 232
Pema Trinley, 67, 206
Pemagatshel, 269–70
Pemagatshel dzong, 269
permits, 188, 189
  visits to religious monuments, 50
Petsheling monastery, 67, 248
personal safety, 11
Phajo Drugom Shigpo, 65–6, 104, 148,
  163, 179, 181, 185
Phajoding monastery, 184–5
Phanri Zampa, 186
pharmacies, 33, 168
Phibsoo Nature Sanctuary, 280
Phobjika valley, 203, 219
Phongme valley, 267
photography, 37
Phuentsholing, 188, 189
pilgrimage sites, 136, 192, 249
police
  checkpoints, 188, 189, 195, 209, 270
  traffic, 163
population, 11, 14, 51, 163
post offices, 156, 169, 268
postal system, 30
Pra (Prakhar) village, 224
prayer flags, 135, 161, 180, 188, 191, 207
prayer walls, 178
prayer wheels, 179, 228, 262
prices
  handicrafts, 95
  medical evacuation, 274
  tours, 19
  trekking, 274
printing, 180, 212, 294
promotions, social, 127

Punakha, 192–4
Punakha *dzong*, 50, 68, 91, 109, 177, 192–3, 194, 198
Punakha trek, 278
Punakha valley, 191, 278
pundo (game), 290

R

Radi temple, 50
Radhi valley, 267
rattan ware, 47, 98
relics, 193
religion (*see also* Tantric Buddhism)
    practice of, 104–5
    rituals, 101, 103, 105, 128
    schools of, 65–6, 104
    symbols of, 14
religious books, 87
religious dances, 112–3, 116–7, 120, 260
religious festivals, 108–9, 206, 266
religious monuments, see monuments, religious
religious music,121
religious objects, 101, 103
purchase and export of, 29
'religious series', 123–4
religious texts, 172, 212, 228, 249
'religious treasures' (see also *tertons*), 65, 229, 249, 250
Renewable Natural Resources building, 226, 228
Rennie, Surgeon, quoted, 291
restaurants, 153, 165, 183, 189, 199, 257, 262
    Chinese, 168
    Indian, 165, 168, 187, 189
    log cabin, 187, 191
    Tibetan, 213
    Western, 168

rice fields, blessing of, 157
Rieffel, Robert, 271
Rigne School, *see* School of Traditional Arts
Rigsum Gonpa, 267
Rigzin Goeden, 248
Rikey Jigdrel, 180
Rinchenzoe Pass, 207, 279
Riserboo Hospital, 269
Rodong La Pass, 58, 266, 276
roads, 32, 52, 70
    Central Bhutan, 219, 221, 223, 225–6, 228, 248, 250
    Eastern Bhutan, 255–6, 257, 258–9, 261, 263, 266–70
    maintenance camps, 202, 255
    Western Bhutan, 161, 186–8, 189, 191–2, 195, 202–3, 206–7, 209
Royal Advisory Council, 74
Royal Institute of Management, 161
Royal University of Bhutan, 161, 183
Royal Society for Protection of Nature, 203, 280
rugs, 48

S

Sacred Lake of Mebartsho, *see* Mebartsho gorge
safety, *see* personal safety
saints, 66–7, 136, 142, 221
Sakteng Nature Sanctuary, 280
Samdrup Jongkhar, 270
Samtengang trek, 278
Samtenling monastery, 66, 223
Sangye Gyatso, 140
Sangye Lingpa, 172
scarves, ceremonial, 49, 159, 282
scholars, 66–7
School of Traditional Arts, 180, 266–7

schools, 70, 269
sculpture, 86–7
Sekargutho temple, 244
Sendhaka, King, 217, 228, 233, 241, 243
Shabdrung Jigme Choegyel, see Jigme
   Choegyel
Shabdrung Ngawang Namgyal, see
   Ngawang Namgyal
Shakya Rinchen, 185
Shalikhar dzong, 269
Shangri–la, 11
Shangkyeme Drogon, 216
Sharchopas, 59
sheep, 53, 58, 248, 252
Sheldrup Oezer, 136, 184
Shelging Karpo, 233
Sherab Gyeltsen, 131, 133, 142
Sherab Singye, 185
sherey parey (game), 290
Sherubtse College, 259, 268
Shingkar monastery, 66
Shingkhar village, 252
Shongar dzong, 256
shopping (see also bargaining, markets),
   44, 168–9
silverware, 46, 97, 98, 145
Simtokha (Semtokha) dzong, 68, 86,
   183–4, 189
Sinchu La Pass, 186
Sinto Raja, see Sendhaka
Sirigang village, 186
slate, engraved, 47, 86, 145, 171
Snowman trek, 279
soksom (sport), 290
Sombrang monastery, 253
Sonam Drugel, 245
Sonam Zangpo, 191, 270
songs, 121

Songsten Gampo, 61, 131, 160, 224
Southern Bhutan, 52
sports, 42, 290
   facilities, 165, 169, 173
stamps, postage, 30, 49, 145
state clergy, 68, 75, 177
stationery shops, 168
statistics, 79
statues, 131, 133, 145, 181, 188, 189, 199,
   222, 229, 238, 239, 243, 245, 248,
   253, 258, 263
   clay, 194, 240, 253
   local attitudes toward, 81
   loss of, 137
   metalworked, 183
   recent, 251
Sugiura, Mrs (Japanese), commemorated,
   183
supermarkets, 168
supplies, see equipment and supplies
swimming pools, 42, 156, 169
Swiss bakery, 164
Swiss farm, 226

T
Ta dzong (watch tower), 144, 211, 213
Ta Rimocen temple, 250
Tachogang Lhakhang, 156
tailors, 49
Taktichu, 187
Taktshang Lhakhang, 133, 135–7
Taktshang Oezergang, 137
Taktshang Ugyen Tsemo, 137
Taktshang Zandropelri, 137
Tala monastery, 184
Talo monastery, 91
Tamshing Jagar, 268
Tamshing monastery, 67, 226

Tamshing temple, 82, 229, 231–2
Tang valley, 219, 248–52
Tango monastery, 91, 179
Tantric Buddhism, 14, 65, 99–101, 104, 172
Tashichoedzong, 50, 176–8
tea, 36, 41, 49
    ceremony, 236–7
tea houses, 135, 164
telephone services, 30, 156, 171, 225
television, 78
temples, 90–1
    Central Bhutan, 211, 212, 216, 219,
        222–4, 228, 238–43, 245, 250, 253,
        254
    Eastern Bhutan, 258, 260, 262, 263, 267
    visits by foreign tourists to, 50
    Western Bhutan, 131, 133, 138, 142, 156,
        160, 178–9, 181, 189, 192, 193, 206,
        207
Tenpe Nyima, 66, 179, 223, 224, 245, 269
tertons ('discoverers of religious treasures'),
    65, 172, 221, 228, 249, 253
Tenzin Drugda, 138, 193
Tenzin Legpe Dondrub, 206
Tenzin Rabgye, 66, 136, 179, 195, 199, 244,
    262
Textile Museum, 97, 169
textiles, see fabrics
Thadra monastery, 185
Thailand, imports from, 169
Thangbi Lhakhang, 239–40
thangkas (religious banners), 29, 44–5, 82,
    108, 144, 180
Thangthong Dewachen nunnery, 180
Thangton Gyelpo, 66, 138, 142, 144, 160,
    180, 262
Tharpaling monastery, 66, 221, 222–3

Thimphu, 42, 44, 163–5, 168–9, 171–3,
    176–8, 179–81
    maps, 162, 166–7
Thimphu dzong, 91, 109
thongdroel (appliquéd thangka), 108, 198,
    248, 260, 261, 262
Thowadra monastery, 252
Thugse Dawa Gyeltsen, 224
Thumsing La, 58, 255
Tibet, 51, 61, 65, 67, 69, 70, 90, 100, 181
    invasion by, 68
time zone, 32
tobacco, 37
Tonshinkha village, 186
Torsa Reserve, 280
tour operators, 20–1, 24, 30, 275
tourism, 10, 19, 28, 76
Tourism, Department of, 19, 28
tourists, areas closed to, 270
traditions, 14, 15, 281–3
Trashi Wangmo (pen–name of author), 108
Trashi Yangtse dzong, 50, 263, 266
Trashi Yangtse village, 266
Trashigang, 261–2
Trashigang dzong, 91, 261, 262
Trashigang nunnery, 185
travel agents, see tour operators
"Travellers and Magicians" (movie), 209
travellers' cheques, 30
Treaty of Sinchula, 69
trekking, 160, 271, 274–6, 278–9
Trongsa village, 211, 213
Trongsa dzong, 93, 109, 209, 211–3
trulkus (reincarnations), 64, 104
Trumshing La National Park, 280
Tsang Desi, 67
Tsanglalo (language), 59, 256

Tsangpa Gyare Yeshe Dorje, 61, 65, 104, 113, 142, 181, 193, 222
Tsenkharla castle, 263
tshechus, see religious festivals
Tshering Penjor, 152
Tshokye Dorje, 117, 251
Tsilung temple, 228
Tsondru Gyeltsen, 243
Tsulag Gyatso, 185
Turner, Samuel, quoted, 236–7

U

Ugyen Pelri, 145, 152
Ugyen Wangchuck, 69, 70, 144, 173, 211, 212, 223, 238, 242, 244
    crowned, 193
    paintings of, 260
    relations of, 69, 212, 241, 244, 245
Umze Tenzin Drugye, 239
university, *see* Royal University of Bhutan
Ura La Pass, 252
Ura temple, 50
Ura valley, 219, 252–4
Ura village, 254

V

Vaccinations, 32
vehicles, 164
visas, 28, 29
Voluntary Artists Studio, 81

W

Walks, 179, 184–6, 207, 228, 240
Wang Chhu River, 53, 186, 187
Wangchuklo *dzong*, 160
Wangduchoeling *dzong*, 50
Wangduchoeling palace, 50, 228, 244
Wangduephodrang, 91, 109, 191, 195, 199
water, drinking, 32

weaving, 97, 219, 224, 258, 267, 269
Web–sites, 31, 81, 305
Western Bhutan, 50, 56, 129–209
White, J Claude, quoted, 157
wine, 37
women, 192, 278, 288
    clothing, 45, 248
woodwork, 47, 98, 266, 267
World Wide Fund for Nature, 280
'wrestling', 290

X

Xylography, 180, 212, 294

Y

Yadi, 259
yak–herders, 58, 59, 207, 278
yaks, 203, 207, 251
Yongla monastery, 269
Yonphula Lhakhang, 268
Yonphula pass, 268
Yonten Thaye, 177, 266
Younghusband, Colonel Francis, 70
Yutong La Pass, 58, 219

Z

Zangdopelri temple, 50, 189, 206, 268
Zhemgang *dzong*, 216
Zhemgang region, 213, 216
Zhidar, 211
Zugne village, 224